PRENTICE HALL
LITERATURE

PENGUIN EDITION

Reader's
NOTEBOOK
TEACHING GUIDE

Grade 9

PEARSON

Prentice
Hall

Upper Saddle River, New Jersey
Boston, Massachusetts

Copyright © 2007 by Pearson Education, Inc., publishing as Pearson Prentice Hall, Boston Massachusetts 02116. All rights reserved. Printed in the United States of America. This publication is protected by copyright, and permission should be obtained from the publisher prior to any prohibited reproduction, storage in a retrieval system, or transmission in any form or by any means, electronic, mechanical, photocopying, recording, or likewise. For information regarding permission(s), write to: Rights and Permissions Department, One Lake Street, Upper Saddle River, New Jersey 07458.

ISBN 0-13-165409-8

5 6 7 8 9 10   10 09 08

Contents

Reader's Notebook

Answers to Part 1

Answers to Part 2

Reader's Notebook Adapted Version

Answers to Part 1

Answers to Part 2

Reader's Notebook English Learner's Version

How to Use the *Reader's Notebooks*

Share the same selection with all your students!

STEP 1

Introduce instruction using *Prentice Hall Literature* Student Edition

- Use the Background information
- Introduce the Literary Analysis and Reading Skill
- Preview the vocabulary words

STEP 2

Develop instruction with targeted reading support
Choose the *Reader's Notebook* that meets each student's needs

Reader's Notebook
- For average readers
- Full-length selections
- Interactive reading support for all selections
- Vocabulary and pronunciation guides
- All selections on audio CD

Adapted Version
- For struggling readers
- Selection adaptations and authentic text
- Enhanced design for easier readability
- All adapted selections on audio CD

English Learner's Version
- Specialized vocabulary and reading support
- Focus on idioms, colloquialisms, and cultural information
- All adapted selections on audio CD

STEP 3

Conclude instruction using *Prentice Hall Literature* Student Edition

- Present the unabridged selection and instruction in the student edition
- Have students read along with the audio CDs
- Use the scaffolded Thinking About the Selection questions

To the Teacher

As you face the challenge of heterogeneous classes, you will find a wide variety of abilities and strengths among your students. The *Reader's Notebook*, the *Reader's Notebook Adapted Version*, and the *Reader's Notebook English Learner's Version* that accompany your *Prentice Hall Literature* anthology are aimed at students who have difficulty with their grade-level textbook. You can use the *Notebooks* to keep your classes reading the same selections but getting the instruction and reading support at the appropriate level. These books provide extended support for those students who need more guidance with reading skills and strategies, literary analysis, and critical thinking skills.

Factors that Affect Reading Success

Four key factors influence students' ability to achieve reading success. These factors, alone and in combination, determine how well a student will learn, grow, and succeed as a reader. To understand the students in your classroom, consider these factors:

(a) **Kinds of Learners** Consider each student's background, previous learning experiences, and special needs. In addition to students who read fluently at grade level, you may find a mix of the following learning characteristics in your classroom:

- *Students who speak a language other than English at home* Unlike their fully fluent counterparts, these students often speak English only at school. This situation leaves them limited hours in which to learn the grammar, vocabulary, idioms, and other intricacies of English.

- *Students who have recently moved to this country* These students may be highly capable students without the specific language skills to function academically in English.

- *Students with learning disabilities* These students may have cognitive, behavioral, social, or physical challenges that make reading more difficult.

(b) **Kinds of Skills and Instruction** Students' reading ability is influenced by the skills they bring to the task. Students must master the skills of decoding, activating and building prior knowledge, and making connections among experiences and new information. Other factors include a student's knowledge of the English language and vocabulary and a student's ability to apply reading comprehension strategies.

Active reading, including the practice of summarizing, questioning, setting a purpose, and self-monitoring, is key to successful reading. For those students who have not yet developed such skills, your classroom instruction is critical. You should model such skills and encourage students to practice them. Through practice, students should be able to internalize the strategies of active reading.

(c) **Kinds of Texts** Just as students and their backgrounds and skills vary, so do the texts presented in a language arts curriculum. The grade-level language arts classroom curriculum traditionally addresses fiction, nonfiction, poetry, and drama. Each of these forms presents unique challenges to students. Each writer and selection also presents challenges in the difficulty of the concepts addressed or in the coherence of the writing. For example, you may find that students are more comfortable with narratives than with expository writing. Focused reading strategies that you model and reinforce can help students tackle texts that are more dense or difficult for them to master.

(d) **Classroom Environment** The classroom environment affects everything and everyone within it. Research suggests that students learn best in a friendly, respectful setting categorized by these criteria:

- Students feel a sense of safety and order.
- They feel comfortable taking risks.
- They understand the purpose and value of the tasks presented.
- They have high expectations and goals for learning.
- They feel accepted by their teachers and peers.

Students performing below grade level may be especially self-conscious. Therefore, these criteria are key to helping students take full advantage of the opportunities the classroom affords. Set up your classroom as a caring yet on-purpose environment that helps students achieve.

Researchers encourage teachers to be truthful with students about the work it will take to build and master abilities in the language arts. Tell your students that improving reading, writing, speaking, and listening takes a great deal of practice. You need to be prepared to provide direct instruction, guided practice, specific feedback, coaching, and more. Then, encourage your students to understand their responsibilities as active, self-directed learners as well.

The Special Education or Special Needs Student

Your classroom may have a number of special education or special needs students—young people who begin the year three or more years below grade level and yet do not qualify for special education services. Special education and special needs students have difficulty in organizing and categorizing new information during instruction. They may have trouble in the following areas:

Memory
- ordering or arranging information
- classifying information
- grasping a main idea or "big picture"
- using long-term memory to make meaningful connections or connecting to prior knowledge

Attention
- focusing attention on the most important elements of a presentation or a selection

By presenting specific focused strategies and interactive review and extension activities, you can provide these students with full access to the language arts curriculum.

Another category of deficiency in special education readers is the ability to apply learning strategies to a variety of situations. Special education and special needs students often have these weaknesses:

Learning Strategies
- a lack of effective or efficient strategies for completing academic tasks such as taking notes, responding to literature, or writing a focused paragraph
- a limited set of learning strategies from which to draw
- difficulty in self-monitoring—they often don't know which strategies to use or when a strategy is not working

Many of these students are underprepared; their deficiencies are generally based on their lack of experience, not on any biological difference. When these students learn effective strategies, they can improve their academic performance. You need to provide direct instruction to explicitly show them how, when, and why to use each strategy.

Overview of Components for Differentiated Instruction

Prentice Hall Literature: Penguin Edition includes an array of targeted resources for special needs students. Fully integrated, these materials help teachers identify student needs or deficiencies, teach to the varying levels in a classroom, and provide the quality that literature teachers expect.

As your main resource, the *Annotated Teacher's Edition* provides a lesson plan for every selection pairing. In addition to teaching notes and suggestions, the *Annotated Teacher's Edition* also includes cross-references to ancillary material such as the *Reader's Notebook*, the *Reader's Notebook Adapted Version*, and the *Reader's Notebook English Learner's Version*. *Differentiated Instruction* notes help teachers direct lessons to the following groups of students: special needs students, less proficient readers, English learners, gifted and talented students, and advanced readers.

The **Reading Kit** has three parts, each designed to help you address the needs of students with varying ability levels.

- *Part 1: Practice and Assess* includes worksheets for every selection to build reading proficiency.

- *Part 2: Everyday Reading Strategies* provides direct instruction to improve students' comprehension and interpretation.

- *Part 3: Classroom Management for Differentiated Instruction* presents research-based, classroom-tested strategies for engaging students of all ability levels in learning activities and class discussions.

Success Tracker is an online intervention system that allows you to monitor progress and intervene before students take your state standardized test.

- *Assess:* Students take a Diagnostic or Benchmark test online.

- *Diagnose:* Based on assessment results, Success Tracker automatically diagnoses student mastery level for each skill tested.

- *Remediate:* Customized assignments are made for each student based on the skills mastered. Assignments can be made automatically or customized by the teacher.

- *Report:* Color-coded reports make it easy for you to monitor progress on your standards.

Several components—**Vocabulary and Reading Warm-Ups, Selection Tests,** and **Graphic Organizer Transparencies**—are offered in two versions, Level A and Level B. This allows you to customize to the individual ability levels of your students.

- *Vocabulary and Reading Warm-Ups* for every selection include word lists, exercises, and reading passages.

- *Selection Tests* for every selection include multiple choice and essay questions.

- *Graphic Organizer Transparencies* support the skills taught in the student edition.

The **Reader's Notebook** is a consumable component. The book contains instructional support for all the selections and the full text of approximately half of the selections from the student book. Questions prompt students to interact with the text by circling, underlining, or marking key details. Write-on lines in the margins also allow for students to answer questions. You can use this book in place of the student book to help students read interactively.

The **Reader's Notebook Adapted Version** is another consumable component. This book uses the same format and contains the same selections as the *Reader's Notebook*. However, the selections are abridged and appear in a larger font size. The questions are targeted toward special education students. You can use this book as a supplement to or in place of the student book for certain selections to enable special education students to experience the same literature and master the same skills as on-level students.

The **Reader's Notebook English Learner's Version** is a third consumable component. This book uses the same format and contains the same selections as the *Reader's Notebook*. Again, the selections are abridged and appear in a larger font size. The questions are targeted toward English learners. You can use this book as a supplement to or in place of the student book for certain selections to enable English learners to experience the same literature and master the same skills as students who are native English speakers.

Listening to Literature Audio CD This component features professional recordings of every selection in the *Reader's Notebook*. To support student reading, you can play the selections, in part or in full, before students read them.

Reader's Notebook Adapted and English Learner's Version Audio Program These components feature professional recordings of every adapted selection in the *Reader's Notebook Adapted* and *English Learner's Versions*. The recordings include the explanatory bridges along with the lines of original text. As with the *Listening to Literature Audio CD*, you can support student reading by playing selections, in part or in full, before students read them.

The Listening to Literature Audio CD and the *Reader's Notebook Adapted and English Learner's Version Audio Program* can be used to support reading fluency. As you play the CDs, have students read along, either silently or aloud.

Spanish/English Summaries Audio CD Audio summaries in both English and Spanish are provided for every selection. You can play these selection summaries for struggling readers, special education students, and English learners before they read the actual texts.

About the *Reader's Notebook*, the *Reader's Notebook Adapted Version*, and the *Reader's Notebook English Learner's Version*

The *Reader's Notebook* is designed to support students who are reading on level or one grade level below level. The *Reader's Notebook Adapted Version* and the *Reader's Notebook English Learner's Version* are designed to support your special needs and special education students.

Part 1: Skills Instruction and Complete Selections (*Reader's Notebook*)

Part 1 will guide students as they interact with the selection from *Prentice Hall Literature*. Skills instruction is included for every selection that appears in *Prentice Hall Literature*. In addition, many of the selections from *Prentice Hall Literature* appear in the *Reader's Notebook* in their entirety. The selections that appear include the more accessible selections, the most frequently taught selections, and many examples of narrative and expository writing.

Part 1: Skills Instruction and Selection Adaptations with Excerpts of Authentic Text (*Reader's Notebook Adapted and English Learner's Versions*)

Part 1 will guide special needs students and English learners as they interact with the selections from *Prentice Hall Literature*. Part 1 in the *Reader's Notebook Adapted Version* and the *Reader's Notebook English Learner's Version* provides larger print summaries of literature selections with passages from the selections.

Prereading pages

The **Build Skills** page is based on its parallel in *Prentice Hall Literature*. It introduces the same literary element and reading skill addressed in the textbook and provides a graphic organizer to make the information more accessible.

The **Preview** page will help your students get the general idea of the selection and therefore be better equipped to understand it. A written summary, along with an image or illustration, previews the selections before students read. The Reading/Writing Connection provides sentence starters that help students think about the big idea behind the selection. It also helps build student vocabulary by using vocabulary that is introduced in the student edition. The Note-taking Guide helps students organize the main ideas of the selection, and helps them track their understanding.

Selection pages

The **selection** pages in the *Reader's Notebook* present the selections as they appear in the student edition. The selection pages in the *Reader's Notebook Adapted Version* and the *Reader's Notebook English Learner's Version* present the text in a larger font size. Interspersed among blocks of authentic text, these two Notebooks also provide summaries of episodes or paragraphs to make the selections more accessible to your students.

The *Take Notes* feature provides questions to accompany the selections. These questions make active reading strategies explicit, asking students to look closely at the text to analyze it in a variety of ways. Notes with a pencil icon prompt students to underline, circle, or otherwise note key words, phrases, or details in the selection. Notes with write-on lines offer students an opportunity to respond in the margin to questions or ideas. These notes offer focused support in a number of ways:

Literary Analysis notes provide point-of-use instruction to reinforce the literary element introduced on the Build Skills page. By pointing out details or events in the text in which the literary element applies, these notes give students the opportunity to revisit and reinforce their understanding of literature.

Reading Skill notes help students practice the skill introduced on the Build Skills page. These notes guide students to understand when, how, and why a skill is helpful.

Stop to Reflect notes ask students to reflect on the selection or on a skill they are using. By encouraging students to solidify their own thinking, these notes help to develop active reading skills.

Reading Check notes help students confirm their comprehension of a selection. These notes help to make explicit a critical strategy of active reading.

Read Fluently notes provide students with concrete, limited practice reading passages aloud with fluency.

THESE INSTRUCTIONAL NOTES ARE SPECIFIC TO THE READER'S NOTEBOOK ENGLISH LEARNER'S VERSION:

Vocabulary and Pronunciation notes guide students in understanding prefixes, suffixes, roots, and words with multiple meanings. In some cases, they explain how specific words are pronounced in English.

Culture notes explain an aspect of American culture that might be unfamiliar to English Learners. They may focus on an aspect of popular culture or on an event or a concept of historical significance.

Build English Skills notes help students in understanding the nuances of the English language, such as idioms, contractions, verb tenses, and difficult sentence constructions.

Post-reading Pages

The *Apply the Skills* pages ensure students' comprehension of the selection. Written in simple language, they assess students' understanding of the literary element and the reading skill. In addition, they offer a scaffolded guide to support students in an activity based on the writing lesson in the student edition of the grade-level textbook. Students are also provided with additional support for an extension activity based on either the Listening and Speaking activity or the Research and Technology activity in the student edition.

Using the *Notebooks*

Classroom Management:

When you are planning lessons for heterogeneous classes, the *Reader's Notebooks* offer you an opportunity to keep all the students in your class reading the same selection and studying the same vocabulary, literary element, and reading skill but also to get the support they need to succeed. At the outset, assign appropriate *Notebooks* to the students and have them write their names in them. Students very quickly assume ownership as they complete the interactive format of the *Notebooks*. The books become a personalized "response journal" and study guide for tests as they move through the selections.

Here are some planning suggestions for using these books in tandem with the grade-level volume of *Prentice Hall Literature:*

Use the *Annotated Teacher's Edition* and the *Student Edition* of the grade-level textbook as the central text in your classroom. The *Annotated Teacher's Edition* includes *Differentiated Instruction* notes throughout each selection. In addition, it identifies when use of the *Notebooks* is appropriate.

Accountability:

Collect the *Notebooks* at intervals that you choose. For example, you may decide to review students' work in the *Notebooks* once weekly. Have students mark a page completed during that time period with a sticky note, which can be used as a tab. This tab makes it easy for you to open the *Notebook* quickly to the specific page, check for the accuracy and thoroughness of the work on selected questions, and award points or a grade.

Absent students:

Use the *Reader's Notebook* for students who will be absent during discussions or for homebound students. These students will be in step with the rest of the class in terms of concepts, strategies, and standards covered during their absence.

Teaching the Genre

At the beginning of each unit of the *Reader's Notebook*, the *Reader's Notebook Adapted Version*, and the *Reader's Notebook English Learner's Version* are two pages devoted to genre instruction. These pages

- describe the most important elements of a particular genre.

- provide definitions for key terms, such as *mood* or *setting*.

Teachers can use these pages as an overview for the Model Selection and for the other selections that follow. Use these steps:

- Review the key terms with students before they read.

- Then, ask them to locate these elements in the selections as they read.

- Finally, reinforce the genre instruction by using the questions on the Apply the Skills page following the first selection in each unit. Each of these questions has students apply their knowledge of genre to the specific selection.

The graphic organizers on the genre page single out certain characteristics of the genre and present them in an easy-to-read format. A sample genre page and graphic organizer are shown here.

A concise definition is provided for setting, *a key term.*

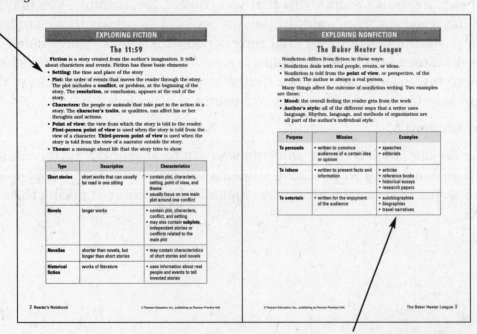

This chart ties the main purposes of nonfiction to real-life examples.

Teaching the Penguin Authors

Penguin Selections

In the student edition of *Prentice Hall Literature: Penguin Edition*, a contemporary Penguin author serves as a guide for each unit. This author introduces the genre or theme of the unit, introduces his or her selection in the unit, annotates and answers questions about that selection, and introduces and annotates a sample of his or her writing. Penguin authors also discuss literature, writing, and their own lives on the DVD that accompanies the textbook.

In the section entitled "Teaching the Penguin Selections," you will find ideas for using the commentary by Penguin authors as you teach their selections in the *Reader's Notebook*, the *Reader's Notebook Adapted Version*, and the *Reader's Notebook English Learner's Version*. The Penguin selections, which are the Model Selections, appear in their entirety in the *Reader's Notebook* and in abridged form in the *Reader's Notebook Adapted Version* and the *Reader's Notebook English Learner's Version* together with almost all the same features that accompany other selections:

- **Preview page**, with a Summary of the selection and a Note-taking Guide

- **Interactive questions** in the margin of the selection

- **Vocabulary words** defined (with pronunciations) where they first appear

- **Reader's Response** question at the end of the selection

- **Apply the Skills** page, with critical thinking questions

However, instead of the page headed Support Your Writing and Extend Your Learning, Penguin selections have a special Research the Author page, which guides students in learning more about the Penguin author:

RESEARCH THE AUTHOR

Oral Report

Create an **oral report** to discuss McCracken's interest in libraries, documents, and research. The following bullets will help you find information for your report.

- Read some of the author's other works. *Niagara Falls All Over Again, The American Child,* and *Here's Your Hat, What's Your Hurry?* are fictional pieces, and her essays appear in the collections *Family: American Writers Remember Their Own* and *A Few Thousand Words About Love.*

What I learned from McCracken's fiction and nonfiction:

_____

_____

- Search the Internet.

What I learned from information about McCracken:

_____

_____

- Watch the video interview with Elizabeth McCracken. Use it and your source material to answer these questions.

1. What did you learn about McCracken's library background? How did her background affect her writing?

_____

_____

2. What did you learn about McCracken's interest in documents?

_____

_____

16 Reader's Notebook   © Pearson Education, Inc., publishing as Pearson Prentice Hall.

Teaching the Penguin Selections

You can use the commentary by Penguin authors in the student edition to help students read the Penguin selections in the *Reader's Notebook*, the *Reader's Notebook Adapted Version*, and the *Reader's Notebook English Learner's Version*.

Before students begin reading the Penguin selection, show them the interview with the author on the DVD. You might want to guide their viewing by asking individuals or groups to focus on different topics. These topics might include the author's

- life experiences,
- ideas about writing,
- ideas about literature, or
- perspectives on the selection that he or she wrote.

Then, have students summarize for the class the information they learned about their topic.

As students read the selection, use the Penguin author's commentary in the student edition to motivate them and reinforce their learning. Following are some suggestions for using this material with specific pages in the *Reader's Notebook*, the *Reader's Notebook Adapted Version*, and the *Reader's Notebook English Learner's Version*.

Preview page

- Explain to students that the Penguin author introduces his or her selection in the student edition. Point out to them that in this introduction, the author often explains how, why, and when he or she wrote the selection.

- Read this introduction—or passages from it—aloud to students before they read the Summary on the Preview page in the *Reader's Notebook*, the *Reader's Notebook Adapted Version*, and the *Reader's Notebook English Learner's Version*.

- Briefly discuss with students some of the author's insights. If appropriate, ask students to look for evidence to support these insights as they read the selection.

Selection

- Tell students that the author comments on specific passages in his or her selection. These comments appear in notes headed by the author's name and located in the margin of the selection.

- Have students mark in the *Reader's Notebook*, the *Reader's Notebook Adapted Version*, and the *Reader's Notebook English Learner's Version* the passages where the author's comments appear in the student edition.

- Ask students to pause in their reading when they reach the marked passage and refer back to the student edition to read the author's comment.

- If appropriate, ask students to circle or underline in the *Reader's Notebook*, the *Reader's Notebook Adapted Version*, and the *Reader's Notebook English Learner's Version* words or phrases that illustrate or support what the author says.

- When students have finished reading the selection, read aloud one or more of the questions and author responses on the page that follows the selection in the student edition. Then, have students formulate their own questions for the author. Consider having students work in pairs to pose and answer these questions. First, one student can pose a question and the other can answer *as* the author. Next, they can switch roles.

Research the Author

- Introduce this page in the *Reader's Notebook*, the *Reader's Notebook Adapted Version*, and the *Reader's Notebook English Learner's Version* by reviewing with students the sources of information about the author on the DVD and in the student book. Do not forget to mention the Writing Workshop page on which the Penguin author introduces and annotates a draft of his or her writing.

- Questions on the Research the Author page sometimes require Internet research. Review with students the use of key words to do such research. Also, remind them that the most reliable Web sites are sponsored by universities, encyclopedias, and other reputable organizations. Sites created by individuals may not have accurate information.

- To achieve closure, have students relate what they have learned about the author to the selection they have just read. Also, if they are not already prompted to do so by a question on this page, have them use their research to create a list of Further Readings by the same author.

Teaching Part One: The Selections and Informational Materials

The Selections
PRETEACH with the Full Class

Anticipate the reading. Use the *Motivation* activity provided for the selection in the *Annotated Teacher's Edition*. These activities vary and may include discussion questions, anticipation guides, or graphic organizers that will help students focus their attention on the important ideas presented in the selection.

Preview the selection. To help students see the organization of a selection, or to help them get a general idea of the text, lead a quick text prereading or "text tour" using the textbook. Focus student attention on the selection title, the art accompanying the text, and any unusual text characteristics. To build connections for students, ask them to identify links between the selection and other works you have presented in class or to find connections to themes, activities, or other related concepts.

Build background. Use the Background information provided in the *Student Edition*. Whether explaining a historical time period, a scientific concept, or details about an idea that may be unfamiliar to students, this instruction presents useful information to help all students place the literature in context.

Build connections. Use the *Connecting to the Literature* feature in the *Student Edition* to help students find relationships between their own life experiences or reading and the selection they are about to read. Direct average students to complete the *Expressive Vocabulary* task in the Connecting to the Literature section. Direct struggling readers, special education students, special needs students, and English learners to the *Preview* page of the *Notebooks*. Work with them to complete the *Reading/Writing Connection* task on that page.

Focus vocabulary development. The *Student Edition* provides a list of vocabulary words included in each selection. Instead of attempting to cover all of the vocabulary words you anticipate your students will not know, identify the vocabulary that is most critical to talking and learning about the central concepts. However, for the words you do choose to teach, work to provide more than synonyms and definitions. Using the vocabulary notes in the *Annotated Teacher's Edition*, introduce the essential words in more meaningful contexts: for example, through simple sentences drawing on familiar issues, people, scenarios, and vocabulary. Guide students in internalizing the meanings of key terms through these familiar contexts and ask them to write the definitions in their own words. Look at the following examples of guided vocabulary instruction:

> Point out the word *serene* and explain that it means "calm or peaceful." Then, provide the following scenarios and ask students to determine whether the situations are *serene* or not: an empty beach at sunset *(yes)*; a basketball playoff game *(no)*. You might also ask students to provide their own examples of *serene* situations.

Point out the word *interval* and explain that it means "the period of time between two events or points of time." Ask students to identify the interval between Monday and Wednesday *(two days)* and the interval between one Monday and the next Monday *(one week)*.

You might also take the opportunity to teach the prefix *inter-*, meaning "between." Then, discuss with students the following group of words:

interview (a meeting between two or more people);

interstate (between two or more states);

international (between nations);

intervene (to come between two sides in a dispute).

Separate the class to introduce the skills. For average students, introduce the *Literary Analysis* and *Reading Skills* using the instruction in the *Student Edition* and the teaching support in the *Annotated Teacher's Edition*. Have struggling readers, special education students, special needs students, and English learners put their textbooks aside. Direct these students to the *Notebooks* to begin study of *Literary Analysis* and *Reading Skills*.

PRETEACH Using the *Notebooks*

Introduce skills. All versions of the *Reader's Notebooks* provide the same literary analysis and reading skills concepts as the *Student Edition*. The *Adapted* and *English Learner's* versions do so with simplified language and basic sentence structures. Use the *Build Skills* page in the *Notebooks* along with teaching support from the *Annotated Teachers' Edition* to introduce the skills to struggling readers, special education students, special needs students, and English learners.

Reinforce the key ideas. Use the *Summary* presented on the *Preview* page for every selection in the *Notebooks*. The summary will give students a framework to follow for understanding the selection. Use this tool to build familiarity, but do not use it as a replacement for reading.

Introduce note taking. Prepare the students to use the *Note-taking Guide* that appears on the *Preview* page for every selection. Each note-taking guide focuses on a specific aspect of the selection. For example, the guide may help students keep track of details in a poem, trace the plot of a story, or track the line of reasoning in an essay. Tell students that taking notes can help them focus their reading and better understand a selection. It will also allow them to gather information that will help them later as they answer questions or write about a particular selection.

Present audio summaries. The *Spanish/English Summaries on Audio CD* can reinforce the main idea of a selection and provide extra support for students whose first language is Spanish.

Provide decoding practice. Because many struggling readers, special education students, and English learners lack strategies for decoding bigger words, give them guided practice with the vocabulary words for the selection. Using the list from the *Student Edition*, model a strategy for decoding polysyllabic words. First, show students how to break the word into parts and then put the parts back together to make a word.

> For the words *mimic* and *frightening*, ask students to draw a line under each word part as they pronounce it.
>
> *mim ic*　　　*fright en ing*

Using this strategy, you can encourage students to look for familiar word parts and then break the rest of the word down into its consonant and vowel sounds. By building this routine regularly into your preteaching instruction, you reinforce a key reading skill for your students.

Prepare for lesson structure. To build students' ability to complete classroom activities, examine your lesson to see what types of language functions students will need to participate in. Look at these examples:

> If students are being asked to make predictions about upcoming paragraph content in an essay, review the power of transition words that act as signals to meaning. Rather than teaching all transitions, limit your instruction to the ones in the passages. Identify the key transition words and point out their meaning. In addition, teach students some basic sentence patterns and verbs to express opinions. Model for students statement patterns such as the following:
>
> *I predict that . . .*
>
> *Based on this transition word, I conclude that . . .*

TEACH Using the *Notebooks*

Read the selection. The three versions of the *Reader's Notebook* allow you to teach the same selections to students who demonstrate differing levels of achievement. Average achieving students in your class may read the selection in the *Student Edition*. The *Reader's Notebooks* provide a range of other options as you work with struggling readers, special education students, special needs students, and English learners:

- Students reading just at or below grade level may benefit from the extra guidance provided in the *Reader's Notebook* version of the selection.

- Have your special education and special needs students and English learners read the adapted version of the selection in the *Reader's Notebook Adapted Version* or *Reader's Notebook English Learner's Version*.

- If the *Reader's Notebook* does not include the selection, have students read the text in the *Student Edition*.

Whenever possible, give your struggling readers, special education and special needs students, and English learners individualized attention by pairing them with aides, parent volunteers, or student peers.

Set purposes and limits. To keep students focused and motivated and to prevent them from becoming overwhelmed as they read a selection, clearly establish a reading purpose for students before assigning a manageable amount of text. Once you identify a focus question or a purpose, revisit the question occasionally as students read. You can do this with a brief whole-group dialogue or by encouraging students in pairs to remember the question. In addition, your effective modeling will also provide the scaffolding for students to begin internalizing these strategies for effective reading.

Model your thinking. Describe and model strategies for navigating different kinds of text. Use the questions raised in the side notes as a starting point. Then, explain how you arrive at an answer. Alternatively, ask a student to explain his or her responses to classmates.

Reinforce new vocabulary. Present key words when they occur within the context of the reading selection. Review the definition as it appears on the page. Then, make the words as concrete as possible by linking each to an object, a photo, or an idea.

Build interactivity. The side notes in the *Notebooks* are an excellent way to encourage student interactivity with the selections. To build students' ability to use these notes, model several examples with each selection. These are not busy work; they are activities that build fluency and provide the scaffolding necessary for student success.

Whenever possible, get students physically involved with the page. Many side-note questions invite students to use highlighters or colored pencils to circle, underline, or number key information. In addition, some students may find that using a small piece of cardboard or heavy construction paper helps to focus and guide their reading from one paragraph or page to the next.

Vary modes of instruction. To maintain student attention and interest, monitor and alternate the mode of instruction or activity. For example, alternate between teacher-facilitated and student-dominated reading activities. Assign brief amounts of text at a time, and alternate between oral, paired, and silent reading.

Monitor students' comprehension. As students use the side notes in the margins of the *Notebooks*, build in opportunities to ensure that students are on purpose and understanding. Consider structured brief conversations for students to share, compare, or explain their thinking. Then, use these conversations to praise the correct use of strategies or to redirect students who need further support. In addition, this is an excellent chance for you to reinforce students' use of the *Note-taking Guide* and provide models of effective study notes for students to emulate.

Reinforce the reading experience. When students read the selection for the first time, they may be working on the decoding level. If time allows, students should read the selection twice to achieve a greater fluency and comfort level.

APPLY THE SKILLS: Post-reading Activities

Invite reader response. Have students using the *Reader's Notebooks* complete the *Reader's Response* question following the selection.

Conduct a full-class discussion. When students have finished reviewing the selection—whether in the *Notebook* or in the grade-level textbook—include all students in your class in a post-reading analysis. To guide an initial discussion, use the *Respond* question in the *Thinking About the Selection* section in the textbook. You will find that questions such as the following examples will provide strong springboards for classroom interaction:

Respond: What advice would you have given the mother and daughter? Why?

Respond: What questions would you like to ask the writer about her experience?

Respond: Do you find the boy's actions courageous, touching, or silly? Explain your response.

Encourage students to support their answers to these questions with evidence from the text or their own lives. In addition, invite students to respond appropriately to classmates' ideas. These questions will lead students from simply getting the gist of a selection to establishing a personal connection to the lesson content.

Direct student analysis with scaffolded questions. When you are ready to move students into more challenging critical thinking questions, have your average-achieving students use the instruction and questions in the grade-level textbook. Have students performing just at or one grade below reading level use the questions in the *Reader's Notebook*. Have struggling readers, special education students, special needs students, and English learners use the questions on the *Apply the Skills* page in the *Reader's Notebook Adapted Version* and *Reader's Notebook English Learner's Version*.

- Questions in the *Notebooks*, written in simpler language and providing more explicit support, will be more accessible to students currently achieving below grade level. Students will be able to apply concepts at their own level.

- Some special education or special needs students or English learners may be prepared to answer questions in the grade-level text. The two-part questions in the *Thinking About the Selection* section are written to build and support student analysis. For the first part of the question, students use lower-level thinking skills to identify information or to recall important details in a selection. For the second part, students use a higher-level thinking skill based on the answer to the first part.

Look at these examples of scaffolded questions from the grade-level textbooks:

(a) **Recall:** Why does the boy tell his father to leave the sickroom?
(b) **Infer:** What does this reveal about the boy?

(a) **Recall:** Why does the boy think he will die?
(b) **Interpret:** What is the meaning of the story's title?

Reinforce literary analysis and reading skills. Have students complete the *Literary Analysis* and *Reading Skills* questions on the *Apply the Skills* pages. Depending on the students' individual capabilities, determine whether students will use the questions in the grade-level textbook or the simplified versions in the *Notebooks*.

Reinforce writing, listening and speaking, or research and technology skills. Once students have completed the *Literary Analysis* and *Reading Skills* questions, assign the *Writing Lesson* and *Extend Your Learning* activities. Based on the activities presented in the grade-level text, the versions in the *Notebooks* provide guided, step-by-step support for students. By giving students supported opportunities to show their reading comprehension, writing, and listening and speaking or research and technology skills, you maintain reasonable expectations for their developing academic competence.

Model expectations. Make sure that students understand your assessment criteria in advance. Provide models of student work, whenever possible, for them to emulate, along with a non-model that fails to meet the specified assessment criteria. Do not provide exemplars that are clearly outside of their developmental range. Save student work that can later serve as a model for students with different levels of academic preparation.

Lead students to closure. To achieve closure, ask students to end the class session by writing three to five outcome statements about their experience in the day's lesson, expressing both new understandings and needs for clarification.

Encourage self-monitoring and self-assessment. Remember to provide safe opportunities for students to alert you to any learning challenges they are experiencing. Consider having students submit anonymous written questions (formulated either independently or with a partner) about confusing lesson content. Later, you can follow up on these points of confusion at the end of class or in the subsequent class session.

EXTEND Using the Student Edition

Present the unabridged selection for students who read the adapted version. Build in opportunities for students to read the full selection in the grade-level textbook. This will allow them to apply familiar concepts and vocabulary and stretch their literacy muscles.

Play an audio reading of the unabridged selection. Use the *Listening to Literature Audio CDs.* Students who read the adapted version may benefit from reading along while listening to a professional recording of the selection. Encourage students to use their fingertips to follow the words as they are read.

Revisit and reinforce strategies. Recycle pre- and post-reading tasks regularly so that students can become more familiar with the task process and improve their performance. If they are constantly facing curricular novelty, special education and special needs students never have the opportunity to refine their skills and demonstrate improved competence. For example, if you ask them to identify a personality trait of an essential character in a story and then support this observation with relevant details in an expository paragraph, it would make sense to have them write a similar paragraph in the near future about another character.

Show students how to transfer skills. Consider ways in which students can transfer knowledge and skills gleaned from one assignment/lesson to a subsequent lesson. For example, discuss with students the ways in which they can apply new vocabulary and language strategies outside of the classroom. In addition, demonstrate the applicability of new reading and writing strategies to real-world literacy tasks. Include periodic writing tasks for an authentic audience other than the teacher, such as another class, fellow classmates, local businesses, family, etc.

Offer praise and encourage growth. Praise students' efforts to experiment with new language in class, both in writing and in speaking.

Reading Informational Materials

The *Reader's Notebook*, the *Reader's Notebook Adapted Version*, and the *Reader's Notebook English Learner's Version* present unabridged versions of all of the Reading Informational Materials features from the student book. As with other selections, questions prompt students to interact with the text in a variety of ways, helping them gain competence in reading informational materials such as newspaper articles, business documents, and product directions and warranties.

The prereading page for each selection previews the type of informational material in the lesson and presents the reading skill that is addressed in the student edition.

The selection pages include many of the same types of side notes that appear with other selections. Additional **Reading Informational Materials** notes focus on specific features of informational materials.

In the *Reader's Notebooks*, an **Apply the Skills** page follows each selection. This page provides additional support for students by focusing on reading comprehension, reading skills, and timed writing activities.

Part 2: Helping Students Use the Turbo Vocabulary Pages

The Turbo Vocabulary pages are located in Part 2 at the end of each *Notebook*. These pages provide ways for students to work with the vocabulary in the selections and to record new vocabulary words they come across in their reading. The Turbo Vocabulary section contains the following types of worksheets.

Word Roots, Prefixes, and Suffixes

Two-page charts give roots, prefixes, and suffixes that will help students improve their vocabulary. The chart gives the meaning of the word part and an example. Space is provided in the chart for students to write in other word parts that they come across in their reading. Point out to students words that contain these word parts as you read in class.

Using a Dictionary

These pages teach students how to read a dictionary entry. Practice working with dictionary entries is provided.

Word Study Cards

Use these word study cards to break big words into their parts. One card is filled out as an example and the rest are blank for students to write in words they want to examine more closely. Make sure that the words students choose to break down can be broken down. Help students choose words with meaningful prefixes and suffixes.

Denotation and Connotation

Understanding the connotation of words can help students determine a writer's purpose and tone. These exercises will help students be aware of more than the word's denotation, or dictionary definition.

Academic Vocabulary Words

The *Reader's Notebook* lists ten academic vocabulary words for each unit. The *Adapted* and the *English Learner's* versions list five words for each unit. Exercises are provided that will help students learn to spell and use the academic vocabulary words. Most units have a place where students can write other academic words that they come across in their reading. Make sure that students pick high-use academic words to add to their lists.

Words in Other Subjects

This page provides students with a place to write down academic words that they come across in other subjects. Many academic words can be used across disciplines. Help students record and define important words for study in other subjects. An example sentence will help reinforce the meaning.

Vocabulary Flash Cards

The first set of these cards gives Vocabulary Builder words from Unit 1. The front of the card shows the word. The back shows the definition, the part of speech, and an example sentence. Students should use the blank cards provided to study words from other units. Students can test themselves using these cards or test each other.

Vocabulary Fold-A-List

The first list uses Vocabulary Builder words from Unit 1. Students can test themselves by filling in the definition of each word and then folding the paper over to check their definitions. The other side of the list provides definitions for which students can fill in the appropriate words. Once again, by folding the paper over, they can check their answers. Blank Vocabulary Fold-A-List pages are provided for studying words in other units.

Commonly Misspelled Words

The word lists on these pages cause problems for many people. You may wish to assign some of the words to be studied with flash cards or fold-a-lists. The pages can also serve as a reference for students to look up words before writing them. Blanks are provided on the second page for students to add words that they frequently misspell.

Word Attack Skills

This section helps students to look for vowel-consonant patterns in words. Learning these patterns will enable to students to read longer words. Guide students to find the appropriate patterns to fill in the chart.

Mnemonics

Mnemonic devices can be very helpful in remembering how to spell words. They can also aid in remembering meaning. Work with students to make up mnemonic devices for words they have trouble with. Divide students into groups so that they can work together to create mnemonic devices.

Communication Strategies (*Adapted* and *English Learner's Versions*)

Learning how to communicate in a classroom setting does not come naturally to most students. Give them these sentence starters and phrases to help them discuss more effectively. Prompt students to use these phrases when answering or asking questions so that they become more natural.

Idioms (*English Learner's Version*)

An idiom is one of the hardest things for a non-native speaker to learn in a foreign language. Point out idioms in the readings for your English Learner students. Have them record and write sample sentences for the idioms in the chart provided.

Vocabulary Bookmarks

Students can cut out these bookmarks and use them to mark their place in their reading. They should record unfamiliar words that they come across on the bookmarks. Students can review those words using Flash Cards or Fold-A-Lists.

Vocabulary Builder Cards

These pages provide a place for students to record new vocabulary words that they encounter in the selections. Remind students to use these pages. Periodically, you may want to allow volunteers to share original sentences that contain the vocabulary words they have chosen.

ANSWERS TO UNIT 1

from The Giant's House
Elizabeth McCracken

"Desiderata"
Elizabeth McCracken

p. 4 Note-taking Guide
Sample response:
What Character Thinks: He wants to find a cure for his condition. He is impatient with Peggy for playing dumb.
What Others Say about Character: Giant describes him.

p. 5 Activate Prior Knowledge
Students may say that *gigantic, enormous, myth and folklore, Cyclops, Goliath, Hercules, Titan, Jack and the Beanstalk,* and *monstrous in strength and anger* come to mind.

p. 5 Fiction
Students should underline "first months of 1955."

p. 5 Fiction
Sample response: She pays attention to the kinds of books that library patrons check out. She is careful not to draw the wrong conclusions when people ask questions.

p. 6 Fiction
Students might underline the following: "I was certain that I could find more," "I got that familiar mania," "a good librarian is not so different from a prospector," "whole brain a divining rod," "blind faith in finding, even when hopeless," "it's out there—I can feel it," and "God wants me to find it."

p. 6 Stop to Reflect
Sample response: People connect *giant* with something strange and abnormal. Peggy does not want James to think of himself in this way.

p. 6 Fiction
Peggy has a problem figuring out what James really wants to know, not just what he says he wants to know. She also has a problem finding the information for him.

p. 6 Reading Check
Students should circle "height," "stature," "anthropometry," and "giant."

p. 7 Fiction
Sample response: The narrator is not part of Anna Swann's life. Anna Swann turns up in Peggy's research of "giants."

p. 7 Stop to Reflect
Sample response: She found the most information under the heading "human abnormalities." She does not want James to feel as if he is an oddity like the two-headed people described in the book.

p. 7 Fiction
Students should circle "worst book," "best book," "a terrible phrase," and "not exactly information, but interesting."

p. 8 Fiction
Sample response: Peggy's actions indicate that she is caring and kind.

p. 8 Fiction
Sample response: His conflict seems to be that he wants to find a cure for his height, which is impossible. He seems to be embarrassed by his height.

p. 8 Reading Check
Students should underline "Cures."

p. 9 Fiction
Students should circle the following: "Medicine, or operations, or something"; "That was a lie, I knew we didn't"; "Really, you should ask your doctor"; "I've asked a lot of doctors." Sample response: No matter how adults try to protect them, young people have to learn to accept what makes them unique. They can't change that.

p. 9 Reader's Response
Students may say that they would feel as if they could never get lost in a crowd and that people would always be looking at them. Some students might be worried that others would not get beyond physical appearances to learn about their true personalities.

p. 10 Note-taking Guide
Sample response:
To entertain: Martha's letters about serving The Dollies chicken are entertaining.
To persuade: Family papers are a useful part of a family's genealogy.
To reflect: Paper collections force a person to draw conclusions based on incomplete information.

p. 11 Activate Prior Knowledge
Students may say that a shopping list would tell them what people were eating or how much money they had. They might say that an old family letter would reveal information about a parent when he or she was younger.

p. 11 Nonfiction
Students should underline the following: "research on early ancestors and personal remembrances"; "stories, poems"; "letters she wrote to God"; "collection of family letters"; "diplomas of relatives"; "diaries"; "laundry lists."

p. 11 Stop to Reflect
Sample response: It helps her learn the truth, which lies somewhere in the middle of the two accounts of the same event. Hearing the story from different points of view allows her to understand more about the people involved in the story.

p. 12 Nonfiction
Students should list "litigious," "petty," and "vindictive."

p. 12 Nonfiction
Students should circle the following: "attorney," "small businessperson," "died at home at the age of 90." Students should double underline the following: "worried and somewhat doubtful person," "wonderful and complex woman," "didn't want to tell us in her diary anything she hadn't told us already."

p. 12 Reading Check
Students should underline "the major frustration is how incomplete everything is, how incomplete *people* are if you try to meet them this way."

p. 13 Nonfiction
Sample response: Some facts are that she read the horoscopes of everyone she might see during a single day, she believed in fortune cookies, she told her own fortune, and she bought lottery tickets.

p. 13 Nonfiction
Students may say that she is trying to show the broad range of family papers that she and other family members collect. Others may say that showing the competition between herself and her brother indicates that her purpose is to entertain.

p. 13 Nonfiction
Students should underline "quiet people."

p. 14 Nonfiction
Students should circle the following: "one of the most beautiful love letters I've ever read, full of delight for her person and for their love together"; "I never imagined my grandfather, my quiet careful grandfather, was the sort of man who'd write any kind of love letter, never mind this kind"; "I wondered whether she took it out and reread it from time to time, or whether she'd forgotten where she'd put it."

p. 14 Reading Check
Students should underline "Another letter. I'll put it with the others."

p. 14 Stop to Reflect
Sample response: The letter enables the author to see an entirely different side of her grandparents.

p. 14 Reader's Response
Some students will say that it has inspired them to begin collecting photographs and writings in order to keep a family history. Other students will be uninterested.

p. 15 Apply the Skills
1. Sample response: Peggy is not satisfied with the job she does for James. She likes to help people find information, rather than look it up for them. In James's case, though, Peggy looks up information because she cannot bring herself to say the word *giant*.
2. **Graphic Organizer**
Sample response:
Research Question: Can medicine stop a person's growth? How do very tall people deal with their problems?
Possible Sources: medical journal, Web site for tall people
3. Sample response: James's problem is affected by the setting of the story because

physical differences were not as accepted in 1955 as they are today. There were far fewer medical treatment options, and not much information was available in the small-town library.

4. Sample response: McCracken's main purpose is to reflect on the importance of documents and artifacts in learning about family history.

"The Washwoman"
Isaac Bashevis Singer

"New Directions"
Maya Angelou

p. 17 Graphic Organizer
Sample response:
"The Washwoman"
Detail: "That winter was a harsh one."
Question: Why does the author mention this detail?
Prediction: The bad weather will make it hard for the washwoman to do her job.
Verification: The prediction was accurate.

"New Directions"
Detail: "She placed stones in two five-gallon pails and carried them. . ."
Question: Why does the author mention this detail?
Prediction: She will carry food to the factories so that she can sell it.
Verification: The prediction was accurate.

p. 18 Reading/Writing Connection
Sample response: When people accomplish a difficult task, they may feel more confident. They want to demonstrate that they can finish the task. When people confront their problems, they become stronger.

p. 18 Note-taking Guide
Sample response:
Circle 1: cares for son
Circle 3: is not bitter about her life
Circle 4: is hardworking and dedicated to her job

p. 19 Apply the Skills
1. Sample response: She is dedicated to her work. It is important for her to finish what she starts.
2. Sample response: The author could have included information about her family history or what she does other than washing laundry.

3. **Graphic Organizer**
Sample response:
The Washwoman: She is small, old, and wrinkled; she does her work well and gives people a good price; she is not angry with her son.
The Washwoman's Son: He is rich; his mother embarrasses him; he does not invite her to his wedding.
4. Sample response: Prediction: The washwoman will not survive her walk home in the cold weather. Details: The washwoman is in bad health. The weather is rough, and it will be hard for her to make it home.

p. 21 Reading/Writing Connection
Sample response: When people initiate a change, they must prepare for the unexpected. To transform their lives, they must be willing to take risks. Later, they can analyze the result in order to measure their success.

p. 21 Note-taking Guide
Sample response:
Circle 1: resourceful
Circle 3: determined
Circle 4: reliable

p. 22 Activate Prior Knowledge
Students may say that they worked through a problem by keeping a positive attitude and thinking of the future.

p. 22 Literary Analysis
Students should underline "two toddling sons, very little money, a slight ability to read and add simple numbers. To this picture add a disastrous marriage and the burdensome fact that Mrs. Johnson was a Negro." Sample response: It moves the story forward because it is clear that Annie must find a way to take care of herself and her children.

p. 22 Reading Skill
Students may predict that Annie will use her cooking skills to provide for her family. Students might circle the following: "decided she would not go to work as a domestic"; "no possibility of being hired at the town's cotton gin or lumber mill"; "she could mix groceries well enough to scare hungry away and from starving a man."

p. 23 Reading Skill

Sample response: The author mentions this detail to give information about Annie's character. Annie's determination may pay off later.

p. 23 Stop to Reflect

Students may say that Johnson's achievement suggests that people can rise above circumstances. They might say that as long as the spirit is unbroken, it will find a way to survive.

p. 23 Reading Check

Students should circle "In years that stall became a store where customers could buy cheese, meal, syrup, cookies, candy, writing tablets, pickles, canned goods, fresh fruit, soft drinks, coal, oil, and leather soles for worn-out shoes."

p. 24 Literary Analysis

Students may say that Angelou uses Annie's story to show human potential. Sample response: The details about the obstacles Annie faces and her hard work to overcome them show what one can accomplish with work and initiative.

p. 24 Reader's Response

Students may find Annie's determination, creativity, and courage inspiring.

p. 25 Apply the Skills

1. Sample response: Annie is a smart businessperson. She knows how to plan ahead and how to attract customers.
2. Some students may say taking a new direction often can lead to a better life, so it is worth the risk of failure. Others may say that some new directions are too scary and not worth the risk.
3. **Graphic Organizer**
Sample response:
Annie Johnson: She will not leave her children. She is a good cook. She makes meticulous plans for her business.
Annie Johnson's Husband: He wants to study religion and preach. He is interested in studying with a minister who has an unmarried daughter. He takes most of the family's money when he leaves.
4. Sample response: She will make food and sell it to the factory workers. The factory workers will not be able to resist the smell

of the fresh meat pies. Annie will build a successful business.

Reading Informational Materials: Instructions: Recipes

p. 28 Reading Recipes

Sample response: Ingredients are needed before doing the steps in the recipe.

p. 28 Reading Skill

Students should circle "diced," "chopped," "minced," "thawed," and "cooked." These signal words tell readers what to do with the ingredients before combining them.

p. 28 Stop to Reflect

Sample response: Reading the recipe will help readers understand the amount of work the main character had to do.

p. 29 Stop to Reflect

Sample response: The sauce may not thicken as well if the ingredients are added first.

p. 29 Reading Check

Students should underline "In a separate saucepan, melt the butter or margarine over medium heat."

p. 29 Reading Skill

There are four steps.

p. 29 Reading Informational Materials

Sample response: Photographs and drawings of the steps would make it easier to follow. Numbering the steps would also make it easier to follow.

p. 30 Apply the Skills
Thinking About the Instruction

1. The finished turnovers are a half-moon shape.
2. Dipping the fork in flour when crimping the edges will help keep the fork from sticking to the dough.

Reading Skill

3. You need three tablespoons of celery.
4. You should whisk the sauce continually.
5. The last thing you are supposed to do before baking the pies is cut a slit in the top of each turnover.

"Sonata for Harp and Bicycle"
Joan Aiken

"The Cask of Amontillado"
Edgar Allan Poe

p. 31 Graphic Organizer
Sample response:
"Sonata for Harp and Bicycle"
Prediction: Jason will sneak into the building after quitting time.
Outcome: He climbs the fire escape and gets in.
Analysis of Prediction: The prediction was accurate.

"The Cask of Amontillado"
Prediction: Fortunato's love of wine will lead him into danger.
Outcome: A cask of amontillado brings Fortunato to his destruction.
Analysis of Prediction: The prediction was accurate.

p. 32 Reading/Writing Connection
Sample response: A good detective must anticipate what a criminal will do. Detectives can expose criminals by setting traps. A detective will not eliminate anything that seems suspicious while searching for clues.

p. 32 Note-taking Guide
Sample response:
Circle 1: a fire escape
Circle 2: a bicycle bell
Circle 3: the echoing sound of music
Circle 5: two eyes carved out of air
Circle 6: Ashgrove's new hair color

p. 33 Activate Prior Knowledge
Students may suggest the adventures of Sherlock Holmes. The main character is a smart, daring person who solves the mystery. The main character often has a sidekick.

p. 33 Literary Analysis
Sample response: The first sentence creates suspense by making readers wonder why no one is allowed in the building after 5 o'clock.

p. 33 Reading Skill
Students may predict that the new assistant will enter the building after 5 o'clock to find out what happens there at night. Students may underline "Why not?" and "But that was not the real reason."

p. 34 Literary Analysis
Jason wants to know the whole truth of the Grimes Buildings and Miss Golden will not tell him.

p. 34 Reading Skill
Students should circle "what she chiefly wanted was Mr. Jason Ashgrove, but he had not realized this yet." Sample response: There will be a romance between Jason and Miss Golden.

p. 34 Stop to Reflect
Sample response: Jason is curious and a little impatient. Miss Golden is frightened.

p. 35 Literary Analysis
Students should underline "'—fire escape,'" "'it's to do with a bicycle. A bicycle and a harp.'" Sample response: Foreshadowing builds on the suspense of the story by making the reader wonder what will happen next.

p. 35 Literary Analysis
Students might say that Jason carefully enters the building, which makes them think that something strange could happen at any moment.

p. 35 Reading Check
Students should underline "the words were lost" and "shaking her head."

p. 36 Reading Skill
Students may predict that Jason will encounter ghosts in the Grimes Buildings.

p. 36 Literary Analysis
Sample response: The passage is part of the rising action because it is still describing the central conflict.

p. 36 Reading Check
Students could underline "bell," "tinkle," "a long ring," "volley of rings together," and "waft of ice-thin notes."

p. 37 Reading Skill
Students may say that their predictions were correct. Reading on provided them with more information to verify their predictions.

p. 37 Stop to Reflect
Students may suggest that they would be afraid if they met a ghost. Others may say that meeting a ghost would be interesting.

p. 37 Literary Analysis

Students could circle "Miss Golden," "She would miss me," and "the syllables Berenice Golden lingered in the air." Sample response: The information foreshadows a romantic relationship between Jason and Berenice.

p. 38 Literary Analysis

Sample response: When Berenice tells Jason that he is doomed because he met the Wailing Watchman, it increases the suspense of the story by making readers wonder what could happen to Jason and why he is doomed.

p. 38 Reading Skill

Students may predict that Jason will try to help the ghosts resolve the conflict.

p. 38 Reading Check

Students should circle "his impeccable dark cut had turned to a stippled silver."

p. 39 Stop to Reflect

Students may say they thought Daisy probably felt very sad, and may have felt that it was her fault that Heron jumped off the balcony.

p. 39 Reading Skill

Students may suggest that Jason will try to arrange a meeting between the two ghosts.

p. 39 Reading Check

Students should circle "And anyone who meets the ghost of William Heron will himself, within five days, leap down from the same fatal fire escape."

p. 40 Reading Skill

Students may predict that he will give one bunch of roses to Miss Bell and the other to Berenice. He would give one to Miss Bell to try to resolve the conflict between her and Heron. He would give the other to Berenice because there is a romantic relationship growing between them.

p. 40 Literary Analysis

Sample response: This information foreshadows a possible meeting between Miss Bell and Heron.

p. 40 Stop to Reflect

Some students may say that it is worth the risk because he doesn't want to die now that he's started a relationship with Berenice.

p. 41 Literary Analysis

The resolution is that Miss Bell and Heron are reunited, and Jason breaks the curse by jumping off the fire escape with a parachute.

p. 41 Reading Skill

Students may say that their prediction that Jason and Berenice would start a relationship was proven correct. They might point to the fact that Jason and Berenice kiss and jump off the fire escape together as events that verify their predictions.

p. 41 Reading Check

Students should underline "We can go now."

p. 41 Reader's Response

Students may like the supernatural elements of the story. Others may find the romantic story unconvincing.

p. 42 Apply the Skills

1. Sample response: Miss Golden is more concerned. She assumes the curse cannot be escaped and is not aware of Jason's plan to try to break it.
2. Sample response: If Heron had not killed himself, he would have seen Miss Bell the next day. She would have explained about the alarm. They could have had a happy life together. Making rash decisions sometimes causes misunderstanding and hardship.
3. **Graphic Organizer**
Sample response:
Rising action: Jason hears hints about the fire escape, bicycle, and harp. Jason enters the Grimes Buildings at night.
Climax: Jason puts the wine and the roses outside the door of room 492.
Falling action: Jason and Ms. Golden leap from the fire escape.
4. Students may have predicted that someone was haunting the building and riding a bicycle.

p. 44 Reading/Writing Connection

Sample response:
1. Reading a scary story lets people safely participate in scary or dangerous situations.
2. A scary setting helps contribute to the overall mood of a story.
3. A reader can interpret a scary story by analyzing the author's purpose.

p. 44 Note-taking Guide
Sample response:
Event 2: Fortunato goes with Montresor to his palace. They wander through caves filled with wine bottles and bones.
Event 3: Montresor gets Fortunato drunk as they walk deeper into the caves.
Event 4: Montresor chains Fortunato to the wall of a small room. He walls up the room and leaves him to die.

p. 45 Apply the Skills
1. Sample response: Fortunato is proud that he knows so much about wine. His vanity makes him eager to judge the wine. Montresor appeals to this vanity.
2. Sample response: Montresor feels that Fortunato has insulted and injured him.
3. **Graphic Organizer**
Sample response:
Rising Action: Montresor invites Fortunato to the vaults to try his wine. Montresor chains Fortunato to the wall.
Climax: Montresor thrusts his torch into the crypt and hears only the jingling of the bells on Fortunato's costume.
Falling Action: Montresor replaces the bones to cover the crypt's entrance.
4. Students may have predicted that Montresor would use Fortunato's interest in wine to exact his revenge.

from A White House Diary
Lady Bird Johnson

"My English"
Julia Alvarez

p. 47 Graphic Organizer
Sample response:
from **A White House Diary**
Text Feature: title
Insight About Purpose: The title suggests a day-by-day or hour-by-hour account of personal experience.

"My English"
Text Feature: title
Insight About Purpose: The title suggests a personal relationship with the language.

p. 48 Reading/Writing Connection
Sample response: The words of Martin Luther King Jr. motivate me to seek justice in the world. The actions of Dr. King illustrate his philosophy of nonviolence. For me, these actions evoke feelings of courage and resolve.

p. 48 Note-taking Guide
Sample response:
Circle 2: fear
Circle 3: sympathy
Circle 4: sorrow
Circle 5: stress
Circle 6: anguish

p. 49 Activate Prior Knowledge
Students may say that many people keep diaries to record thoughts and feelings and reflect on the significance of events. A diary entry is a private place to express powerful emotions and personal thoughts.

p. 49 Reading Skill
Sample response: This subhead suggests that the author's purpose is to reflect and comment on the events that took place at this specific place and time.

p. 49 Literary Analysis
Sample response: At the time of the assassination, the author could not conceive that something so horrible could happen to the President. The events of the day had been happy and festive.

p. 49 Reading Check
Students should underline "HOSPITAL."

p. 50 Literary Analysis
Sample response: The phrase set off with dashes that refers to earlier information and the different words she uses to describe the Secret Service men's actions reinforces the writer's confusion and anxiety.

p. 50 Reading Skill
Sample response: The author included these names to suggest the closeness of those in the President's inner circle. It showed how the President's assassination impacted those people.

p. 50 Literary Analysis
Students should underline "remarkably calm and quiet." Sample response: Mrs. Johnson would notice these details because, as his wife, she was extremely close to Mr. Johnson. She was especially worried about his condition during this time.

p. 51 Literary Analysis

Sample response: The short, choppy sentences create a sad voice.

p. 51 Reading Skill

Sample response: The author's purpose was to show how deeply Kennedy's death affected those around him.

p. 51 Reading Check

Students should underline "I think it was from Kenny's face that I first knew the truth and from Kenny's voice that I first heard the words "The President is dead."

p. 52 Reading Skill

Students should underline "dress was stained with blood," "one leg was almost entirely covered with it," "her right glove was caked," "caked with blood," and "immaculate woman exquisitely dressed, and caked in blood." Sample response: The details help to show Mrs. Kennedy's shock and grief. They also emphasize the horror of what has happened.

p. 52 Literary Analysis

Sample response: Mrs. Johnson doesn't know what to say to Mrs. Kennedy. She feels sorry for her. The section also suggests that Mrs. Johnson and Mrs. Kennedy are not close.

p. 52 Reading Check

Students should circle "I want them to see what they have done to Jack."

p. 53 Stop to Reflect

Sample response: This comment means that he handles himself well under pressure. This would be a good quality because President Johnson was able to stay calm under pressure. As President, he may experience many pressures.

p. 53 Reader's Response

Students may say that reflection allows them to consider the significance of events in their lives. Others may say that reflection does not play a major part in their lives.

p. 54 Apply the Skills

1. Sample response: Mrs. Kennedy wants the nation to see evidence of the brutality of the assassination.
2. Sample response: It is a powerful comment. It makes Mrs. Kennedy's feelings clear.

3. Graphic Organizer

Sample response:
Word choice: "that immaculate woman exquisitely dressed, and caked in blood"
Attitude: "I went up to her, put my arms around her"
Sentence structure: "We got in. Lyndon told the agents to stop the sirens. We drove along as fast as we could."
4. Sample response: The general purpose was to inform readers about the assassination. Her diary offers details about events, the setting, and people's feelings.

p. 56 Reading/Writing Connection

Sample response:
1. In a democracy, people may debate ideas about the government without worrying about being punished.
2. Demonstrating against the government is often against the law in a dictatorship.
3. In a dictatorship, people are deprived of the right to speak out about abuses of their freedoms.

p. 56 Note-taking Guide

Sample response:
Spanish, Negative Memory: "I grew insecure about Spanish. My native tongue was not quite as good as English . . ."
Spanglish, Positive Memory: "*Butter, butter, butter, butter.* All day, one English word . . . But would you be needing some butter on your bread?"
Spanglish, Negative Memory: "At school, a Spanish word would suddenly slide into my English . . . 'Do you mean a *swing?*'"
English, Positive Memory: "I learned not to hear it as English, but as sense . . . I relaxed in this second language."

p. 57 Apply the Skills

1. Sample response: The teacher at Carol Morgan School took a more technical approach. She focused on teaching vocabulary and grammar.
2. Sample response: Her parents spoke English when they did not want the children to understand them. English kept Alvarez out of the conversation.

3. Graphic Organizer

Sample response:
Word Choice: "another strange tongue emerged from my papi's mouth or my mami's lips"

Attitude: "Supposing, just supposing . . . My mind would take off, soaring into possibilities . . . ."

Sentence Structure: "I thought about the snow. I saw how it might fall on the hills . . . on people out late walking on the streets . . . ."

4. Sample response: Her purpose was to inform and entertain. She wanted readers to know what it was like to learn English. She also wanted them to enjoy reading about her experience.

Reading Informational Materials: Spanish/English Dictionaries

p. 62 Apply the Skills
Thinking About the Spanish/English Dictionary

1. You would look under the heading Vowels in the Key to Spanish Pronunciation.
2. The Note on Spanish Gender would give you this information.

Reading Skill

3. The masculine form of the noun means *boundary mark* or *landmark.* The feminine form means *headless nail* or *brad.* Therefore, using one for the other would completely change the meaning.
4. Sample response: First, find the entry by looking up the keyword. Then, read the entry to find the part of speech. The italicized letter or letters immediately following the keyword shows you what the part of speech is.

"The Secret Life of Walter Mitty"
James Thurber

"Uncle Marcos"
Isabel Allende

p. 63 Graphic Organizer
Sample response:

"The Secret Life of Walter Mitty"

Story Event or Detail: Walter Mitty forgets what his wife wants him to purchase.

Possible Importance: Walter Mitty is so involved in his daydreams that he has trouble remembering details about his real life.

Author's Purpose: to show that Walter Mitty is out of touch with real life

"Uncle Marcos"
Sample response:

Story Event or Detail: Uncle Marcos performs strange exercises at night. He sleeps during the day in a hammock.

Possible Importance: Uncle Marcos is an unusual person.

Author's Purpose: to reveal Uncle Marcos's unique character.

p. 64 Reading/Writing Connection
Sample response: Daydreaming can enhance life by making it more interesting. A daydream might derive from real life events. Sometimes daydreams project a person's real-world experience into an imaginary world.

p. 64 Note-taking Guide
Sample response:

Daydream: Mitty is a surgeon saving a patient's life; Mitty is a criminal standing trial in a courtroom; Mitty is a pilot on a dangerous mission.

Reality: Mitty parks the car to buy overshoes; Mitty buys the biscuits and waits for his wife in a chair; Mrs. Mitty goes on another errand.

p. 65 Activate Prior Knowledge
Students may say they think about being a great athlete, singer, writer, actor, or mountaineer, or about becoming someone who is already famous.

p. 65 Literary Analysis
Students may say that the Commander is a flat character because he is a typical hero. They may underline "We're going through"; "He wore his full-dress uniform, with the heavily braided white cap pulled down rakishly over one cold gray eye"; "The Old Man ain't afraid of Hell.'"

p. 65 Reading Skill
Sample response: The phrase suggests that the author's purpose is to reveal the differences between the real world and the unseen, imaginary landscape of Mitty's mind.

p. 66 Literary Analysis
Sample response: Mrs. Mitty is a flat character. Readers only see her harping on Walter.

p. 66 Reading Skill

Sample response: In real life Walter Mitty is timid and uncertain. In his daydream others are uncertain, and he is in charge. The author's purpose is to show how Mitty wishes he could be.

p. 66 Stop to Reflect

Sample response: Mitty wants excitement, admiration, and respect.

p. 67 Literary Analysis

Sample response: Students should circle "They're so cocky" and "they think they know everything." Students may suggest that these statements show Mitty is insecure, or that he looks down on garagemen.

p. 67 Reading Skill

Sample response: The author's purpose may be to draw attention to Mitty's fumbling, forgetful nature in real life.

p. 67 Reading Check

Students should underline "Back it up, Mac! Look out for that Buick!"

p. 68 Stop to Reflect

Sample response: It is exciting and dangerous to think about being on trial. Mitty's daydreams allow him to find the excitement and danger he doesn't have in his real life.

p. 68 Reading Skill

Students may suggest that the author's purpose is to show how much Mitty wishes for excitement and danger. It may also be to show that Mitty has some pent-up frustration.

p. 68 Reading Check

Students should circle "Puppy biscuit."

p. 69 Reading Skill

Sample response: Mitty's daydreams are exciting. His daydream characters are adventurous and daring. Thurber uses Mitty's daydreams to show the human desire for adventure and escape from everyday life.

p. 69 Stop to Reflect

Some students may say that Mitty is not brave or forward in daily life. His daydreams allow him to be something he is not.

p. 69 Literary Analysis

Sample response: Mitty's responses show that he is a round character because he is standing up to his wife. His response "Does it ever occur to you that I am sometimes thinking," shows that some of the bravery and confidence from his daydreams is affecting his real life.

p. 70 Stop to Reflect

Sample response: People imagine doing things in daydreams that they may be too afraid to do in real life. They can do things in daydreams that might be dangerous, or might require them to be brave in a way that they really are not.

p. 70 Reader's Response

Some students may reply that they feel sorry for Mitty. He seems unhappy with his life, and his wife does not understand him. Others may think his character is funny or that a timid person gets what he deserves.

p. 71 Apply the Skills

1. Sample response: In his fantasy life, Mitty is landing a plane, doing surgery, testifying in court, fighting a war, and facing a firing squad.
2. Sample response: The tasks of Mitty's daily life are boring and dull. The tasks of Mitty's imaginary life are exciting.
3. **Graphic Organizer**
Sample response:
Detail from Daydream:
2. "Give me a fountain pen."
3. "Mitty let the man have it. . . ."
4. "We only live once, Sergeant."
5. "He faced the firing squad."
Desired Character Trait:
2. resourcefulness
3. gallantry
4. fearlessness
5. heroism
4. Sample response: Thurber's purpose may have been to show the positive effects of imagination in the face of everyday troubles and defeats.

p. 73 Reading/Writing Connection

Sample response: One event that may evolve is my brother's skateboarding story. People might enhance the details of the story to make it seem more exciting. People might alter the reality of the event by exaggerating actual events.

p. 73 Note-taking Guide

Sample response:

Box 2: Marcos's flying machine carries him over the mountains.

Box 3: Marcos and Clara have great success telling fortunes.

Box 4: Marcos dies of an African plague during his travels.

p. 74 Apply the Skills

1. Sample response: Clara's reaction shows her faith and positive attitude. It may also suggest her innocence about death and her belief in her uncle's powers of magic.

2. Sample response: People can learn that their successes depend on their own attitudes. Be adventurous; be yourself; develop your sense of wonder; seek adventure; be unique.

3. **Graphic Organizer**

Sample response:

Project or Adventure: performs alchemy; takes trips around the world; builds flying machine

Character Traits: curiosity; adventurous; inventiveness

4. Sample response: Uncle Marcos never allows failure or the attitudes of others to discourage him. Allende's purpose may have been to encourage readers to be true to themselves.

"The Jade Peony"
Wayson Choy

p. 78 Note-taking Guide
Sample response:

Plot: Grandmama resists going into hospital; she takes home remedies to treat her illness; Grandmama makes windchimes out of found objects; Grandmama and Sek-Lung hide collections under her bed until rest of family is out; Sek-Lung has missed school because of lung infection, but Grandmama educates him; Grandmama works on her last windchime; Grandmama dies of complications from pneumonia; Sek-Lung discovers that she has left him her prize possession, a peony carved out of jade.

Conflict: Grandmama's collection process embarrasses other members of family; Sek-Lung's fear and sorrow at losing Grandmama; the family's ties to its Chinese heritage versus its desire to be modern and Canadian; the other children's dislike of learning Mandarin

Characters: Grandmama: 83; artistic; treasures memories of the past, particularly of the juggler who gave her the jade peony; believes in signs. Sek-Lung: 8; illness has kept him at home; close ties with Grandmama. Two brothers, sister, father, and stepmother.

Setting: Keefer and Pender Streets, Vancouver, Canada; Grandmama dies in September

p. 79 Activate Prior Knowledge
Sample response: An older adult can play a supportive role for a young person. He or she can teach the young person skills or lessons about the past.

p. 79 Short Story
Students should circle "Vancouver" and "Canadians."

p. 79 Short Story
Sample response: The grandmother is stubborn, decisive, and old-fashioned. She believes in Chinese home remedies. She is tied to the past. Sample response: The conflict is internal because it is past versus present and Eastern versus Western ways of life.

p. 80 Short Story
Students should circle "wrinkled brow"; "wet with fever"; "small body seemed even more diminutive"; "palm felt plush and warm"; "the slender, old fingers boney and firm"; and "magically strong was her grip."

p. 80 Stop to Reflect
Sample response: Grandmama keeps the jade peony because it reminds her of the juggler. She can think of him and their time together every time she touches the pendant.

p. 80 Reading Check
Students should underline "promising to return."

p. 81 Short Story
Sample response: She is important to them, and they love her. However, they are embarrassed about the way she acts.

p. 81 Short Story
Sample response: The father is torn between being embarrassed by his mother and not wanting to be disrespectful of her. He is also concerned about her safety and the safety of Sek-Lung, who accompanies her.

p. 81 Reading Check
Students should underline "the back alleys of Keefer and Pender Streets, peering into our neighbors' garbage cans."

p. 82 Short Story
Students should underline "when the family was away at school or work, we brought them out and washed every item"; "Our greatest excitement"; and "she became my spiritual playmate." Sample response: Both are adventurous and detail-oriented. They appreciate small, insignificant things.

p. 82 Stop to Reflect
Sample response: They are sacred pieces because they are from a church. Also, Sek-Lung and his Grandmama had an abundance of beautiful pieces to choose from.

p. 82 Reading Check
Students should circle "My juggler . . . he never came back to me from Honan."

p. 83 Short Story
Sample response: The three older children go to a separate school to learn Mandarin Chinese in addition to the Cantonese that

they already speak. The children complain about learning a language that will not serve them well in the modern world. The children do not complain about learning Western languages like French, Latin, or German because these languages may be more useful to them in the future.

p. 83 Stop to Reflect
Sample response: Grandmama teaches him about the traditions of the past as well as the family history. She also teaches him how to prepare for death.

p. 83 Reading Check
Students may circle "Grandmama went on rocking quietly in her chair," "she complimented my mother on her knitting," "made a remark about the 'strong beauty' of Kiam's brushstrokes," and "All this babbling noise was her family torn and confused in a strange land: everything here was so very foreign and scientific."

p. 84 Short Story
Grandmama says that her spirit will be drawn to the windchime after she dies. Then, she will be able to come back to the house and tell her family goodbye.

p. 84 Stop to Reflect
Sample response: Grandmama's movements mesmerize the narrator. Her skill amazes him.

p. 84 Reading Check
Students should circle "That is my body fighting with Death. He is in this room now."

p. 85 Short Story
Sample response: The windchimes are a symbol of Grandmama's spirit because the chimes hold so many memories for her.

p. 85 Short Story
It reveals that he paid attention to even the smallest details about his grandmother. It shows that he felt a very strong connection to her.

p. 85 Stop to Reflect
He works harder so that he can fight off Death with his grandmother. He also wants to make sure that the chime is finished before she dies.

p. 86 Stop to Reflect
Sample response: She will remain in his memory. Every time he looks at the windchime, he will remember her and what she taught him.

p. 86 Short Story
Sample response: The white cat symbolizes the juggler from Grandmama's past. He had white hair and pink eyes, as well. Grandmama thinks he has finally come back to her.

p. 86 Stop to Reflect
Sample response: He is probably very upset. He knows that she is gone and that he will never see her alive again. He probably feels very lonely and afraid.

p. 87 Short Story
Sample response: The theme of this story is that family and traditions are important. A person must blend the past and the present together in order to be a complete person. Young people should honor older people for what they can teach. Sample response: The theme is implied. Choy never says that people should honor and respect the past. However, his relationship with his grandmother shows the theme. This relationship helps him understand who he is and what life is all about.

p. 87 Reading Check
Students should circle "Instead, caught between my fingers, was the small, round firmness of the jade peony."

p. 87 Reader's Response
Some students may agree that people should listen to their families' teachings. They may say that the past stays alive in memories, in the traditions that are handed down, and in objects passed along from one generation to the next. Without families to pass on memories, traditions, and objects, each generation would be lost. Other students may not agree and say that each person is new and different and must learn everything on his or her own.

p. 88 Apply the Skills
1. Sample response: Making windchimes was a recreation of Grandmama's past. Not only was she maintaining tradition in creating the chimes, but she was also using fragments from the past to make them.
2. Sample response: Sek-Lung supports and understands Grandmama's activities. He is happy to be included in the process. The father understands what she is doing, but it bothers him that she is not more modern in her approach to things. The rest of the family is embarrassed by her activities.

3. Graphic Organizer

Sample response:

What It Says: The family waits for a sign.

What It Means: Grandmama's rest is peaceful, and her family is safe.

Why It Is Important: These signs or omens signify the attachment to and belief in the past.

4. Sample response: The theme is that the past is important because it forms people's characters and a culture's shared understanding. Students should explain how the chart did or did not affect their understanding of the story's theme.

"American History"
Judith Ortiz Cofer

"The Most Dangerous Game"
Richard Connell

p. 90 Graphic Organizer

Sample response:

"American History"

Detail: The door was painted green, the color of hope.

Question: Why might a writer describe a door as having the color of an emotion?

Inference: The door stands for opportunity.

"The Most Dangerous Game"

Detail: The island that Rainsford swims to is described as forbidding.

Question: Why would an island be described this way?

Inference: This island must hold something evil.

p. 91 Reading/Writing Connection

Sample response:

1. A natural disaster can transform peoples' lives.

2. Bravery and kindness emerge when people go through a crisis.

3. People define themselves as survivors after living through a hurricane.

p. 91 Note-taking Guide

Sample response:

Story Detail 2: Even though she gets straight A's, the honors classes are not open to Elena.

Conflict 2: Elena is viewed as low class.

Story Detail 3: President Kennedy has just been killed, but Elena can't help but feel

excited about the time she is going to spend with Eugene.

Conflict 3: Elena's mother thinks that Elena is disrespectful. She warns Elena that she is headed for heartbreak.

Story Detail 4: Eugene's mother asks Elena whether she lives "there" in the El Building.

Conflict 4: Eugene's mother does not want Elena spending time with her son.

p. 92 Apply the Skills

1. Sample response: Elena thinks her home is large and noisy. She thinks Eugene's home is quiet and comfortable.

2. Sample response: Elena's tears are just for herself because she feels her personal pain more than she feels the pain of the national tragedy.

3. Graphic Organizer

Sample response:

Elena vs. another person: Elena's conflict with her mother's expectations of her occurs when Elena chooses to go to Eugene's house instead of going to church.

Elena vs. herself: Elena is bothered by her inability to "feel the right thing" for the dead president.

4. Sample response: One inference is the love that people had for the president. This inference is based on their anguish. Another inference is Elena's respect for learning. This inference is based on her interest in reading. A third inference is Eugene's mother's prejudice. This inference is based on her treatment of Elena.

p. 94 Reading/Writing Connection

Sample response:

1. I do not want to contemplate what could happen if a dangerous game became real.

2. Some people tried to simulate death and destruction.

3. Opponents might utilize real weapons to win the game.

p. 94 Note-taking Guide

Sample response:

Event 2: Rainsford meets Ivan and Zaroff on a nearby island.

Event 3: Rainsford refuses to hunt men and becomes the one who is hunted.

Final Event: Rainsford kills Zaroff.

p. 95 Activate Prior Knowledge
Students may suggest that playing a game with unfamiliar rules was confusing at first. They may say that they had to take time to learn how to play the game.

p. 95 Reading Skill
Sample response: The name suggests that the island is a deadly place for ships and sailors.

p. 95 Literary Analysis
Students may underline "The best sport in the world," "Not for the jaguar," "Who cares how a jaguar feels?" and "Perhaps the jaguar does." Sample response: Rainsford does not care about the feelings or fate of the animals. Whitney is sympathetic.

p. 95 Reading Check
Students should underline "the hunters and the huntees."

p. 96 Stop to Reflect
Sample response: Superstitions make people avoid certain situations. For instance, if you were superstitious about the number 13, you might be wary about taking an elevator to the thirteenth floor.

p. 96 Reading Check
Students should circle "someone had fired a gun three times."

p. 96 Reading Skill
Sample response: Someone or something is in danger or needs help.

p. 97 Literary Analysis
Sample response: Rainsford is confronted with the danger of the sea.

p. 97 Reading Skill
Sample response: Students may infer that Rainsford keeps his composure during a crisis. He does not panic.

p. 97 Reading Check
Students should underline "a high screaming sound, the sound of an animal in an extremity of anguish and terror" and "pistol shot."

p. 98 Reading Skill
Students may infer that Rainsford is an experienced outdoorsman.

p. 98 Literary Analysis
Students should list three of the following: "weeds were crushed down," "moss was lacerated," "one patch of weeds was stained crimson," and "it was an empty cartridge."

p. 98 Reading Check
Students should circle "All he knew was that he was safe from his enemy, the sea."

p. 99 Reading Skill
Students may infer that few, if any, visitors knock at this door.

p. 99 Reading Check
Students may circle "enormous," "lofty," "pointed towers," "palatial chateau," and "set on a high bluff."

p. 99 Reading Skill
Students should underline "He was dressed in uniform, a black uniform trimmed with gray astrakhan" and "Then Rainsford saw the man's free hand go to his forehead in a military salute, and he saw him click his heels together and stand at attention." Students may infer that Ivan has been in the military.

p. 99 Literary Analysis
The tension is resolved when Zaroff arrives.

p. 100 Stop to Reflect
Many students' impressions of the general will be positive at this point in the story. They might mention that he is polite and speaks with sophistication. They also might point out that he welcomes Rainsford into his home and offers Rainsford his own clothing to wear. However, some students might see the general's unusual looks and offhand remarks about "savage Cossacks" as warning signs.

p. 100 Reading Skill
Sample response: Zaroff is familiar with Rainsford's hunting abilities and seems to be excited about their shared interest in hunting. Rainsford can infer that the general is happy to welcome a fellow hunter to the island.

p. 100 Reading Check
Students should underline "I've read your book about hunting snow leopards in Tibet, you see."

p. 101 Literary Analysis
It was an external conflict. It was between the general and another character—the buffalo.

p. 101 Reading Skill
Sample response: Zaroff is a tough, determined man. He can handle a great deal of physical pain.

p. 101 Reading Check
Students should circle "Whenever he looked up from his plate he found the general studying him, appraising him narrowly."

p. 102 Reading Skill
Sample response: Students may infer that the animal he hunts is quite unusual. Some students may infer that Zaroff hunts other men.

p. 102 Reading Check
Students should underline "it was imprudent for an officer of the Czar to stay there."

p. 102 Reading Skill
Students may infer that Zaroff feels no guilt about hunting living things. He has no fear about hunting, either.

p. 103 Stop to Reflect
Students may agree with Zaroff. They may have grown bored with an activity when it was no longer challenging to them.

p. 103 Literary Analysis
Zaroff is struggling with a feeling within himself. He is losing interest in the only thing he loves.

p. 103 Reading Check
Students should underline "Hunting was beginning to bore me!"

p. 104 Reading Skill
Student will catch on at different points in the scene. They might circle "'But no animal can reason" or "Hunting? General Zaroff, what you speak of is murder.'"

p. 104 Literary Analysis
Rainsford realizes that Zaroff hunts men for sport. Conflict grows between the two men because Rainsford believes that this sport is murder.

p. 104 Reading Check
Students should circle "courage," "cunning," and "reason."

p. 105 Stop to Reflect
Students probably will disagree with Zaroff's philosophy. They may point out that this philosophy lacks compassion and understanding for the plights of others.

p. 105 Reading Skill
Zaroff tricks sailors. They think that the lights mean a clear and safe channel is ahead.

p. 105 Reading Check
Students should underline "They can reason, after a fashion. So they are dangerous."

p. 106 Stop to Reflect
Sample response: Zaroff calls the sailors "specimens" because he does not think of them as human beings. He hunts them like animals.

p. 106 Literary Analysis
Sample response: Either decision—to hunt or to face Ivan—is deadly. The internal conflict would be choosing whether to die quickly by Ivan's hands or whether to prolong their death in the hopes of escape.

p. 106 Reading Check
Student should underline "'They're from the Spanish bark San Lucar that had the bad luck to go on the rocks out there.'"

p. 107 Reading Skill
Most students will infer that the new heads are human heads. They may infer this on the basis of the previous conversation between Zaroff and Rainsford.

p. 107 Stop to Reflect
Students may say that their impression of Zaroff has changed. They no longer find him friendly, polite, or sophisticated. He is not a gentleman. He is a ruthless killer.

p. 107 Literary Analysis
He is restless and cannot quiet his thoughts. His conflict is internal because he is struggling with his own feelings.

p. 108 Literary Analysis
Students should circle "The general raised his thickets of eyebrows; he seemed hurt" and "General Zaroff's face suddenly brightened." Sample response: Zaroff's response to Rainsford's feelings will produce an external conflict.

p. 108 Reading Skill
Students may infer that Rainsford feels trapped and afraid. He probably is panicking.

p. 108 Reading Check
Students should underline "Last night I detected traces of my old complaint" and "Ennui. Boredom."

p. 109 Reading Skill
Students may infer that Lazarus was pulled into the quicksand and died.

p. 109 Stop to Reflect
Sample response: Zaroff wants the hunt to be as challenging as possible. He does not want it to be boring.

p. 109 Reading Skill
Sample response: The knife is for protection and self-defense. Rainsford is expected to survive in the wilderness in order to play the game.

p. 109 Reading Check
Students should underline "'I'll cheerfully acknowledge myself defeated if I do not find you by midnight of the third day,' said General Zaroff."

p. 110 Literary Analysis
Rainsford is trying to outwit General Zaroff.

p. 110 Reading Skill
Students may infer that Rainsford is confident in his skills.

p. 110 Stop to Reflect
Sample response: Rainsford is unable to fall asleep because he is nervous about his survival. He is also watchful. He does not want to be caught by Zaroff.

p. 110 Reading Check
Students should circle "fox" and "cat."

p. 111 Reading Skill
Students should circle "a smile spread over his brown face," "Very deliberately he blew a smoke ring," and "walked carelessly away."

p. 111 Stop to Reflect
Zaroff walks away because he wants the game to last longer. He wants to be challenged.

p. 111 Literary Analysis
Sample response: Rainsford is experiencing the struggle to stay calm. He feels terror, but he does not want it to get the better of him.

p. 112 Stop to Reflect
Sample response: Zaroff has found a worthy opponent. He is impressed with Rainsford.

p. 112 Literary Analysis
Some students may say that Zaroff is winning because he escapes the traps set for him and continues the hunt. Others may think Rainsford is winning because he has harmed Zaroff.

p. 112 Reading Check
Students should underline "Death Swamp."

p. 113 Reading Skill
He infers that he has successfully trapped the general. His inference is wrong. He has only trapped one of the dogs.

p. 113 Literary Analysis
Rainsford knows that the dogs are drawing near. He has only a short time to think of a way to get away from the dogs.

p. 113 Reading Check
Students should underline "It was the baying of a pack of hounds."

p. 114 Literary Analysis
Rainsford must decide whether to wait to be caught by Zaroff and his hounds or to jump into the sea. Either choice is almost certain death.

p. 114 Reading Skill
Sample response: The author may want readers to think that Rainsford has leaped to his death.

p. 114 Reading Check
Students should circle "But Ivan was not. The knife, driven by the recoil of the springing tree, had not wholly failed."

p. 115 Literary Analysis
The conflict is resolved through a hands-on fight between the two men. Rainsford wins.

p. 115 Reading Skill
Students may infer that Rainsford is at peace. He has successfully overcome his enemy and won the game.

p. 115 Reading Check
Students should circle "'I am still a beast at bay . . . Get ready, General Zaroff.'"

p. 115 Reader's Response
Many students will be satisfied with the outcome of the story. Readers often naturally sympathize with Rainsford because of Zaroff's extreme behavior.

p. 116 Apply the Skills
1. Students may like Rainsford's courage, intelligence, and self-control under pressure. They may not like his attitude about hunting.

2. Sample response: Zaroff forces Rainsford to be the prey of a hunt. If Rainsford hunts, he will certainly think about the prey's experience.

3. **Graphic Organizer**
Sample response:

Rainsford vs. nature: almost drowning at start of story; almost dying in jungle and swamp

Rainsford vs. himself: not panicking when thrown from boat; controlling anxiety during hunt

4. Sample response: Whitney's desire to relate to the animals shows that he is a more sensitive man than Rainsford.

Reading Informational Materials: Signs and Instructions

p. 119 Reading Signs and Instructions
Students should circle the small falling person in the sign and underline the words "CAN CAUSE SERIOUS INJURIES OR DROWNING."

p. 119 Reading Skill
Sample response: Students may say that the picture does give a clear message because they can clearly see that a person is sucked under by a huge wave. They may say that the words "WARNING" and "HIGH SURF" should be as big as they are because they attract attention and relay the main message quickly.

p. 119 Stop to Reflect
Sample response: The subheadings divide the information into sections and tell what each section will address. A person on the beach might not want to take much time to read the information. These subheadings help readers organize and read information quickly.

p. 119 Reading Check
Students should circle "twenty-five feet plus" and "fifteen feet plus."

p. 120 Reading Skill
Sample response: The sign shows a person swimming in rough water. The sign is a little unclear. Someone may have to read the words to understand what the sign means.

p. 120 Reading Check
Students should underline "YOU COULD BE SWEPT AWAY FROM SHORE AND COULD DROWN."

p. 120 Reading Informational Materials
Sample response: Signs and instructions should be easy to understand because everyone needs to be able to read the message. Some people cannot read difficult text. Some people will not take the time to read a sign with too many words.

p. 121 Apply the Skills
Thinking About the Sign and Instruction
1. Sample response: The simple pictures suggest danger without need for words.
2. Sample response: People who are very good surfers and who are familiar with big waves might be safe.

Reading Skill
3. Sample response: Large, powerful waves are the danger shown in the first sign.
4. Sample response: A "strong current" is water that is moving so quickly that it can overpower people who are trying to walk or swim against it. It is dangerous because people can be swept into deep water, and then they could drown or be seriously injured.

"The Gift of the Magi" O. Henry

"The Interlopers" Saki

p. 122 Graphic Organizer
Sample response:
"The Gift of the Magi"
Detail: Jim is shocked when he sees Della's hair.
My Experience: People are often speechless when something happens that they do not expect.
Inference: Jim was not expecting Della to cut her hair, so his gift may be something that she can use in her hair.

"The Interlopers"
Detail: The two men are alone when they get caught under the tree.
My Experience: It would take time to find people in a large forest. It would take even longer if you did not suspect that something was wrong.
Inference: The two men will not be rescued.

p. 123 Reading/Writing Connection

Sample response:

1. Some people might adjust the amount they spend on gifts.

2. A person can embody love simply by doing a special favor for a loved one.

3. Someone can emphasize love by giving a family member a treasured possession.

p. 123 Note-taking Guide

Sample response:

Della Action: Della sells her hair to buy the chain.

Unexpected Result: Della receives combs for hair she no longer has.

Jim Christmas Gift Idea: hair combs

Action: Jim sells his watch to buy the combs.

Unexpected Result: Jim receives a watch chain for a watch he no longer has.

p. 124 Activate Prior Knowledge

Students may list several types of sacrifices. For example, they may have sacrificed free time by taking a job to be able to afford something they wanted. They may have given up something they were accustomed to, such as new clothes or video games.

p. 124 Literary Analysis

Della only will be able to afford an inexpensive present for Jim. Students may underline "One dollar and eighty-seven cents" or "sixty cents of it was in pennies."

p. 124 Reading Skill

Sample response: Jim wants to be successful. He wants people to respect him.

p. 124 Reading Check

Students should circle "One dollar and eighty-seven cents. And the next day would be Christmas."

p. 125 Stop to Reflect

Students may say that people give expensive gifts because they think it shows how much they care. Others may say that people want to give expensive gifts because they want to show off.

p. 125 Reading Skill

Sample response: Della may be planning to do something with her hair to earn money. She may cut and sell it. Students may underline "she pulled down her hair and let it fall

to its full length," "the other was Della's hair," and "Hair Goods of All Kinds." Students may suggest that from their knowledge and experience they know that people are willing to make sacrifices when they love someone.

p. 125 Reading Check

Students could circle "Twenty dollars a week doesn't go far. Expenses had been greater than she had calculated."

p. 126 Stop to Reflect

Della feels excited. She is happy that she cut her hair for Jim's present. Students may suggest that they have had similar experiences. They may say they felt excited as well.

p. 126 Reading Skill

Students may say that Della is nervous about how Jim will feel about the way she looks. Students may underline "If Jim doesn't kill me . . . " on this page and "Please God, make him think I am still pretty" on the next page.

p. 126 Reading Check

Students should circle " Will you buy my hair?" "I buy hair," or "Twenty dollars."

p. 127 Reading Skill

Jim is shocked by Della's haircut.

p. 127 Reading Skill

Students may infer that Jim keeps asking about Della's hair because he planned a gift that has something to do with her hair.

p. 127 Reading Check

Students should underline "Please God, make him think I am still pretty."

p. 128 Literary Analysis

Jim's gift is ironic because Della cannot use the combs on her short hair.

p. 128 Reading Skill

Sample response: He realizes how ironic the situation is. He appreciates how much she loves him.

p. 128 Reading Check

Students should circle the paragraph that begins "Don't make any mistake, Dell."

p. 129 Literary Analysis

The ending is a surprise because neither Della nor the reader knows that Jim has sacrificed something, too.

p. 129 Stop to Reflect
Sample response: The author does not really think they are foolish, though they might appear that way to others. The couple is foolish in many respects, such as being financially irresponsible. But they are wise in love.

p. 129 Reader's Response
Some students may think they are foolish to spend the money. Other students may think that spending the money is wise because it shows that they are willing to sacrifice for each other.

p. 130 Apply the Skills
1. Della's action shows that she is generous and self-sacrificing.
2. Sample response: Wisdom is the understanding that some things, such as love and kindness, are more important than money or expensive things.
3. Sample response: This situational irony conveys the idea that life is not predictable. It also shows that gifts are not the most reliable means for showing someone that you love them.
4. Students may be familiar with characters who were in love from books, television, or movies. These characters were willing to sacrifice for each other, as well.

p. 132 Reading/Writing Connection
Sample response:
1. To end a feud, the groups involved could <u>participate</u> in a peace conference.
2. A court could <u>verify</u> which of the feuding parties owns the <u>land</u>.
3. Participants could <u>focus</u> more on ending rather than fighting the <u>feud</u>.

p. 132 Note-taking Guide
Sample response:
Detail: The two families have hated each other for three generations.
What the Reader Expects: Ulrich and Georg will never be able to resolve their conflict.
What Actually Happens: They resolve their conflict.
Detail: Ulrich offers to end the feud.
What the Reader Expects: Georg will refuse Ulrich's offer.
What Actually Happens: Georg agrees to end the feud. The men decide to become friends.

Detail: Nine or ten figures respond to their cries for help.
What the Reader Expects: The men will be rescued. They will surprise everyone when they announce that they are friends.
What Actually Happens: The figures are wolves.

p. 133 Apply the Skills
1. Georg does not accept the court's decision.
2. Sample response: Their present situation makes the two men realize that their dispute is a waste of time.
3. Sample response: One message is that people should resolve their differences while they have the opportunity.
4. Sample response: Saki probably intended readers to infer that the men are proud and stubborn. He may have also wanted readers to infer that the unexpected situation makes the men see how good their lives could have been without the feud.

"The Necklace"
Guy de Maupassant

"Rules of the Game"
Amy Tan

p. 135 Graphic Organizer
Sample response:
"The Necklace"
Narrator's comments: "She suffered constantly, feeling that all the attributes of a gracious life, every luxury, should rightly have been hers."
What They Show About the Character: Madame Loisel makes herself miserable because she was not born rich.
Character's thoughts and words: " . . . there's nothing more humiliating than to look poverty-stricken among a lot of rich women."
What They Show About the Character: She is very sensitive about her appearance and social status.
Character's actions: "She remained in her evening dress, too weak to go to bed, sitting crushed on a chair, lifeless and blank."
What They Show About the Character: She falls apart in a crisis.
Character's appearance: "Disheveled, her skirts askew, with reddened hands, she spoke in a loud voice . . ."

What They Show About the Character:
The hard work and poverty she endures have made her indifferent to her appearance.
What others say or think about the character: "Why, I thought you'd be pleased, dear. You never go out and this would be an occasion for you, a great one!"
   What They Show About the Character: She is difficult to please. Even a party invitation makes her dissatisfied.

"Rules of the Game"
Narrator's comments: " . . . she asked without a trace of knowing how wicked I was being"
What They Show About the Character: The narrator's comments reveal that Waverly is being sarcastic.
Character's thoughts and words: "I read the rules and looked up all the big words in a dictionary . . . I studied each chess piece, trying to absorb the power each contained." "By my ninth birthday, I was a national chess champion."
What They Show About the Character: Waverly's thoughts and words reveal her intelligence.
Character's actions: "I raced down the street, dashing between people, not looking back as my mother screamed shrilly, "Meimei! Meimei!"
What They Show About the Character: Waverly's actions show how Waverly argues with her mother.
Character's appearance: "In my crisp pink-and-white dress with scratchy lace at the neck, one of two my mother had sewn for these special occasions . . . "
What They Show About the Character: Waverly's special dresses for tournaments show her mother's involvement in her life.
What others say or think about the character: "Is shame you fall down nobody push you.'"
What They Show About the Character: Waverly's mother thinks that Waverly is talented enough to play in competitions.

p. 136 Reading/Writing Connection
Sample response:
1. Some people think expensive things identify them as having a successful and happy life.

2. Buying expensive items may cause some people to exceed their financial limits.
3. Many people think that expensive possessions will help them obtain admiration from others.

p. 136 Note-taking Guide
Sample response:
Box 2: She goes to the party and loses the necklace
Box 3: The Loisels replace the necklace and work ten years to pay for it.
Final Event: Madame Loisel learns the secret of the necklace.

p. 137 Activate Prior Knowledge
Students may describe feeling upset, panicked, and regretful.

p. 137 Literary Analysis
Sample response: The author says that the young woman is attractive but poor.

p. 137 Reading Check
Students may circle "feeling that all the attributes of a gracious life, every luxury, should rightly have been hers"; "the poverty of her rooms . . . caused her pain"; "she dreamt of thick carpeted reception rooms"; and "she dreamt of great drawing rooms."

p. 137 Literary Analysis
The comment reveals that the husband is a happy and contented person.

p. 138 Reading Skill
These visits fill her with despair because she wants her life to be like her friend's life.

p. 138 Stop to Reflect
Students may say that Madame Loisel should give up her desire for riches. She should not pretend to be something she is not. She will only set herself up for more unhappiness.

p. 138 Reading Skill
The husband is surprised because he thought that his wife would be excited to go to the party.

p. 138 Reading Check
Students should circle "I haven't a thing to wear. How could I go?"

p. 139 Literary Analysis
He loves his wife. He is willing to make great sacrifices for her happiness.

p. 139 Reading Skill

Students may underline "I hate not having a single jewel, not one stone, to wear." Sample response: What will she do about not having a jewel to wear?

p. 139 Reading Check

Students should circle "That didn't satisfy her at all."

p. 140 Literary Analysis

Students should underline "her heart started beating with overwhelming desire," "her hands trembled," and "gazing at herself ecstatically." Sample response: This indirect characterization shows that Madame Loisel desires nice things. She loves seeing herself wearing fine jewelry.

p. 140 Reading Skill

Sample response: What will happen when the evening is over and she has to return to the reality of her life?

p. 140 Reading Check

Students should circle "She felt this and wanted to escape quickly so that the other women, who were enveloping themselves in their rich furs, wouldn't see her."

p. 141 Stop to Reflect

Sample response: The wife is sad that her wonderful evening is over. The husband is sad because he has to get up early for work, and he knows that he will be tired.

p. 141 Reading Skill

Sample response: What will happen if they cannot find the necklace? Students may underline "He got up, thunderstruck."

p. 141 Reading Check

Students should circle "She took off her wraps before the mirror so that she could see herself in all her glory once more. Then she cried out. The necklace was gone; there was nothing around her neck."

p. 142 Literary Analysis

Sample response: Monsieur Loisel's efforts to recover the necklace show that he is a determined man of action. Madame Loisel's depression and inactivity show that she does not respond well to a crisis.

p. 142 Reading Skill

Sample response: They must replace the necklace.

p. 142 Reading Check

Students should circle "He would borrow the rest."

p. 143 Reading Skill

Students should underline "Mightn't she have taken Madame Loisel for a thief?"

p. 143 Literary Analysis

Sample response: Madame Loisel has accepted the hard work she has to do. She is less concerned with her looks and her place in society. Students may circle the passage beginning with "Madame Loisel came to know the . . . " and ending with " . . . of her pitiful funds."

p. 143 Reading Check

Students should underline "They dismissed the maid; they moved into an attic under the roof."

p. 144 Literary Analysis

Sample response: Madame Loisel's attitude and appearance have changed tremendously. However, she still fondly remembers the party from so long ago. This passage is an example of indirect characterization. The writer describes Madame Loisel's behavior, thoughts, and physical appearance.

p. 144 Reading Skill

Sample response: Seeing Madame Forestier reminds Madame Loisel of the cause of her hardships.

p. 144 Stop to Reflect

Students may suggest that she wanted Madame Forestier to know what the Loisels endured to replace the necklace.

p. 145 Literary Analysis

Sample response: The author shows Madame Forestier as kind and compassionate. She feels bad that the Loisels worked so hard to replace imitation diamonds.

p. 145 Reading Check

Students should circle the last paragraph of the story.

p. 145 Stop to Reflect

Sample response: Madame Forestier should sell the diamond necklace and repay Madame Loisel. Madame Loisel and her husband deserve to live comfortably after ten years of unnecessary work.

p. 145 Reader's Response

Many students will enjoy the irony of the situation. They may reply that they do not like people who pretend to be something they are not or who are too proud to admit to a mistake. Other students may feel sorry for Madame Loisel. They may think that the consequences were too severe.

p. 146 Apply the Skills

1. Sample response: Monsieur Loisel is much less selfish and much more loving than his wife.
2. Sample response: Madame Loisel loses her charm and beauty. She becomes old before her time. She also learns to work hard.
3. Sample response: Madame Loisel is interested in material possessions and appearances. She is selfish. An example of indirect characterization is her selfish use of the money her husband saved. She uses the money to buy herself a new dress for the party.
4. **Graphic Organizer**
Sample response:
Causes: She is invited to a party; she does not want to look poor.
Effects: She looks beautiful at the party; she loses the necklace; she lives in poverty in order to repay the cost of the necklace.

p. 148 Reading/Writing Connection

Sample response: Games can induce feelings such as satisfaction, anger, or happiness. These feelings may initiate friendships that cross age or culture barriers. Games can also evoke conflicts that divide friends or family members.

p. 148 Note-taking Guide

Sample response:
Event 2: Waverly learns to play chess.
Event 3: Waverly wins many tournaments.
Climax: Waverly runs away when she and her mother quarrel.
Resolution: She thinks about her next move in this mother-daughter conflict.

p. 149 Apply the Skills

1. Sample response: She pretends to be weaker than she is.
2. Sample response: Waverly will win the game of doing what she wants to do. She has learned from her mother.

3. The conversation is an example of indirect characterization. Waverly's mother does not realize that Waverly is being wicked. Her mother tells her that the Chinese do the best torture. These remarks show the cultural and generational differences between the two people.
4. **Graphic Organizer**
Sample response:
Causes: Two causes for her success are her intelligence and her mother's teachings.
Effects: Three effects of her success are increases in self-confidence, her status, and her mother's pride.

"Blues Ain't No Mockin Bird" Toni Cade Bambara

"The Invalid's Story" Mark Twain

p. 151 Graphic Organizer

Sample response:
"Blues Ain't No Mockin Bird"
Cause: The twins ask whether the man in the story jumped.
Mental Picture: Granny stares at the twins.
Effect: Granny gets angry about the twins' responses to her story.

"The Invalid's Story"
Cause: The smell in the train becomes overwhelming.
Mental Picture: Thompson's face is buried in a handkerchief. The narrator's face has no color.
Effect: The men smoke cigars to try to cover up the smell.

p. 152 Reading/Writing Connection

Sample response: I would intervene if I saw someone abusing an animal. Laws should oblige people to respect animal rights. I write letters to a newspaper to promote the protection of endangered animals.

p. 152 Note-taking Guide

Sample response:
Beginning Event: The two men offend Granny.
Box 2: Granddaddy arrives.
Box 3: Granddaddy brings down the hawk.
Box 4: Granddaddy disables the camera.
Box 5: The cameramen back off.
Final Event: Granny goes back to making cakes.

p. 153 Activate Prior Knowledge
Students may describe a disapproving scowl or a glare that the older person has.

p. 153 Literary Analysis
The use of the words *ain't* and *no* and the dropping of the final *g* in words show that this story is written in dialect.

p. 153 Reading Skill
Students may suggest that Granny's smile, eyebrow movement, and way of saying "Good mornin" help them visualize the camera crew's effect on her.

p. 153 Reading Check
Students should underline "They're makin movie pictures."

p. 154 Stop to Reflect
Sample response: These two men do not seem like they are individuals.

p. 154 Literary Analysis
The dialogue shows that the men are disrespectful of Granny. She feels insulted and angered by the men.

p. 154 Reading Check
Students should underline "Granny said nuthin."

p. 155 Literary Analysis
Students should circle "hatin," "standin," and "wonderin."

p. 155 Reading Skill
Students should underline "people wouldn't pay her for things like they said they would," "Mr. Judson bringin us boxes of old clothes and raggedy magazines," and "Mrs. Cooper comin in our kitchen and touchin everything and sayin how clean it all was." Sample response: Moving makes Granddaddy angry.

p. 155 Reading Check
Students should underline "About this lady Goldilocks who barged into a house that was't even hers."

p. 156 Literary Analysis
Sample response: It probably means he would have slapped her on the side of the head.

p. 156 Reading Skill
Students should underline "Cathy say it's because he's so tall and quiet and like a king. And people just can't stand it." People tend to

abuse Granddaddy. Sample response: They cannot bear his formidable presence.

p. 156 Reading Check
Students should circle the sentence "So he nails the bird to the toolshed door, the hammerin crackin through the eardrums."

p. 157 Reading Skill
The arrival of the hawk frightens the film crew. Granddaddy stands straight and watches the hawk. He does not appear to be afraid.

p. 157 Stop to Reflect
Students should look at "'Good day, gentlemen'" and circle "Like he'd invited them . . . it was time to go." Sample response: Granddaddy's greeting confuses the men because, although he is being calm and polite, he is still asking them to leave.

p. 157 Reading Check
Students should circle "Granddaddy Cain straight up and silent . . . the hammer off his wrist."

p. 158 Literary Analysis
Smilin and Camera are engaged in dialogue. Sample response: The dialogue shows they are nervous and afraid of Granddaddy.

p. 158 Stop to Reflect
Sample response: Granddaddy has every right to ruin the film. The film crew did not get permission to come on their land and film.

p. 158 Reading Skill
Sample response: By visualizing the scene, one can see the men trying to gather the spilled film as they back away. The men's reaction shows that Granddaddy's opening of the camera has made them nervous and afraid.

p. 158 Reading Check
Students should circle "We puttin together a movie for the food stamp program . . . filmin all around these parts."

p. 159 Reading Skill
Tyrone puts up his hand so that Cathy will notice him and possibly place him in her story.

p. 159 Reading Check
Students should underline "There's this story I'm goin to write one day."

p. 159 Reader's Response

Most students will probably sympathize with the family because their rights are being violated. Some students may have sympathy for the two men because, although they go about it wrong, they are trying to do their job.

p. 160 Apply the Skills

1. Some students may choose Granddaddy because he is tall and dignified. Other students may choose the narrator because she is perceptive.

2. **Graphic Organizer**

Sample response:

Hawks and Cameramen: The cameramen swoop down on people. They are frightening and threatening. They stay together.

Hawks and Granddaddy: Granddaddy is threatening. He tries to protect his mate and drive away the threatening men.

What the Hawks Represent: The hawks represent Granny and Granddaddy. The intruders have walked onto Granny's property (as into a hawk's territory). Granddaddy, her mate, is trying to protect her.

3. The grammar shows dialect by the phrase "always got," instead of "have," and "teaches steady," instead of "steadily." The spelling shows dialect with the *g* dropped from "somethin."

4. Sample response: The men have taken motion pictures of his family.

p. 162 Reading/Writing Connection

Sample response: Seeing how characters analyze a problem might help readers deal with real-life situations. A reader might focus on how the characters find a solution. Finding humor in these stories can verify the importance of keeping a sense of humor.

p. 162 Note-taking Guide

Sample response:

2: The coffin is switched with a box of guns and a block of cheese.

3: The narrator and Thompson stand on the platform to avoid the smell.

p. 163 Apply the Skills

1. Thompson says the corpse "wants to travel alone" because it is creating the bad smell.

2. The contrast between a serious and a harmless source of the odor is humorous.

3. Graphic Organizer

Sample response:

Sad Details: The narrator's good friend died. The dead man's parents are sad.

Humorous Details: The narrator and Thompson mistake the cheese odor for the smell of a dead body. Thompson gasps over the box near the cheese.

Evaluation: The story is funny because of all of the confusion and drama a simple cargo mix-up causes.

4. Students might say that the dialect makes the speaker come alive. The dialect makes the characters and setting more vivid because it makes them seem more realistic.

5. The smell makes the men leave the car.

Reading Informational Materials: Brochures

p. 166 Reading Skill

Students should circle the map and the hours and admission information. Sample response: They are located next to each other to help people easily find the information needed to visit the museum.

p. 166 Stop to Reflect

Brochures often are meant to persuade people to come to a place. The maps help people get to the place.

p. 166 Reading Brochures

Sample response:

Barber Junction: Visitors can get tickets here.

Roundhouse: Visitors can see trains, exhibits, videos, and working shops here.

Spencer Shops: This section gives a history of the museum location.

p. 167 Reading Skill

Students should write "A" next to "The Museum." Students may write "B" next to "Barber Junction," "The Robert Julian Roundhouse," or "Historic Spencer Shops." Students may write "C" next to "Spencer Shops' mission was . . ." or "Southern Railway was one of the first U.S. rail systems . . ."

p. 167 Reading Check

Students should underline "While the museum is young—founded in 1977—the story of the Spencer Shops reaches back more than one hundred years."

p. 167 Reading Brochures

Sample response: The man in the picture seems happy. His happiness could make the museum seem like a fun place to visit.

p. 167 Reading Informational Materials

Sample response: This brochure shows the reader the different activities that they could choose from when visiting the museum.

p. 168 Apply the Skills
Thinking About the Brochure

1. Sample response: Placing learning opportunities earlier would leave the reader wondering what there was to learn about.
2. Sample response: This building was chosen so that people could both learn history about trains and see train repairs taking place.

Reading Skill

3. Sample response: It is a good idea to put the map on the front page because it is easily and quickly seen there. The map is more useful to the reader on the first page.
4. You would look under the heading "Learning Opportunities."

ANSWERS TO UNIT 3

"Before Hip-Hop Was Hip-Hop"
Rebecca Walker

p. 171 Note-taking Guide
Sample response:
Circle 1: Hip-hop helped bridge the gap between different cultures.
Circle 2: The revolution of hip-hop affected music, fashion, and dance.
Circle 3: Hip-hop created new words and slang.
Circle 4: Hip-hop taught her creativity, community, and self-confidence.

p. 172 Activate Prior Knowledge
Students may say that Ronald Reagan was President, followed by George Bush. They may say that they think of slap bracelets, neon-colored clothing, home video and cable television, *Sixteen Candles* and *The Breakfast Club*, MTV, moonwalking, the Phillies winning their first World Series, the Rubik's Cube, video games, designer jeans, Smurfs, or Cabbage Patch dolls. Some of the music from the era includes Bruce Springsteen, Devo, Duran Duran, and Madonna.

p. 172 Nonfiction
Students should underline "kids," "they'll," "spit out," "EO," "ATL"; "West Side," "glossiest," "flossiest," "can't," "latest 'steelo,'" "cocked," "old school," and "sodas." Sample response: Walker chose informal English to reflect the language of hip-hop culture.

p. 172 Reading Check
Students should underline "The vast empire of hip-hop amazes me because I knew hip-hop before it was hip-hop. I was there when it all began."

p. 173 Nonfiction
Sample response: She wants her readers to get an idea of how broad her tastes in music were—from rock to heavy metal to soul to disco. Her love of many kinds of music shows that she was open to different styles.

p. 173 Nonfiction
Sample response: The author's tone is friendly and conversational. By asking and answering her own question and by saying that others "looked at you like you were crazy," she is speaking to her readers as peers.

p. 173 Stop to Reflect
Students may say that they take their friends with them to buy clothes so that they can get their opinion. Students may also say that their friends introduce them to new music and new bands.

p. 174 Nonfiction
Sample response: Both examples show the unexpectedness of what the author encountered in hip-hop culture. The author did not expect the reserved Asian American girl to sneak a bright red sweatsuit under her coat. In the same way, she did not expect the preppy boy to support all religions.

p. 174 Nonfiction
Sample response: She uses expository, narrative, and descriptive writing. She wants to explain and inform about hip-hop culture. She also wants to tell the story of how after-school and weekend activities led to its development. She describes the dancers so that readers will be able to "see" the dancers even if they have never seen breakdancing.

p. 174 Reading Check
Students should underline "the way they infused their words with attitude and drama, moving their hands and heads as they spoke," "the way many of them walked and ran and joked with each other with confidence and bravado" and "what they wore and how they wore it."

p. 175 Nonfiction
Students could underline "breakers," "poppers and lockers," "moonwalked," "breaking," "capping on," "hipping," "dope," and "fresh." Sample response: The slang adds to her informal, friendly approach. Readers understand that the author and the reader are equals.

p. 175 Nonfiction
Sample response: Walker describes how hip-hop was about more than music. The hip-hop culture affected clothes, language, and where people spent time.

p. 175 Stop to Reflect
Students may suggest that other forms of art, such as painting and sculpture, bring people together. Students may also suggest that helping others who are less fortunate will bring many people together.

p. 176 Stop to Reflect

Students may agree with Walker and say that they do not like hip-hop music because it is sometimes violent and sometimes contains foul language. Students may describe hip-hop as a series of fast beats that repeat underneath one or more voices that are speaking very quickly and often in rhyme.

p. 176 Nonfiction

Students may say that Walker does not mention examples of good hip-hop today. She seems to label all hip-hop as pre-packaged. This would make her view a biased one.

p. 176 Reading Check

Students should circle "art could bring people together and make them forget their differences," "how good it could feel to move with a 'posse,'" "I could express myself and communicate with others through what I wore and how I walked and what music I liked," "it doesn't take money or a special degree to transform the grit and drive and hardness of the city into something beautiful," "Loyalty. Community. Self-confidence. Creativity," and "more about real life than anything I learned that year in class."

p. 177 Nonfiction

Students may underline "I hope that they will remember that hip-hop was born without a formula and without a lot of expensive props or violent undertones," "I hope they will think about what it takes to create culture that is unique and transcendent and honest," and " . . . and I hope they begin to dream about crating a new world for themselves."

p. 177 Reader's Response

Students may say that they enjoyed Walker's descriptions of the music, dancing, and clothing. They may say that the cultural history of the 1980s interests them. They may never have realized that hip-hop was so old or that it had such an interesting beginning.

p. 178 Apply the Skills

1. Sample response: Hip-hop bridged the gap by giving Walker and her friends common interests.
2. Sample response: It was important for Walker and her friends to express themselves in this way because it taught them how to bring people together and how to communicate with others.
3. Sample response: The tone is personal, passionate, joyous, and nostalgic. Her tone comes through when she states that she was there when hip-hop began. It also comes through in her descriptions of the wonderful times she and her friends shared.
4. Sample response: Walker has an informal, direct, and friendly style.

Graphic Organizer

Sample response:

Level of Formality: talks about kids not knowing the impact of their ideas; talks about her personal feelings

Word Choice: slang, contractions; brand names; musical groups and their recordings; uses "I"

Sentence Patterns: direct, short sentences; tendency to provide multiple examples in one sentence; asks and answers her own questions

"A Celebration of Grandfathers"
Rudolfo A. Anaya

"On Summer"
Lorraine Hansberry

p. 180 Graphic Organizer

Sample response:

"A Celebration of Grandfathers"
Question: What does Anaya feel about old people?
Detail/Answer: Old people have much to teach us.
Main Idea? We should respect old people.

"On Summer"
Question: How do Hansberry's feelings about summer change as she grows older?
Detail/Answer: She begins to see the beauty of summer's gentle sunsets and long days.
Main Idea? Summer is "the noblest of seasons."

p. 181 Reading/Writing Connection

Sample response:
1. Older people can help people appreciate the values of the past.
2. Talking to older people can help people clarify their own values.
3. Older people often demonstrate a respect for the land.

p. 181 Note-taking Guide

Sample response:

What was the author's grandfather like?
Wise, spoke to the point, actively involved in life

Why are elders valuable? They work hard, are connected to the earth, have faith and inner strength, teach us valuable lessons

How are elders viewed now? They are supposed to look and act like young people.

p. 182 Activate Prior Knowledge

Students may say that a grandparent or older person has affected their lives by teaching them a respect for hard work and effort. Because life was not so easy in the past, a grandparent or older person may have taught them never to take life for granted or the opportunities that have been presented to them.

p. 182 Reading Skill

Sample response: Details that support Anaya's main idea include that they knew the value of nurturing, they knew the sensitivity of the earth, they contributed to society, and they were respected for their contributions.

p. 182 Literary Analysis

Students may say that the author creates a tone of admiration and respect for his elders. Students may underline "they knew the rhythms and cycles of time" and "they shared what little they had."

p. 183 Reading Skill

Sample response: Some details that support the author's point include "All worked with a deep faith," "they meant what they said," and "They helped each other through the epidemics and the personal tragedies."

p. 183 Literary Analysis

Students should circle "fiestas," "abuelitos," "llano," "pueblo," and "curandera." Sample response: Anaya's use of Spanish words shows that he is comfortable using Spanish and takes pride in his language and culture.

p. 183 Stop to Reflect

Some students may say that time moves slowly when they are bored, which is a negative thing. Others may see some good in a slower pace of life, which allows them to think more deeply, enjoy simple pleasures, and notice the world around them more.

p. 183 Reading Check

Students should underline "magical time of childhood stood still" and ". . . the pulse of the living earth pressed its mystery into my living blood."

p. 184 Reading Skill

Sample response: The main idea is that the grandfather draws strength from his connection with the earth and with life.

p. 184 Literary Analysis

Sample response: The syntax emphasizes how impressive and strong the grandfather appears to the little boy.

p. 184 Reading Check

Students should underline "for I was to learn the ways of a farmer."

p. 185 Literary Analysis

Students may circle "esteem," "respect," and "venerable."

p. 185 Reading Skill

Sample response: The main idea is that young people will lose a part of their humanity as they lose the old values.

p. 185 Reading Check

Students should underline "You will live in a new time, the time of the gringos."

p. 186 Literary Analysis

Sample response: The syntax emphasizes the changes that come with aging.

p. 186 Stop to Reflect

Students may point out that now the grandson is the one to help the grandfather and to teach him to have patience.

p. 186 Reading Skill

Sample response: Details supporting his being an extraordinary man are that he could break a wild horse and ride far distances and that he could dance all night and work all the next day. Details supporting his being ordinary are that he helped his neighbors, married, and raised children.

p. 186 Reading Check

Students should underline "Small things bothered him," "he shouted or turned sour when his expectations were not met," "he was returning to that state of childhood," and "wishes and desires were now wrapped in a crumbling old body."

p. 187 Stop to Reflect

Students may agree with Anaya's description of the way old people are portrayed in the media because they may think that the media does not offer a realistic view of old people. The media does not praise the wisdom and contribution of the elderly, and they insist on keeping the elderly young. Other students may disagree with Anaya and claim that the media offer a realistic view of old people.

p. 187 Literary Analysis

Students should underline "leaves falling from the tree" and "autumn of life."

p. 187 Reading Skill

Sample response: The main idea is whether the values of the old ones will become neglected and wash away, just as the adobe has done.

p. 188 Stop to Reflect

Students may say that they connect the sounds and smells of holiday dinner with their family because they spend holidays with their family.

p. 188 Reader's Response

Students may say that the "old ones" in their lives are different from the "old ones" in Anaya's life. The old people they know were, or continue to be, part of the young culture. They fight old age and are angry with growing old. Living in an age of technology, they are not connected to the land like the "old ones" Anaya describes. Other students may say that their "old ones" are similar to Anaya's and that they learn new things from them about the past.

p. 189 Apply the Skills

1. Sample response: The old ones Anaya remembers are strong, wise, and independent. Modern mass media show images of old people who appear youthful, lively, and healthy. Anaya offers a more realistic view of old people.
2. Sample response: Anaya believes that old people should be treated with patience and care because growing old can be painful and damaging.
3. **Graphic Organizer**
Sample response:
Diction: Buenos días le de Dios, abuelo; ancianos; authentic lives
Tone: admiration, respect, affection
Style: serious, thoughtful, informal

4. Sample response: Young people should respect old people because the elders are strong and wise and have something important to share.

p. 191 Reading/Writing Connection

Sample response:
1. The older members of my family embody stories from the past.
2. The pictures of our celebrations signify happy memories.
3. I react with pride when I see my family together.

p. 191 Note-taking Guide

Sample response:
As a Child: It is a mistake. It is excessive. It is an overstatement. It is too stark.
As an Adult: It is noble. It is life at its apex. It has the gentlest nights and the longest days. It is beauty. She has respect for it.

p. 192 Apply the Skills

1. Sample response: It is a memory of a specific summer. Hansberry's memories of her grandmother provide a contrast to her description of the woman in Maine.
2. Sample response: She considers summer noble because it represents life in its most complete form.
3. **Graphic Organizer**
Sample response:
Diction: "life at the apex," "gentlest nights," "noblest of the seasons"
Tone: respectful, admiring, affectionate
Style: thoughtful, solemn, formal
4. Sample response: Hansberry did not like summer as a young person, but she learned to appreciate it as an adult.

"The News"
Neil Postman

"Single Room, Earth View"
Sally Ride

p. 194 Graphic Organizer

Sample response:
"The News"
Details 1: Dramatic video is often shown to keep viewers' attention.
Details 2: The news anchor is chosen because he or she "looks" the part.
Main Idea: Television news cannot cover all of the news adequately because of its nature as entertainment.

"Single Room, Earth View"
Details 1: One moment she could see fires in Africa, and then she could see ice flowing in the Antarctic.
Details 2: The eddies and spirals in Earth's water eventually become visible.
Main Idea: Seeing the world from the space shuttle creates a new perspective on Earth.

p. 195 Reading/Writing Connection
Sample response: I rely on news Web sites to find out about current events. These sources clarify details and help me understand what is happening in the world. These sources also indicate how events will affect me in the future.

p. 195 Note-taking Guide
Sample response:
Newspapers: show many articles at the same time
Television News: shows stories in sequence
Both: supply news of the world

p. 196 Apply the Skills
1. Students may suggest that the comparison reveals that the news broadcast is an artificial order imposed on the real world. Real events appear "dramatized" on television news. This makes television news seem like a play.
2. Sample response: Time limits prevent the day's news from being covered sufficiently. The viewer gets only a series of impressions.
3. **Graphic Organizer**
Sample response:
Description:
Example: description of planes landing on an aircraft carrier
Effect: This example illustrates how moving images on television can hold the audience's attention.
Comparison/Contrast:
Example: comparison of the size of a television screen to the size of a movie-theater screen
Effect: This example illustrates why dramatic moving images are more important on television.
Cause and Effect:
Example: The need for television news stories to keep all viewers results in brief stories that have widespread appeal.

Effect: This example illustrates why it is impossible for television news to cover news stories adequately.
4. Sample response: The main idea of "The News" is that television news has time limitations and must appeal to a wide audience. As a result, it gives a false impression of the world.

p. 198 Reading/Writing Connection
Sample response:
1. I had to alter my feelings about the city when I saw it from the Empire State Building.
2. Looking at something up close can emphasize how complex it is.
3. The sight of the moon seems to contradict what I thought the moon's surface looked like.

p. 198 Note-taking Guide
Sample response:
Geographical Sites: Ganges River, Persian Gulf
Human-Made Structures: cities, Great Wall of China, bridges, airports
Natural Occurrences: hurricane clouds expanding, ice floes jostling, volcanoes smoldering
Environmental Problems: oil spills, air pollution, destruction of forests

p. 199 Activate Prior Knowledge
Students may say that Earth is very blue because most of its surface is water. They may say that because they can see the landmasses, it looks just like a globe. They may also point out weather patterns such as hurricanes.

p. 199 Reading Skill
Sample response: The space traveler is a giant step farther away. A space traveler can see typhoons forming, volcanoes smoking, and meteors streaking to Earth. The islands look just like they do on globes, according to the astronauts.

p. 199 Reading Check
Students should underline "In orbit, racing along at five miles per second, the space shuttle circles the Earth once every 90 minutes."

p. 200 Literary Analysis
Sample response: The description appeals mainly to sight.

p. 200 Stop to Reflect
Some students may say that seeing the Caribbean from space would be the most interesting. They may like to watch hurricanes form and move across the ocean.

p. 200 Reading Check
Students may underline "Indian Ocean," "Cape Hatteras," and "Cape Cod."

p. 201 Literary Analysis
Sample response: She is describing the effects of pollution. She is pointing out that pollution is getting worse and that the environment is becoming more damaged.

p. 201 Reading Skill
Students should underline "right lighting conditions," "intricate patterns in the oceans—eddies and spirals become visible," and "subtle differences in water color and reflectivity."

p. 201 Literary Analysis
Sample response: Scientists can study the ocean eddies from space much more easily than from a boat.

p. 202 Literary Analysis
Sample response: She compares the lights to twinkling stars.

p. 202 Reading Skill
Sample response: The details include ghostly clouds, bright reflections on water, and the moonlight flowing with the Mississippi River.

p. 202 Stop to Reflect
Students may say that it would be hard to adjust sleeping and eating schedules in space.

p. 202 Reading Check
Students should circle "the magnificent displays of lightning that ignite the clouds at night."

p. 203 Stop to Reflect
Students may say that there is no gravity in space and that changes the perspective of the astronauts. Students may also say that because the astronauts are so far away, the moon and Earth movements might look very different.

p. 203 Reader's Response
Students may be surprised by some of the smaller human-made features that are visible from space.

p. 204 Apply the Skills
1. Sample response: Ride thought that she could almost see geological forces working in the way the theories say they work.
2. Students may say that the way they think about Earth is very different. The essay may have given them a new sense of the unity and fragility of the planet Earth.
3. **Graphic Organizer**
Sample response:
Description:
Example: the description of the view of the Hawaiian Islands from space
Effect: The example conveys the sense of awe that is experienced by viewing Earth from space.
Comparison/Contrast: comparison of the appearance of Earth from space in 1973 with the view in 1983
Effect: The example emphasizes the changes that have taken place on Earth.
Cause and Effect: the effects of pollution on the Earth's environment
Effect: The example illustrates the various types of damage that have been done to the environment.
4. Sample response: The main idea is that space travel offers an amazing view of the world.

Reading Informational Materials: Technical Documents

p. 206 Graphic Organizer
Sample response:
Narrative text
Information Provided: basic facts
Diagrams
Information Provided: names and locations of parts as well as an overall view of the shuttle
Lists or statistics
Examples: the *Shuttle Statistics* list

p. 207 Reading Technical Documents
Students should write the following:
1. Length; 2. Height; 3. Wingspan; 4. Weight; 5. Maximum cargo to orbit; 6. SRB separation; 7. External Tank Separation; 8. Orbit.

p. 207 Reading Skill
Sample response: At the end of a mission, the space shuttle weighs 104,326 kilograms (230,000 pounds).

p. 207 Stop to Reflect
Sample response: A technical document might start with history and background to help familiarize readers with the topic.

p. 207 Reading Check
Students may underline "The space shuttle is the world's first reusable spacecraft," "The shuttle launches like a rocket," and "Each of the three space shuttle orbiters now in operation—Discovery, Atlantis and Endeavour—is designed to fly at least 100 missions."

p. 208 Reading Skill
The *Endeavour* was delivered in May 1991.

p. 208 Stop to Reflect
Sample response: The last two paragraphs tell how NASA has worked to make the shuttle safer and more reliable. They describe the improvements made to the shuttle since 1992.

p. 208 Reading Check
Students should circle "All of the components are reused except for the external fuel tank, which burns up in the atmosphere after each launch."

p. 209 Reading Technical Documents
Sample response: By looking at the diagrams, one can tell that the space shuttle is made up of at least four separate large pieces.

p. 209 Stop to Reflect
Students may say that the *Columbia* accident may cause NASA to prepare even more carefully for each launch.

p. 209 Reading Informational Materials
Students should underline "the safety of the crew." Sample response: NASA has been doing very well with this goal. Although two shuttles have exploded and resulted in loss of life, most of the people who have traveled in space shuttles have returned safely.

p. 210 Apply the Skills
Thinking About the Technical Document
1. Sample response: The author probably discusses the shuttle's launch record because he or she previously mentioned accidents. The launch record shows that the space shuttle is largely a successful design. The author then mentions design improvements to show the progress being made to improve the shuttle.
2. Sample response: The text and the diagram give the reader different kinds of information about the shuttle parts. The text tells what the functions of the parts are. The diagram shows the reader where the parts are located.

Reading Skill
3. *Discovery*, *Atlantis*, and *Endeavour* are now in use.
4. The shuttle's wingspan is 23.79 meters (78.06 feet).

"Carry Your Own Skis"
Lian Dolan

"Libraries Face Sad Chapter"
Pete Hamill

p. 211 Graphic Organizer
Sample response:
"Carry Your Own Skis"
Claim: Be responsible for yourself and your stuff, or you miss out.
Logical? yes
Evaluation: The author shows how being responsible leads to a fuller life.

"Libraries Face Sad Chapter"
Claim: Reading is not an assignment, it is a pleasure.
Logical? no
Evaluation: The author shows how losing library services would deprive children of access to information found in books.

p. 212 Reading/Writing Connection
Sample response: Activities that involve hardship would frustrate people who expect life to be easy. Some people, however, love the challenge of pushing themselves to extremes. They like to display their courage and their ability to face life's hardships.

p. 212 Note-taking Guide
Sample response:
Those Who Carry Their Own Skis: are liked by others; are asked to participate in other activities; are responsible; are not afraid to work hard
Those Who Do Not Carry Their Own Skis: are not always liked by others; are not always asked to participate in other activities; are not responsible; do not like to work hard

p. 213 Activate Prior Knowledge
Students may say that learning to write in cursive was difficult for them. They may say that they are glad now that they learned to do it because it looks nicer when they write.

p. 213 Reading Skill

Sample response: The details show that skiers used wooden skis that were "heavy" and "bulky," they had to walk uphill to the chair lift, and the lodges did not have any luxuries. Then, they had to ride home in their "cold, wet clothes." The words Dolan uses show that skiing was uncomfortable and tiring.

p. 213 Literary Analysis

Sample response: The words "cold, wet, and tired" are all negative words. They make the reader feel Dolan's discomfort. They help the reader see that skiing was not always fun for Dolan.

p. 213 Reading Check

Students should underline "Carry your own skis."

p. 214 Literary Analysis

Students could underline "cold, wet day on the ice-blue slopes"; "freezing in leather boots"; "soggy tuna fish sandwiches"; "sheet of ice disguised as a trail"; "tramping through three feet of snow"; "in near darkness, cold and alone and crying." Sample response: These details are so unpleasant that they make skiing seem like something one would not want to do.

p. 214 Stop to Reflect

Some students will agree that Dolan's mother was reasonable, because she could not carry all of her children's skis for them. Others may say that small children cannot carry skis and that it was inconsiderate to leave small children out of the fun.

p. 214 Reading Skill

Sample response: She supports her claim with the details of how other kids behaved compared with how she behaved. She gives examples such as kids who thought somebody was going to take care of things for them, and girls who did not help out with chores on camping trips.

p. 215 Literary Analysis

Sample response: Her motive might be to convince other people that it is important to "carry their own skis" because she prefers people who are responsible for themselves.

p. 215 Stop to Reflect

Students may say that people who do not take responsibility for themselves annoy them. When others are not responsible, they make more work for responsible people.

p. 215 Reading Skill

Sample response: She shows how being forced to be responsible for her skis, even though she did not like it, taught her that she had to be responsible for other things in life. She would have to be responsible if she wanted to fully enjoy life.

p. 215 Reading Check

Students should underline "When I wasn't responsible for myself or my stuff, I felt lousy."

p. 216 Literary Analysis

Students may underline "hard falls on hard ice," "damp long underwear," and "endless ride home."

p. 216 Reading Skill

Sample response: Yes, she makes the connection by showing how being forced to be responsible for her skis, even though it was unpleasant, taught her that she had to be responsible for other things in life if she wanted to enjoy life to its fullest.

p. 216 Reader's Response

Some students may say that Dolan made them feel guilty because they do not "carry their own skis." Dolan's criticisms of irresponsible people may have angered them. Other students may say that Dolan made them feel proud because they do "carry their own skis." They may have been happy to read about someone who has the same feelings about life as they do.

p. 217 Apply the Skills

1. Sample response: Carrying her own skis taught Dolan to be responsible for herself in order to fully participate in life. This lesson has also guided her in getting a job, paying off her student loans, working hard for the company that was providing her paycheck, meeting her deadlines at work, and keeping appointments and commitments.

2. Some students may agree that taking personal responsibility leads to a fuller life because others are more likely to accept a person who does so. Other students may disagree, saying that avoiding responsibility

may affect a person positively because others will do things for that person.

3. **Graphic Organizer**
Sample response:
Passage: Paragraph beginning "The lesson was simple, really. Be responsible for yourself and your stuff or you miss out"; Paragraph beginning "I like the folks who clear the dishes. . . ."; Paragraph beginning "The funny thing is, some of the worst moments of my childhood were spent on skis. . . ."
Reason or Emotion: She appeals to reason by explaining in a logical way why it was important to "carry your own skis." She appeals to emotion by explaining that she has pleasant feelings about people who take responsibility. She appeals to emotion by explaining that even though she suffered, she did not want to miss out on things.

4. Sample response: The author was convincing because she gave specific examples of people who do accept responsibility and people who do not accept responsibility.

p. 219 Reading/Writing Connection
Sample response: My first library visit did reveal that there are books on every topic. Seeing so many books helped me perceive that the world is a very big place. I knew then that I wanted to dedicate my life to reading books.

p. 219 Note-taking Guide
Sample response:
Circle 2: to check out books
Circle 3: to learn about jobs
Circle 5: to study to become a U.S. citizen

p. 220 Apply the Skills
1. Some students may say that they share Hamill's feelings because they had many happy experiences in a library as a child. Other students may not share Hamill's feelings, saying that people can get information by television, online, or by purchasing books.
2. Sample response: He believes that books feed the mind and imagination.
3. **Graphic Organizer**
Sample response:
Passage: paragraph beginning "We passed into that library . . ."; paragraph beginning "We could live in the South Seas . . ."; paragraph beginning "For those without money, . . ."

Reason or Emotion: He appeals to emotion by remembering how important libraries were to him as a child. He appeals to emotion by explaining how he liked to learn about history. He appeals to emotion with images of poor children getting a free education and growing up to build great things.

4. Students may say that Hamill's arguments are well reasoned and logical. He gives facts about how important libraries are to immigrants. He explains how the city government may be forced to cut services. He explains the importance of libraries today with the cost of books and the lack of good shows on television.

"I Have a Dream"
Martin Luther King, Jr.

"First Inaugural Address"
Franklin D. Roosevelt

p. 222 Graphic Organizer
Sample response:
"I Have a Dream"
Technique: restatement of "never give up"
Purpose: to get people to realize that the struggle is long and needs commitment
Effect: makes listeners believe that there is support for them

"First Inaugural Address"
Technique: repetition of "stricken" in ". . . a stricken nation in the midst of a stricken world . . ."
Purpose: to show that it is not just this country that is having a problem
Effect: People will believe that they are not alone in the world.

p. 223 Reading/Writing Connection
Sample response:
1. When it comes to fairness, Americans embody the meaning of good sportsmanship.
2. Freedom and justice comprise two of the most important American ideals.
3. Most Americans define tolerance as the acceptance of other people and ideas.

p. 223 Note-taking Guide
Sample response:
Whom will it affect? everyone, regardless of race or religion
What will it take? faith in the cause of equality

What will it be like? Inequality will disappear; descendants of slaves and slave owners will eat together; people will be judged by their deeds, not by their skin color; children of all races will join hands as brothers and sisters.

p. 224 Activate Prior Knowledge
Students may say that the United States celebrates the holiday because King was a great civil rights leader and national figure. Some students will be aware of his role in leading the Montgomery Bus Boycott, the protests in Selma, and the March on Washington. Some may be familiar with his philosophy of nonviolence and the fact that he was assassinated.

p. 224 Reading Skill
Students may underline "a great American, in whose symbolic shadow"; "beacon light of hope"; "seared in the flames of withering injustice"; "joyous daybreak"; "long night of captivity"; "sadly crippled"; "manacles of segregation"; "chains of discrimination"; "lonely island"; "an exile in his own land"; "a shameful condition." Students may suggest that the words make them feel sad and angered.

p. 224 Stop to Reflect
Students may know that the Constitution and Declaration of Independence were written in the eighteenth century. They are important documents about freedom and the government from the very beginning of United States history. Students may say that they share King's view that these documents guarantee the rights of all citizens in the United States. They may agree with King that all men are equal and deserve equal treatment.

p. 225 Literary Analysis
Students should underline "Now is the time." Sample response: It helps create a feeling that the time has come for change. This feeling makes people excited and motivated.

p. 225 Reading Skill
Students may underline "fatal for the nation"; "sweltering summer"; "invigorating autumn"; "blow off steam"; "rude awakening"; "neither rest nor tranquility"; "whirlwinds of revolt"; "shake the foundations"; "bright day of justice." Students may suggest that the passage makes them feel excited, eager, and hopeful.

p. 225 Reading Check
Students should circle "with soul force."

p. 226 Literary Analysis
Students may suggest that King is saying that when progress is being made, both whites and African Americans must continue to move forward until the job is done.

p. 226 Stop to Reflect
Students may suggest that Dr. King's dreams did come true because many laws have been passed to make sure that people are not judged by their race or religion. Others may believe that some of his dream was accomplished, but that there is still more work that needs to be done.

p. 226 Reading Skill
Students may suggest that they feel angry that people in America have been judged by the color of their skin. Students may also suggest that the passage makes them feel hopeful for the future.

p. 226 Reading Check
Students should circle "the sons of former slaves and the sons of former slaveowners will be able to sit down together at the table of brotherhood."

p. 227 Literary Analysis
Students should underline "I have a dream." Students may say that this repetition emphasizes that King's dream could be a reality and that he believes strongly in a good future for all the races.

p. 227 Reading Skill
Students may say that his appeals are inspiring and persuasive. They make a listener feel patriotic and want to live up to American ideals.

p. 227 Stop to Reflect
Students may suggest that King would talk about women's rights or the rights of different races. They may suggest that he would fight against religious discrimination or for the rights of women in the workplace.

p. 228 Literary Analysis
Sample response: King is using repetition. Students should underline sentences that include the words "let freedom ring."

p. 228 Reading Skill

Students may say that they believe that this is an appeal to emotion because it talks about many groups that traditionally do not get along well coming together to live in peace.

p. 228 Reader's Response

Students may say that being in the audience at King's speech would have been exciting and inspiring.

p. 229 Apply the Skills

1. Sample response: He reminds everyone that the country was founded on a promise of liberty.

2. Sample response: The mention of these places ties in with his message of equality for everyone across the country.

3. **Graphic Organizer**

Sample response:

Restatement

Example: "the sons of former slaves and the sons of former slaveowners will be able to sit down together at the table of brotherhood," and "little black boys and black girls will be able to join hands with little white boys and white girls and walk together as sisters and brothers"

Effect: The example emphasizes the differences at the time and the hope that things will change in the future.

Repetition

Example: "I have a dream"

Effect: The repetition emphasizes how much King hopes for equality and justice.

Parallelism

Example: "sweltering summer of the Negro's legitimate discontent/invigorating autumn of freedom and equality"

Effect: This emphasizes the contrast between how African Americans are treated and how they should be treated.

4. Students may say that King is effective because the rhetorical devices and emotion-charged language emphasize his ideas.

p. 231 Reading/Writing Connection

Sample response: A speaker's true excitement can evoke excitement in those who are listening. When I hear a person project his or her ideas, I think about what the ideas mean to me. Good ideas stimulate me to make changes.

p. 231 Note-taking Guide

Sample response:

Who is giving this speech? Franklin Delano Roosevelt, the thirty-second president of the United States

Why is he giving this speech? It is his first speech as president. All new presidents give a speech at the inauguration, or swearing-in.

In what year is he giving this speech? 1932

What is the greatest problem for the country at this time? Many people are unemployed and do not have any money to make a living.

What is the main promise that is made in the speech? Roosevelt wants to help people find jobs.

p. 232 Apply the Skills

1. Sample response: He sends the message that the people have been misled and cheated.

2. Sample response: His listeners probably felt encouraged.

3. **Graphic Organizer**

Sample response:

Restatement

Example: "Nature still offers her bounty. . . . Plenty is at our doorstep. . . ."

Effect: The effect is emphasis on optimism and hope.

Repetition

Example: He repeats that he will perform his "duty."

Effect: The repetition helps give listeners a sense that he will do what they expect of a leader.

Parallelism

Example: "on honesty, on honor, on the sacredness of obligations, on faithful protection, on unselfish performance . . ."

Effect: This listing of virtues gives readers a sense of momentum, or forward motion.

Analogy

Example: He compares the state of the nation today with its state in other dark times in the country's history, when good leadership and support of the people pulled the country through.

Effect: This analogy helps give listeners a sense that the country will pull through this tough time, as it has in the past.

4. Sample response: Roosevelt plays to people's feelings when he says, "We are stricken by no plague of locusts. Compared with the perils which our forefathers conquered because they believed and were not afraid, we have still much to be thankful for."

Reading Informational Materials: Historical Research Study

p. 234 Graphic Organizer
Sample response:
Statement: "Only a foolish optimist can deny the dark realities of the moment."
Provable: no
Fact or Opinion: opinion
Statement: *Defending Your Life* was a 1991 movie written and directed by its star, Albert Brooks.
Provable: yes
Fact or Opinion: fact

p. 235 Reading Historical Research Studies
Sample response: This study begins with a quotation to capture the reader's attention. It reminds the readers that the study is about a speech. It includes the famous line, "The only thing we have to fear is fear itself."

p. 235 Stop to Reflect
Sample response: Axelrod starts the article with a description of a popular movie to catch the reader's attention.

p. 235 Reading Skill
Sample response: This statement is an opinion. It is not something that can be proved.

p. 235 Reading Check
Students should underline "First inaugural address, March 4, 1933."

p. 236 Reading Historical Research Studies
Sample response: President Roosevelt is in a wheelchair and looks like he likes dogs. He also likes reaching out to people.

p. 236 Stop to Reflect
Sample response: Axelrod repeats the words "fog of fear" to tie ideas in the study together.

p. 236 Reading Skill
Students may underline "There is no sugar-coating of reality here!" Students may circle "He embarked on this catalog of economic

disasters by defining them as "our common difficulties. . . ."

p. 237 Reading Historical Research Studies
Sample response: Axelrod uses this quotation to support his claim that Roosevelt has revealed the truth to the American people. These are not acts of nature that cannot be overcome. He is not afraid to face these difficulties. He will overcome them.

p. 237 Reading Skill
Sample response: This passage is mostly opinion. It cannot be proved true. It contains mostly Roosevelt's feelings about the problem.

p. 237 Reading Check
Students should underline the sentence that begins, "The fog was lifted and the president's listeners could see the reality . . ."

p. 238 Reading Skill
Students should underline the word "always." Sample response: This word warns that the sentence might be a generalization because it cannot be proved that Roosevelt "always" navigated between the new and the age-old.

p. 238 Stop to Reflect
Students may point out the microphones for CBS and NBC on the edge of the podium. Roosevelt's words were reaching the people over the radio.

p. 238 Reading Historical Research Studies
Sample response: Axelrod uses these transitions to connect ideas and explain his arguments.

p. 238 Reading Check
Students should underline "a generation of self-seekers."

p. 239 Reading Historical Research Studies
Sample response: Axelrod is offering an explanation of the quote below. He is giving it context in the rest of Roosevelt's presidency so that readers will know why the quote is important.

p. 239 Reading Skill
Sample response: Roosevelt is stating an opinion. No one can prove what causes happiness.

p. 239 Stop to Reflect

Sample response: No, he was simply saying everything he wanted to tell the American people. He would probably have been very surprised if he could have known how often his speech would be studied.

p. 240 Reading Skill

Sample response: The phrase tells readers the statement is an opinion. It cannot be proved true.

p. 240 Reading Historical Research Studies

Students should circle "restoring the temple of our civilization"; "happiness lies not in the mere possession of money"; "the mad chase of evanescent profits"; "our true destiny is not to be ministered unto but to minister to ourselves and our fellow men." Sample response: The last sentence says that money will not make people happy, morals and ethics should not be sacrificed to reach monetary goals, and people must help themselves and the people around them.

p. 240 Reading Informational Materials

Sample response: Axelrod did a good job of supporting his thesis with examples. He included many quotations from the speech. He tied those quotations to events in time.

p. 241 Apply the Skills
Thinking About the Historical Research Study

1. Sample response: Axelrod means that people can pay too much attention to their fear. Then, they do not face the problem. Focusing on fear can cause people to think less clearly about possible solutions.

2. Sample response: Axelrod points out how Roosevelt shows his radically new ideas. He connects these new ideas to Roosevelt's plans for the "New Deal." He also points out Roosevelt's age-old and unchanging beliefs with references to the Bible.

Reading Skill

3. Sample response: "Our kind has conquered worse in the past."

4. Sample response: "He began by asking the American people to sweep aside the 'nameless, unreasoning, unjustified terror.'"

"Uncoiling"
Pat Mora

"A Voice"
Pat Mora

p. 244 Note-taking Guide
Sample response:
What is the main image of the poem? giving a speech in front of people
What details support this image? "roars / and rivers leap," "howling / leaves off trees"; "lights on the stage unrelenting," "the only Mexican in the auditorium," "you wanted to hide from those strange faces"

p. 245 Activate Prior Knowledge
Students may compare a storm to an animal, a machine out of control, or an angry person. They may say that the storm might be cold if it were a machine and hot if it were an angry person.

p. 245 Poetry
Students should underline "scratches," "tosses her hair," "snares," "sighs," "spooks," and "spins."

p. 245 Poetry
Mora is using alliteration. The image is of a woman growing tired because of her frantic activity.

p. 245 Reading Check
Students should circle "lightning," "cholla," "hawks," and "butterfly swarms."

p. 246 Poetry
Sample response: The comparisons that involve water ("he floated" and "slow / as a hot river") suggest that the father moves at his own pace, despite the pace of the world around him. The speaker also compares him to a judge without a courtroom. This comparison suggests that he is wise and solemn but out of place.

p. 246 Poetry
Students should underline "You like," "You liked," "You liked," "all the," "all those," "How did I do it?" and "How did I do it." Sample response: Mora emphasizes that the speaker's mother has strong motivations and desires to speak in public. However, she still feels nervous about speaking in public.

p. 246 Poetry
Sample response: "Spunky as a peacock" is a simile. By making this comparison, Mora is saying that the speaker's mother is loud, vibrant, eager to be seen, and proud.

p. 246 Stop to Reflect
Sample response: Mora means that families like to find similarities in their members, particularly over generations. By doing so, they preserve family characteristics, or blood.

p. 247 Poetry
Sample response: Mora uses a simile, comparing the speaker's mother's breath moving through the family to the wind moving through trees. She is trying to say that the wind will always blow through the trees, just as the speaker's mother will always have an influence on the family.

p. 247 Reading Check
Students should underline "You, who are never at a loss / for words, felt your breath stick in your throat / like an ice cube. 'I can't,' you whispered. / 'I can't.'"

p. 247 Reader's Response
Some students may find "Uncoiling" more powerful or appealing because of its vivid imagery. Other students may find "A Voice" more powerful or appealing because it tells a family story and has an important message.

p. 248 Apply the Skills
1. The speaker is describing a desert storm.
2. Sample response: That day's failure taught the speaker's mother that it was important to teach her children to use their voices.
3. Sample response: The storm is wild, powerful, and destructive. The women are frightened and timid but also protective.
4. **Graphic Organizer**
Sample response:
What It Says: The storm sighs; the mother's breath sticks in her throat.
What It Means: The storm produces wind and clouds; the mother cannot make herself speak.
Effect: The image describes the motion of the storm; the image conveys a feeling of fright and helplessness.

Poetry Collection 1
Poetry Collection 2

p. 250 Graphic Organizer
Sample response:
Poetry Collection 1
Example: "Does it dry up / like a raisin in the sun?"
Type: Simile
Meaning or Effect: The simile stresses that when dreams are pushed away, they may lose their power and importance.

Poetry Collection 2
Example: "where mammals and computers / live together in mutually / programming harmony / like pure water / touching clear sky"
Type: Simile
Meaning or Effect: The simile stresses how effortlessly the author wants mammals and computers to live together.

p. 251 Reading/Writing Connection
Sample response:
1. Dreams help people achieve their goals.
2. People can benefit from their dreams by taking steps to make them come true.
3. People who believe in dreams can maintain a positive attitude.

p. 251 Note-taking Guide
Sample response:
Dreams: to show that dreams should be followed
I Wandered Lonely as a Cloud: to lovingly recall an inspiring scene of nature
Meciendo: to compare rocking one's son to God's rocking of nature
Sonnet on Love XIII: to compare the poet's love to the idea of an inventor from long ago

p. 252 Activate Prior Knowledge
Sample response: Nature is a source of inspiration because of its beauty. Most people can relate to imagery associated with the beauty of nature.

p. 252 Reading Check
Students should circle "What happens to a dream deferred?"; "Does it dry up / like a raisin in the sun?"; "Or fester like a sore— / And then run?"; "Does it stink like rotten meat?"; "Or crust and sugar over— / like a syrupy sweet?"; "Or does it explode?"

p. 252 Reading Skill
The first stanza contains one sentence.

p. 252 Literary Analysis
Sample response: One metaphor is "Life is a broken-winged bird / That cannot fly."

p. 253 Literary Analysis
The speaker compares the daffodils to stars in the Milky Way.

p. 253 Reading Skill
The reader should stop reading after "breeze," "dance," and "daffodils."

p. 253 Stop to Reflect
Sample response: The figurative language paints a vivid picture for the reader.

p. 253 Reading Check
Students should circle "The waves beside them danced" and "And then my heart with pleasure fills, / And dances with the daffodils."

p. 254 Reading Skill
This translation contains seven sentences.

p. 254 Literary Analysis
The wind is "wandering" and "loving," and it "rocks the wheat."

p. 254 Reading Check
Students should underline "I rock my son."

p. 255 Literary Analysis
A paradox appears in the first stanza.

p. 255 Reading Skill
Sample response: The sentence ends in line 7.

p. 255 Reading Check
Students should underline "'Give me a place to stand,' Archimedes said, / 'and I can move the world.'"

p. 255 Reader's Response
Sample response: "Dreams" had the strongest effect because of the importance of the theme and the two vivid metaphors.

p. 256 Apply the Skills
1. Sample response: Cherish your dreams. Life is meaningless without dreams.
2. Sample response: The sights and sounds fill the speakers with delight and comfort.
3. Sample response: One example is in "I Wandered Lonely as a Cloud": "A host, of golden daffodils . . . Fluttering and dancing in the breeze."

4. Graphic Organizer

Sample response:

Stanza: "The wind wandering by night / rocks the wheat. / Hearing the loving wind, / I rock my son."

Paragraph: The wind wandering by night rocks the wheat. Hearing the loving wind, I rock my son.

p. 258 Reading/Writing Connection

Sample response:

1. Computers <u>minimize</u> problems by helping people <u>get</u> organized.
2. E-mail allows us to <u>accelerate</u> communication.
3. Some choose to <u>interact</u> with computers instead of people.

p. 258 Note-taking Guide

Sample response:

"Hope" is the thing with feathers—: the characteristics of hope

Much Madness is divinest Sense—: the nature of sanity

The War Against the Trees: how progress destroys nature

p. 259 Apply the Skills

1. Sample response: The comparison suggests that the speaker feels comfortable and safe with computers.
2. Sample response: The image of war shows that the speaker feels that the trees are victims being unfairly attacked.
3. Sample response: The trees in "The War Against the Trees" are described as "great-grandfathers."

4. Graphic Organizer

Sample response:

Stanza: "I saw the ghosts of children at their games / Racing beyond their childhood in the shade, / And while the green world turned its death-foxed page / And a red wagon wheeled, / I watched them disappear / Into the suburbs of their grievous age."

Paragraph: I saw the ghosts of children at their games racing beyond their childhood in the shade, and while the green world turned its death-foxed page and a red wagon wheeled, I watched them disappear into the suburbs of their grievous age.

Reading Informational Materials: Case Studies

p. 261 Graphic Organizer

Sample response:

Details: Matt wants to study computer science and then become a professor; Gil wants to study robotics and explore other areas of robotics.

Generalization: Even people who have similar jobs at one point in their lives can go on to do different things in their futures.

p. 262 Reading Case Studies

Sample response: Readers learn that this case study examines the different paths that can be taken to a career in robotics.

p. 262 Reading Skill

Sample response: People who do not work hard in high school can still succeed in college.

p. 262 Stop to Reflect

Sample response: It makes sense to say that Matt was lucky to get into college because students who do not do well in high school often have trouble finding a college that will accept them.

p. 262 Reading Check

Students should circle "Think you'll never use high school math? Think again . . ."

p. 263 Reading Check

Students should underline "physics, math, science, engineering, communications, and others."

p. 263 Reading Case Studies

Sample response: 1. He went to college to study political science. 2. He took an artificial intelligence class. 3. He took part in robotics competitions.

p. 263 Stop to Reflect

Sample response: It was worth it to give up their summers because they gained experience that helped them get jobs.

p. 264 Reading Case Studies

Sample response: Internships can often present opportunities for jobs.

p. 264 Reading Skill

Sample response: One detail that supports this generalization is "Often internships are the first step through the door."

p. 264 Reading Check

Students should underline "variety" and "you usually get to learn something big and new every few weeks."

p. 264 Reading Informational Materials

Students may say that this case study made them appreciate math class. Other students may say that it had no effect on their feelings about math.

p. 265 Apply the Skills
Thinking About the Case Study

1. Sample response: Gil started working hard in high school. Matt did not start working hard until college.
2. Sample response: Yes; this case study's advice about pursuing a robotics career applies to other fields as well.

Reading Skill

3. Sample response: Matt took classes in psychology, philosophy, and anthropology.
4. Sample response: Matt did not do well in high school. But when he got to college and found a subject that he was interested in, he began to do well in school.

Poetry Collection 1

Poetry Collection 2

p. 266 Graphic Organizer

Sample response:

Poetry Collection 1: "Summer"
Sight: "old men sleeping"
Hearing: "bugs buzzin"
Smell: "daisies"
Taste: "juices dripping"
Touch: "hot"

Poetry Collection 2: "The Bells"
Sight: "twinkle"
Hearing: "tinkle, tinkle, tinkle"
Smell: none
Taste: "rust within their throats"
Touch: "balmy"

p. 267 Reading/Writing Connection

Sample response:
1. I anticipate summer because I love to go swimming.
2. During the fall, we are blessed with a display of colorful leaves.
3. When spring arrives, I can participate in baseball.

p. 267 Note-taking Guide

Sample response:
Summer
Two Events: Bugs fly through the air. Old men sleep.
The Eagle
The topic of the poem: a look at an eagle
Two Events: An eagle stands on a mountain.
Analysis of Baseball
The topic of the poem: the basics of baseball
Two Events: The ball bounces. The fans cheer.

p. 268 Activate Prior Knowledge

Some students may say that winter is their favorite season because they love skiing. Other students may say that summer is their favorite season because they like swimming.

p. 268 Reading Skill

Sample response: "Summer" appeals to all five senses. "Juices dripping" appeals to the sense of taste. "Old men sleeping" appeals to the sense of sight. "Bugs buzzin" appeals to the sense of sound. "Daisies" appeals to the sense of smell. "Hot" appeals to the sense of touch.

p. 268 Literary Analysis

Students should circle "clasps," "crag," "crooked," "close," "lonely," and "lands."

p. 268 Reading Check

Students should underline "He clasps the crag" and "He watches."

p. 269 Reading Skill

This stanza contains four sentences. "Bounces" and "flies" appeal to the sense of sight. "Thuds" and "duds" appeal to the sense of sound.

p. 269 Literary Analysis

Students should circle "thwack."

p. 269 Stop to Reflect

Students may say that it is not necessary to know the rules of baseball in order to enjoy the poem. The sound devices and imagery make the poem enjoyable.

p. 270 Reading Skill

The words "40,000 fans" appeal to the sense of sight because there are so many people. "Exploded" appeals to the sense of sound because the crowd sounds like an explosion.

p. 270 Literary Analysis

Sample response: The consonant sound "t" is repeated frequently. It gives a sense of finality.

p. 270 Reading Check

Students should underline "It's about / the ball, / the bat, / the mitt, / the bases / and the fans" and "It's about / home, and it's / about run."

p. 270 Reader's Response

"Summer" may make students long for summers. "The Eagle" may call to mind thoughts of heroism or independence. "Analysis of Baseball" may make students want to play or watch a baseball game.

p. 271 Apply the Skills

1. Sweat or nectar may be dripping.
2. The eagle is probably watching for something to eat.
3. **Graphic Organizer**
Sample response:
Alliteration
Summer: "bugs buzzin"
Effect: makes the poem more rhythmic
The Eagle: "clasps . . . crag"
Effect: emphasizes the strength of the eagle's grasp
Analysis of Baseball: "ball . . . bat"
Effect: makes the poem more rhythmic
Consonance
Summer: "sweat . . . what"
Effect: strengthens the feeling of wetness
The Eagle: "Ring'd . . . world"
Effect: ties the line together
Analysis of Baseball: "mitt . . . bat"
Effect: makes the poem more rhythmic
Assonance
Summer: "daisies lay"
Effect: makes the daisies seem relaxed
The Eagle: "clasps . . . crag"
Effect: emphasizes the strength of the eagle's grasp
Analysis of Baseball: "take . . . bait"
Effect: makes the poem more rhythmic
4. Sample response: Fluent reading helps readers appreciate the musical quality that the sound devices give the poems.

p. 273 Reading/Writing Connection

Sample response: The buzz of my alarm clock is a trigger that gets me up and moving. It makes me appreciate my daily routine. My alarm clock helps me contemplate how valuable time is.

p. 273 Note-taking Guide

Sample response:
The Bells: different bells
Jabberwocky: the Jabberwock

p. 274 Apply the Skills

1. The ball dropping through the net makes the sound described.
2. Students may say that the poem is at least mocking stories of heroism.
3. **Graphic Organizer**
Sample response:
Alliteration
The Bell: "tinkle, tinkle, tinkle"
Effect: gives the poem a rhythmic quality
Consonance
Slam, Dunk, & Hook: "but a hot"
Effect: quickens the reading pace
Assonance
Jabberwocky: "left it dead"
Effect: makes this line sound depressing
4. Sample response: Fluent reading helps readers appreciate the musical qualities of the poems.

Poetry Collection 1

Poetry Collection 2

p. 276 Graphic Organizer

Sample Response:
Poetry Collection 1
Lines of Poetry: "It looked extremely rocky for the Mudville nine that day; / The score stood two to four, with but an inning left to play."
Details in Lines of Poetry: The team is losing with one inning left to play.
Paraphrase: The Mudville team is losing by two runs. Only one inning remains in the game.

Poetry Collection 2
Lines of Poetry: "Ah, distinctly I remember it was in the bleak December, / And each separate dying ember wrought its ghost upon the floor."

Details in Lines of Poetry: The speaker clearly remembers a December night next to his fire.

Paraphrase: I remember a specific December evening when the fire was casting shadows on the floor.

p. 277 Reading/Writing Connection
Sample response:
1. Some events that evoke happiness are birthdays and graduations.
2. People respond to sad news by trying to stay positive.
3. People can reinforce happiness in others by being a giving person.

p. 277 Note-taking Guide
Sample response:
Casey at the Bat
What Happens Next: Casey gets two strikes.
Final Event: Casey strikes out.
Fifteen
What Happens Next: The boy imagines riding the motorcycle.
What Happens Next: Teenager finds the driver of the bike.
Final Event: The driver rides away.
Twister Hits Houston
Beginning Event: A bad storm is coming.
What Happens Next: The father and mother don't take shelter.
What Happens Next: The tornado rips through the yard.
Final Event: The family survives.

p. 278 Activate Prior Knowledge
Students may say that pressure improved their performance because it sharpened their ability to focus and got their adrenaline flowing. Others may say that they would have performed better without the added pressure.

p. 278 Literary Analysis
The setting of the poem is a baseball field. Students should circle "inning," "second," and "game."

p. 278 Reading Skill
Sample response: To the crowd's surprise, Flynn and Blakey both hit the ball. Flynn is on third base, and Blakey is on second base. The crowd cheers as Casey comes to bat.

p. 279 Literary Analysis
Sample response: The poem's mood is optimistic, confident, and excited.

p. 279 Reading Skill
Students should underline "black with people," "a muffled roar," and "Like the beating of the storm waves on the stern and distant shore."

p. 279 Reading Check
Students should circle "Ten thousand eyes" and "Five thousand tongues."

p. 280 Reading Skill
Sample response: The crowd is angry with the pitcher, but Casey gives the crowd a look to show that they shouldn't worry. He is determined to hit the ball. As he prepares for the last pitch, he hits the plate with his bat. Casey swings hard at the ball.

p. 280 Literary Analysis
Sample response: The mood goes from optimistic to disappointed. Casey has struck out, and the Mudville team has lost the game.

p. 280 Reading Check
Students should circle "Fraud!"

p. 281 Stop to Reflect
Students may say that a poem is an effective way to tell a story because poets normally include only the most important and vivid details. Other students may say that the poetry doesn't allow the author to give enough details and description.

p. 281 Reading Skill
Sample response: The speaker means that he could ride the bike toward the horizon.

p. 281 Literary Analysis
The characters are the speaker and the owner of the motorcycle.

p. 281 Reading Check
Students should underline "South of the bridge on Seventeenth / I found back of the willows one summer / day a motorcycle with engine running."

p. 282 Reading Skill
Sample response: The tornado banged against the door like an angry cat.

p. 282 Literary Analysis
Sample response: The speaker's father is on the front porch when a tornado hits. The speaker's mother is in the kitchen. The storm damages a tree, drops a car into the yard, and bangs the back door of the house. The speaker does not see it happen. The speaker's parents are recalling the events.

p. 282 Stop to Reflect
Students may describe the ferocity of specific storms. They may say that they stayed in their houses and away from the windows during the storms.

p. 282 Reading Check
Students should underline "Papa was on the front porch. / Mama was in the kitchen."

p. 282 Reader's Response
Sample response: "Casey at the Bat" has the most exciting and interesting plot. It has more vivid details than the other poems, and it is suspenseful.

p. 283 Apply the Skills
1. Sample response: He may have been overly confident. He let two pitches go by without swinging. He believes that he can get a hit when he wants.
2. Sample response: No, his behavior is not appropriate. A tornado is very dangerous. One would not sit calmly on the porch and watch it. One would take cover.
3. **Graphic Organizer**
Sample response:
Casey at the Bat
Setting: a ballpark during the ninth inning
Characters: baseball players and fans
Plot: The ballgame is in the ninth inning. The opposing team is winning by two runs. Casey comes to bat. He strikes out.
Fifteen
Setting: the side of a road
Characters: a fifteen-year-old boy, a motorcycle rider
Plot: A fifteen-year-old boy finds an overturned motorcycle on the roadside. He pushes it back on the road. He imagines what it would be like to ride away on it. Instead, he helps the owner get back to his cycle.
Twister Hits Houston
Setting: a family home in Houston;
Characters: Mama, Papa, the speaker
Plot: A speaker is retelling the story of a tornado that strikes the speaker's home. Papa sits on the front porch. Mama is in the kitchen. The storm uproots a big tree. It also drops a car in the yard and bangs the screen door.
4. Sample response: The baseball came flying, but Casey ignored it. He said that it wasn't his style. The umpire called strike one.

p. 285 Reading/Writing Connection
Sample response: Things in my life that evoke happy feelings include my family and friends. I respond to these feelings by spending more time with these people. When I am in a bad mood, I react by not talking.

p. 285 Note-taking Guide
Sample response:
The Horses
Event: The horses come.
Effect: The people are filled with hope.
The Writer
Event: The speaker hears his daughter typing.
Effect: The father stops in the hallway and thinks about his daughter and her life.

p. 286 Apply the Skills
1. Students might describe the speaker's state of mind as horrified or despairing.
2. Sample response: The sounds of his daughter's typing, trying to set her imagination free, remind him of the starling trying to gain its freedom.
3. **Graphic Organizer**
Sample response:
The Raven
Setting: the speaker's room on a night in December
Characters: the speaker and the raven
Plot: The speaker misses his lost love, Lenore. He grows more and more upset by a visiting raven. He asks the raven questions. The raven always answers "Nevermore."
The Horses
Setting: in the future; about one year after the Seven Days' War
Characters: people living in the world and horses
Plot: After a war nearly destroys the world, a community abandons its tractors. The people farm with oxen and plows. Then, one day a herd of horses appears and gives the people hope of a new world.
The Writer
Setting: the speaker's house
Characters: a girl, her father, a bird
Plot: A speaker is listening to his daughter struggle to type a story. He is reminded of when a starling was trapped in her room, struggling to find freedom through an open window.
4. Sample response: One gloomy night, while I tiredly pored over some old books . . .

Reading Informational Materials: Web Sites

p. 291 Apply the Skills
Thinking About the Web Site
1. The link "Nature's Most Violent Storms" provides information about measures schools can take to ensure the safety of students and teachers. The "You are in school" link on the "Weather Safety for Kids" page may also provide safety measures for schools.
2. Category F5 tornadoes have wind speeds greater than 260 mph and cause tremendous damage, such as houses lifted from their foundation and objects as large as cars thrown over 100 meters.

Reading Skill
3. The link "Storm Reports" has information on current storms.
4. It is a government-sponsored weather Web site.

Poetry Collection 1
Poetry Collection 2

p. 293 Graphic Organizer
Sample response:
Poetry Collection 1
Original Lines: "Two roads diverged in a yellow wood, / And sorry I could not travel both / And be one traveler, long I stood / And looked down one as far as I could / To where it bent in the undergrowth;"
Lines in Smaller Sentences: Two roads diverged in a yellow wood. I was sorry that I could not travel both. I was one traveler. I stood a long time. I looked down one as far as I could. I looked to where it bent in the undergrowth.
Paraphrase: There were two roads in the woods. I could not go down both roads. I stood and looked down one of the roads. I looked to where it curved into the bushes.

Poetry Collection 2
Original Lines: "But if I had to perish twice, / I think I know enough of hate / To say that for destruction ice / Is also great / And would suffice."
Lines in Smaller Sentences: But if I had to perish twice, I think I know enough of hate. For destruction ice is also great. It would suffice.
Paraphrase: If I had to die again, I know that hatred can be just as destructive.

p. 294 Reading/Writing Connection
Sample response:
1. People who <u>challenge</u> themselves can achieve great <u>things</u>.
2. Some people refuse to <u>conform</u> because they want to be different.
3. People like to <u>distinguish</u> themselves from those around them.

p. 294 Note-taking Guide
Sample response:
We never know how high we are: rising above fears to achieve wonderful things
Macavity: The Mystery Cat: a cat named Macavity who lives a life of crime

p. 295 Activate Prior Knowledge
Students may say that they like images the most in their favorite poems because they like vivid description. Other students may say that they like poems about subjects they are interested in.

p. 295 Literary Analysis
Students should underline "rise," "skies," "thing," and "King."

p. 295 Reading Skill
Sample response: The speaker takes the other path because it is just as pleasant and a little less worn.

p. 295 Literary Analysis
The rhyme scheme is *abaab*.

p. 296 Literary Analysis
This stanza uses end rhyme. Students should underline "Paw," "Law," "despair;" and "there."

p. 296 Reading Skill
Sample response: You may seek him in the basement. You may look up in the air. But I tell you once and once again, Macavity's not there.

p. 296 Reading Check
Students should underline "For when they reach the scene of crime— / *Macavity's not there!*"

p. 297 Literary Analysis
"Glass" and "past" are an example of both slant and internal rhyme. They both end with an "s" sound, and they are in the middle of the line instead of at the end of the line.

p. 297 Stop to Reflect
Sample response: Macavity is funny because when the police come looking for him he's doing seemingly innocent things like licking his thumbs or doing long division.

p. 297 Reading Check
Students should circle "Foreign Office find a treaty's gone astray" and "Admiralty lose some plans and drawings."

p. 298 Reading Skill
Sample response: He always has an alibi. He has one or two to spare. At whatever time the deed took place, Macavity wasn't there! Macavity always has more than one alibi. He is never around when the crime occurs.

p. 298 Reading Check
Students should circle "There never was a Cat of such deceitfulness and / suavity."

p. 298 Literary Analysis
The rhyme scheme of the last stanza is *aabbccdd*.

p. 298 Reader's Response
Sample response: "Macavity: The Mystery Cat" sounds the best when read aloud. It has an upbeat meter and is humorous.

p. 299 Apply the Skills
1. Graphic Organizer
Sample response:
What Does It Mean? This choice might represent a choice of colleges to attend or a career to follow.
2. Sample response: Cats are mischievous and curious. They get into things, and they can move silently and quickly disappear.
3. Sample response: "We never know how high we are" has a more regular meter. Every other line has the same meter.
4. Sample response: Two roads diverged in a yellow wood. I was sorry I could not travel both and be one traveler. Long I stood and looked down one as far as I could. I saw where it bent in the undergrowth.

p. 301 Reading/Writing Connection
Sample response:
1. Childhood experiences help an individual acquire qualities such as patience.
2. As children grow older, they may alter their views and opinions.

3. Young adulthood is a time when most people cease to depend upon their parents.

p. 301 Note-taking Guide
Sample response:
maggie and milly and molly and may: to describe the characters' self-discovery
The Seven Ages of Man: to describe a person's journey through life

p. 302 Apply the Skills
1. Graphic Organizer
Sample response:
What Does It Mean? Fire works as a metaphor for desire because desire "burns." Ice is fitting for hate because hate is a "cold" emotion.
2. Sample response: Each character is drawn to something that reflects her inner likes or fears.
3. Sample response: The words "severe" and "beard" show both slant rhyme and internal rhyme.
4. Sample response: Maggie found a shell that sang so sweetly she couldn't remember her troubles. Milly befriended a stranded star. Its rays were five languid fingers.

ANSWERS TO UNIT 5

from The Shakespeare Stealer
Gary Blackwood

p. 306 Note-taking Guide
Sample response:
Box 1: Dr. Bright discovers that Widge was caught stealing a sermon.
Box 2: Falconer buys Widge from Dr. Bright and takes him to Bass's house.

p. 307 Activate Prior Knowledge
Some students may not think copying music is a crime because music is available on the radio. Other students may give examples of when stealing seems acceptable—such as when a father steals diapers for a baby or a mother steals food to feed her children.

p. 307 Drama
Sample response: It sets the time period (some 400 years ago) and the place (England). It also establishes that readers and viewers should think of the actions on stage as real.

p. 307 Drama
Students should underline "apothecary," "Berwick-in-Elmet, Yorkshire, c. 1601," "A table at Center contains glass and earthenware jars and beakers," "pot filled with burning pitch," "plumbago pencil."

p. 307 Drama
Students should circle "At various times, this set will represent Dr. Timothy Bright's apothecary, with Widge's living quarters upstairs; Simon Bass's house; and the backstage area at the Globe Theatre."

p. 308 Drama
Sample Response: The stage directions help the actor playing Widge know what actions to take in reaction to Bright's angry comments. The stage directions help readers imagine what is happening on stage.

p. 308 Drama
Sample response: The dialogue reveals details of character (Dr. Bright's temper) and background information on what has occurred before the play begins. Students may underline "You're lying. No, don't bother to deny it. I've the proof here. The rector at Leeds caught you red-handed" and "But . . . if he took away your transcription of his sermon, then . . .

then whose sermon was it that I . . . used as my model last Sunday?"

p. 308 Drama
Sample response: Widge has been Dr. Bright's apprentice for seven years. Bright has received a letter from the bishop, accusing him of stealing other rectors' sermons. Widge was caught in the act of copying, but he was too frightened to tell Dr. Bright about the incident. Dr. Bright is upset that Widge completed the sermon from memory after Widge was discovered.

p. 309 Drama
Sample response: Widge has learned much at Bright's, but he wants to leave.

p. 309 Drama
Sample response: Falconer could be a symbolic death figure. He seems to suggest that something terrible may come. Students may underline "tall figure in a hooded cloak; looking as grim as Death," "he carries a rapier," "We seldom see his face," and "A nasty scar disfigures one side of his face."

p. 309 Reading Check
Students should circle "seems to reach for his rapier, but instead takes a leather-bound book from beneath his cloak."

p. 310 Drama
Students may circle "Oh, two months, perhaps three. Well, let's say four" and "Well . . . one, actually," which reveal information about Dr. Bright. Students may circle "Yes, yes, but how long to learn it" and "How many?", which reveal information about Falconer.

p. 310 Stop to Reflect
Sample response: Dr. Bright is very hard on his apprentice. He has just called Widge incompetent. Widge probably has never received a compliment while working for the doctor.

p. 310 Drama
Sample response: They tell the actor how to react to another character.

p. 311 Drama
Students may say that it gives Bright and Falconer a chance to discuss Widge without Widge leaving the stage.

p. 311 Drama
Students may suggest dimming the lights between leaving Dr. Bright's and arriving in the woods. Students may also suggest that Falconer and Widge move across the front of the stage; behind them, a curtain could open to reveal the woods.

p. 311 Reading Check
Students should circle "(unexpectedly amiable) God rest you, gentlemen."

p. 312 Drama
Students should underline "parsons" and "parsimonious." Sample response: Someone who is parsimonious is extremely stingy. A parson is a member of the clergy. Some parsons may be parsimonious, but the pun implies that all parsons are stingy.

p. 312 Drama
Sample response: He is clever and is skilled in self-defense techniques.

p. 312 Stop to Reflect
Sample response: He probably is impressed by Falconer and is relieved that the robbers will not hurt him.

p. 313 Drama
Sample response: Falconer is an unpredictable man.

p. 313 Drama
Sample response: It is possible that Falconer and Bass are the same person. Bass may use the alias Falconer so that he can conduct his business in secret.

p. 313 Reading Check
Students should underline "Bass is much more approachable and genial, but a prickliness lurks beneath the surface."

p. 314 Stop to Reflect
Sample response: Bass might want Widge to represent himself as someone from the upper class to do his job. Bass might also feel that it reflects poorly on a master to have a rustic apprentice.

p. 314 Drama
Students may underline "Aye," "I ken that," "Nay," "a wight," "'a got very upset wi' me," "small tablebook," and "plumbago pencil."

p. 314 Drama
Sample response: Widge has already been yelled at and then sold as a result of having been caught copying for Dr. Bright, so he might be afraid of being caught and sold again. Widge also seems to wrestle with himself over whether stealing the play is the right thing to do.

p. 314 Stop to Reflect
Sample response: Dr. Bright used the copied sermons because he was too lazy to write his own. Bass admits that his reason is to make money.

p. 315 Stop to Reflect
Sample response: Others will copy the plays if he does not do it. They will not do the job as well as he will. Shakespeare is a poet of quality and deserves better. If his work is borrowed, it should be done properly.

p. 315 Drama
Sample response: Widge will copy the play and run into difficulty. Perhaps he may be caught. Widge may learn about the negative consequence of speed writing.

p. 315 Reading Check
Students should circle "London."

p. 315 Reader's Response
Some students may say that copying the play is wrong because it is stealing. Other students may say that it is similar to copying a videotape, an audiotape, a CD, or a DVD, and that they see nothing wrong with it.

p. 316 Apply the Skills
1. Sample response: Widge has an excellent memory and excellent writing skills. He was able to recall the sermon. He was able to produce a version good enough that Dr. Bright did not know about the incident until he received a letter from the bishop.
2. Sample response: Falconer does not trust Dr. Bright. He wants to see for himself whether the system works and whether Widge can do the job.
3. Students may say that "So help me God and halidom," "You halfwitted hoddypeak," and "nay" are examples of dialogue that show the play takes place in seventeenth-century England.
4. **Graphic Organizer**
Sample response:
Prop: Dr. Bright uses a walking stick.
How It Is Used: Dr. Bright uses it to scare Widge.

What It Shows: Dr. Bright likes to control others, but he yells more often than he hits with his stick.

Prop: Widge uses a notebook and pencil.

How It Is Used: Widge uses these to carry out tasks assigned by Dr. Bright, Falconer, and Samuel Bass.

What It Shows: Although Widge has received lengthy training from Dr. Bright, he has developed further skills on his own. These props represent his confidence in himself.

Prop: Falconer uses a rapier.

How It Is Used: Falconer uses it to look dangerous to Dr. Bright, Widge, and the thieves.

What It Shows: Falconer will serve as protection for Widge when he goes to London.

The Tragedy of Romeo and Juliet, Act I
William Shakespeare

p. 318 Graphic Organizer
Sample response:

Scene: one

Summary of Action: A fight breaks out between servants and relatives of the two families, the Capulets and the Montagues. The prince breaks up the fight. Benvolio finds out that Romeo is sad about a lost love.

p. 319 Reading/Writing Connection
Sample response:

1. Sad events inspire artists to illustrate people's tragic flaws.
2. To contrast perfection and reality, writers give readers detailed descriptions.
3. Composers can emphasize the pain of lost love by making their music sound dreary.

p. 319 Note-taking Guide
Sample response:

Box 2: Romeo and Benvolio attend the Capulets' feast.

Box 3: Romeo and Juliet meet and fall in love.

Final Outcome: Romeo and Juliet discover that their families are enemies.

p. 320 Apply the Skills
1. Sample response: Romeo is moody and romantic. Juliet is an obedient girl. Before meeting Romeo, she has not given much thought to love. They both fall in love easily.
2. Some students may say that Romeo's passion for Rosaline shows the deep feelings teenagers can have. Other students may say the fact that he forgets about Rosaline after meeting Juliet shows that teens' feelings can change quickly. Other students may say that Romeo is too violent in his passions and does not accurately portray teenagers in love.

3. **Graphic Organizer**
Sample response:

Character: Nurse

Dialogue: "Faith, I can tell her age unto an hour."

Reveals: Nurse is devoted to Juliet.

Character: Juliet

Dialogue: "It is an honor that I dream not of."

Reveals: Juliet has given little thought to love.

Character: Lady Capulet

Dialogue: "Younger than you, / Here in Verona, ladies of esteem, / Are made already mothers."

Reveals: Lady Capulet believes that Juliet is old enough to get married.

4. Sample response: "Leave him alone. Who's in charge here, me or you? If you don't leave him alone, my guests will riot. But you want to act macho. Someday that's going to hurt you. Now, settle down!"

The Tragedy of Romeo and Juliet, Act II, Scene ii
William Shakespeare

p. 322 Graphic Organizer
Sample response:

Character: Juliet

Character's Speech: Formal

Character's Action: Juliet wants to protect Romeo from her family.

Character's Rank: Important; Aristocrat

p. 323 Note-taking Guide
Sample response:

Effect/Cause: Romeo promises to send word about his plans to marry Juliet.

Effect/Cause: Romeo goes to ask the Friar for help.

p. 324 Activate Prior Knowledge
Students may say that they know that Romeo and Juliet are young lovers. Some may know their tragic end.

p. 324 Literary Analysis
Students should underline "O, that she knew she were!"

p. 324 Reading Skill
Students should circle "The brightness" and "night."

p. 324 Reading Check
Students should circle "Enters Juliet at a window."

p. 325 Stop to Reflect
Sample response: Names are important because they are symbolic of the blood feud between the two families. Romeo and Juliet wish they had different names because they are in love. They do not care about the feud between their families.

p. 325 Reading Skill
Sample response: Juliet says that a name is not who a person really is. A rose would keep its qualities if it were called something else. Similarly, the qualities that Juliet admires in Romeo would still exist if he were called by another name. Juliet tells Romeo to give up his name and take her in exchange.

p. 325 Literary Analysis
Sample response: In line 57, the stressed syllables emphasize the words "I," "written," "I," "tear," and "word." These words reinforce Romeo's message that he hates his name.

p. 325 Reading Check
Students should underline "My name, dear saint, is hateful to myself / Because it is an enemy to thee."

p. 326 Reading Check
Students may circle "Dost thou love me? I know thou wilt say 'Ay'; / And I will take thee at thy word. Yet, if thou swear'st, / Thou mayest prove false" and "O gentle Romeo, / If thou dost love, pronounce it faithfully."

p. 326 Literary Analysis
Students should place an accent mark over "love," "first," "prompt," "to," "-quire," "lent," "coun-," "and," "lent," "eyes," "am," "pi-," "yet," "thou," "far," "that," "shore," "with," "far-," "sea," "should," "-ven-," "for," "mer-," and "-dise." Sample response: Shakespeare uses this type of verse to separate noble characters and ideas from the more common characters and simpler ideas.

p. 326 Stop to Reflect
Some students may draw parallels with modern love. Juliet is worried that she appears too eager by declaring her love so openly.

She wonders whether she should play "hard to get." Some things have changed since the time of Shakespeare, but these concerns have not. People are still worried about the way girlfriends or boyfriends feel about them.

p. 327 Literary Analysis
Sample response: The split shows the bond between Romeo and Juliet. The lovers are very connected. They are, in a sense, able to finish each other's sentences.

p. 327 Reading Skill
Sample response: "Do not swear at all. Or if thou wilt, swear by thy gracious self, which is the god of my idolatry, and I'll believe thee."

p. 327 Reading Check
Students should circle "th' inconstant moon, / That monthly changes in her circle orb, / Lest that thy love prove likewise variable."

p. 328 Literary Analysis
Sample response: The Nurse's interruption breaks the blank verse. Without the Nurse's interruption, Juliet's words would complete a full line of blank verse.

p. 328 Stop to Reflect
Students may say that modern lovers use "I love you" and call each other "baby" and "sweetheart."

p. 328 Reading Check
Students should circle "send me word tomorrow, / By one that I'll procure to come to thee" and "Tomorrow will I send."

p. 329 Literary Analysis
Sample response: Romeo and Juliet are aristocrats.

p. 329 Reading Skill
Students may underline "nine," "stand," "love," "stay," and "home."

p. 329 Stop to Reflect
Students may say that they remember the love scenes from *West Side Story* and *Grease*. The love scenes in these movies involve two people promising to be together forever.

P. 330 Literary Analysis
Students may say that they paced their reading as though they were reading prose.

p. 330 Reading Check
Students should circle "Hence will I to my ghostly friar's close cell."

p. 330 Reader's Response

Some students may say that they find the characters and the scene romantic and powerful. Others may say that they think that the lovers are a bit melodramatic.

p. 331 Apply the Skills

1. Sample response: The darkness conceals Romeo from Juliet's relatives. It also makes the lovers feel as if they are alone and can reveal their true feelings.

2. Students may say that the romantic words and images, the vivid descriptions, and the poetic expressions of devotion make the audience share the characters' emotions.

3. **Graphic Organizer**

Sample response:

Blank Verse Pattern: Stressed syllables are "words," "Rom-," "and," "night," "-deed." Unstressed syllables are "Three," "dear," "-eo," "good," and "in-".

Key Words: words, Romeo, night

Why are the stressed words important ones? They emphasize Juliet's request.

4. Students should say that there are 19 sentences in lines 1–25.

The Tragedy of Romeo and Juliet, Act III

William Shakespeare

p. 333 Graphic Organizer

Sample response:

Allusion: "Gallop apace, you fiery-footed steeds, / Towards Phoebus' lodging!"

Refers to: the horses that pulled the sun chariot of the god of the sun, Phoebus

Purpose: refers to the sun moving more quickly across the sky; time moving more quickly

p. 334 Note-taking Guide

Sample response:

Effect/Cause: Romeo kills Tybalt.

Effect: Romeo is not allowed to come back to Verona.

p. 335 Apply the Skills

1. **Graphic Organizer**

Sample response:

What Does It Mean? Mercutio means the statement as a curse. He blames both sides for the fight.

2. Sample response: Romeo means that he is a victim of fate.

3. Sample response: Juliet is impatient for the night to arrive so she can be with Romeo.

4. Sample response: Banishment is torture, not mercy, for heaven is where Juliet lives. While every little creature may look upon Juliet, I cannot. I must go. Even flies have it better than I, for they can hear Juliet speak. But I cannot hear Juliet's voice because I am banished. You say that exile is not death, but it is. The damned howl the word *banished* in hell. How can you torture me with the word *banished*?

The Tragedy of Romeo and Juliet, Act IV

William Shakespeare

p. 337 Graphic Organizer

Sample response:

Line of Dialogue: "I met the youthful lord at Lawrence' cell / And gave him what becomèd love I might, / Not stepping o'er the bounds of modesty."

Lines in Smaller Sentences: "I met the youthful lord at Lawrence' cell. I gave him what becomèd love I might. I did not step o'er the bounds of modesty."

Summary of Line: Juliet is telling her father that she met Paris and showed him appropriate affection.

p. 338 Note-taking Guide

Sample response:

What character does: Juliet takes a potion to escape marriage to Paris.

What character thinks: Juliet is sad because of Romeo is gone and because she is being forced to marry Paris.

What others say about character: "A peevish self-willed harlotry it is." "How now, my headstrong?"

p. 339 Apply the Skills

1. Some students may find the advice risky and tricky and say that Romeo and Juliet should have admitted their marriage. Other students may say that, at the time, the plan seemed to be the only option.

2. Sample response: The soliloquy reveals that Juliet is fully aware of the great risks she is taking. However, she is still willing to take them.

3. Graphic Organizer

Sample response:

What Character Thinks: Capulet thinks Juliet is in her bed asleep.

What Audience Knows: The audience knows that Juliet is in a comatose state and cannot be awakened.

4. Sample response: Juliet tells the Friar that she will kill herself if he cannot help her. He must tell her something immediately or she will die.

The Tragedy of Romeo and Juliet, Act V
William Shakespeare

p. 341 Graphic Organizer

Sample response:

Cause: Friar John is unable to deliver the message to Romeo.

Effect/Cause: Romeo believes that Juliet is truly dead.

Effect: Romeo wants to kill himself.

p. 342 Note-taking Guide

Sample response:

Event 1: Romeo buys poison.

Event 2: Romeo goes to Juliet's grave in Verona.

Event 3: Romeo kills Paris.

Event 4: Romeo poisons himself.

Event 5: Juliet wakes to see Romeo.

Event 6: Juliet stabs herself.

Final Event: The Montagues and Capulets agree to stop fighting.

p. 343 Apply the Skills

1. Students may be surprised that Romeo kills Paris because it seems so sudden. Some students may be surprised that Lady Montague dies of grief because Romeo was not dead, he was only banished.

2. Some students will say it is not a fair exchange. The lovers might have stopped the fighting through their marriage. Others may say that two lives may save many more in the future.

3. Graphic Organizer

Sample response:

Romeo and Juliet's Personalities: Romeo: impulsive, hotheaded, melodramatic; Juliet: strong-willed, disobedient

Fate or Chance: the accidental meeting of the two lovers, Tybalt's misunderstanding

of Romeo's presence at the Capulet party, the Friar's plan goes wrong

Other Causes: the feud between the Montagues and the Capulets

4. Sample response: Romeo hurries to Juliet's tomb and meets and kills Paris. Romeo kills himself because he believes Juliet is dead. Juliet awakens to find Romeo dead. She stabs herself. Families, servants, lawmen, and the Prince gather at the tomb. The Friar explains everything. The Prince, Capulet, and Montague meet at the tomb and the two families end their feud.

Reading Informational Materials: Atlases

p. 348 Apply the Skills
Thinking about the Atlas

1. Sample response: Palermo is the largest city in Sicily. No other city in Sicily uses a symbol that shows greater population.

2. Sample response: Sixteen percent of Italy's exports travel by sea.

Reading Skill

1. Students may list Rome, Florence, Venice, or Padova.

2. Sample response: Illegal immigration became a major issue in the 1993 election.

The Inspector-General
Anton Chekhov
Adapted by Michael Frayn

p. 349 Graphic Organizer

Sample response:

Information Provided: Traveler wants to talk about himself.

Conclusion: He thinks he is an important man.

p. 350 Reading/Writing Connection

Sample response: It can be difficult to interpret what others say. The person cannot respond because the person's identity is secret. If he or she chooses to ignore the conversation, he or she might miss something.

p. 350 Note-taking Guide

Sample response:

What character says: "I'll come down on them like a thunderbolt out of the blue. I can just imagine their faces when they hear who I am . . ." "Wheezes? That's not wheezing! That's the way he talks!" "He's never touched a drop!" "I'll take them by surprise."

What character does: tries to sneak up on the towns; drinks vodka; wheezes when he talks; orders the driver to turn around when he realizes the town knows he is coming

What others say about the character: "We know everything about all of them up there!" "Oh, yes, he's a good one, this one." "Creeps around like a cat. Don't want no one to see him, don't want no one to know who he is." "He wheezes away like an old dog so no one can recognize his voice." "He drinks, mind!" "Oh, like a hole in the ground. Famous for it." "His housekeeper . . . Runs circles around him, she does, like a fox round his tail. She's the one who wears the trousers." "He's a blessing from heaven, I'll grant him that." "Oh, he creeps around all right." "He don't make no trouble." "Though if I know the old devil, he's like as not turned around and gone home again himself."

p. 351 Activate Prior Knowledge
Students may suggest feelings of anger or resentment. If they are doing what they should be doing, they might resent someone's distrusting them.

p. 351 Literary Analysis
Sample response: The inspector-general tries to take a town by surprise by hiding his identity. This is humorous because the town already knows who he is.

p. 351 Reading Skill
Sample response: The traveler thinks he is fooling the driver and townspeople. The traveler does not believe that they know anything about him.

p. 352 Reading Skill
Students may underline "he creeps out of his office, so none of them up there see him go," "He hops on a train just like anyone else," and "He wraps himself up from head to toe so you can't see his face." Students may conclude that the driver knows the traveler is really the inspector-general.

p. 352 Literary Analysis
Sample response: Readers know that the traveler is really the inspector-general. This makes the dialogue humorous because the driver is talking about how much the inspector-general drinks, and the traveler does not like it.

p. 352 Reading Check
Students may underline "Hear him coming five miles off!" and "he has a good sleep, he has a good eat and drink—and then he starts."

p. 353 Reading Skill
Students should underline "The Traveler discreetly pushes the traveling bag out of the Driver's sight." Sample response: The traveler does not want to take a chance of the driver seeing his traveling bag, which probably holds a bottle of vodka.

p. 353 Literary Analysis
Sample response: The traveler is trying to hide who he really is to fool the driver. The driver is pretending not to know that the traveler is the inspector-general.

p. 353 Stop to Reflect
Students may say that the driver is cleverer than the traveler. The traveler thinks he is fooling the driver. The driver knows that the traveler is the inspector-general, but he pretends not to know. He tells the traveler that everyone knows the inspector-general is coming.

p. 354 Literary Analysis
Students may underline "Don't want to go running into the Inspector-General, is that it?" Sample response: This sentence shows that the driver is still pretending not to know who the traveler really is. Students may underline: "Though if I know the old devil, he's like as not turned around and gone home again himself." Sample response: It is comic because the driver says he is describing a supposed situation. He is really saying exactly what is happening.

p. 354 Reading Skill
Students may say that they can conclude that the traveler has realized that his disguise has fooled no one. Everyone knows his secrets. He no longer feels he should bother to hide his drinking habit.

p. 354 Reading Check
Students should underline "Doing drinks and refreshments for the Inspector-General!"

p. 354 Reader's Response

Some students may say that they felt bad when someone tried to deceive them. They felt embarrassed and no longer believed they could trust that person. Other students may say that the deception was harmless and was only meant as a joke. They may say that they were not angry.

p. 355 Apply the Skills

1. Sample response: The traveler realizes he is wasting his time trying to find anything wrong, and he is embarrassed to realize that his cleverness has been so transparent.

2. **Graphic Organizer**

Sample response:

Questions: Who sent the anonymous letter?
Details: People in town seem to know that he is coming. Perhaps someone from the town sent the letter.
Understanding of the Play: Students' understanding may change because they understand why someone would want to contact the inspector-general.
Questions: Will the inspector-general ever visit the town again?
Details: The driver and everyone else in the town seem to know who he is and how he operates. The traveler turns around when he realizes that all the people know he is coming.
Understanding of the Play: Students' understanding may change because they understand why the driver might want to convince the inspector-general that he is expected.
Questions: Why does the driver not tell the traveler immediately that he knows who the traveler is?
Details: The traveler thinks he is being sneaky. The driver appears to enjoy the joke.
Understanding of the Play: Students' understanding may change because they realize that the driver could not have affected the traveler so strongly if the driver had been honest.

3. Sample response: The play ends happily because it's humorous that the only harm done is to the inspector-general's pride. The driver's dialogue is witty when he insults the inspector-general to his face and the inspector-general is forced to sit quietly because the inspector-general wants to

protect his identity. The situation is comic because the inspector-general tries to sneak into the town but everyone knows who he is. The play amuses the audience because the audience knows from the beginning that the traveler's disguise is not working.

4. Sample response: The driver is clever and has a sense of humor. He outsmarts the traveler and he is happy without letting the traveler know that he has been discovered.

Reading Informational Materials: Book Review

p. 357 Graphic Organizer

Sample response:

Intent or reasons for writing: to discuss the new translation of Chekov's plays
Bias toward the subject: The writer likes the plays of Chekov. The writer also thinks that many of the translations are unreadable by Americans.
Thorough support for opinions: He uses excerpts from the other translations and the new translation to support his opinion that the new translation makes Chekov more accessible for American audiences.

p. 358 Reading Book Reviews

Sample response: Kirsch's review begins with information about Chekov's life to give background information and identify the controversy.

p. 358 Reading Skill

Students may say that quoting Tolstoy helps Kirsch's credibility because Tolstoy is a famous writer who wrote something about Chekhov's plays. Quoting relevant famous people lends credibility to the review.

p. 358 Reading Check

Student should underline "Like lyric poems, they favor mood over plot; there is no overriding 'problem,' and when problems do appear, the playwright never seems to endorse any solutions."

p. 359 Reading Skill

Students may underline "Chekhov's emphasis on tone and mood, and his faithful re-creation of ordinary conversation with all its hesitations, references, and silences . . . ."

p. 359 Reading Book Reviews

Students may circle "lively"; "colloquial and clear"; "revelation"; "clear away the obscurity and sentimentality"; "The plays that emerge are funnier and more muscular than one might have expected."

p. 359 Stop to Reflect

Sample response: Including quotes is a good way to support his opinion that Schmidt's translation makes sense.

p. 360 Stop to Reflect

Students may circle "Tut-tut." Students may say that they would say "That is not nice" instead.

p. 360 Reading Book Reviews

Sample response: Kirsch thinks Schmidt's work makes sense and that the book should be the first choice for American readers.

p. 360 Reading Informational Materials

Sample response: Chekhov's plays were first written in Russian. Chekhov's plays have been translated into British English.

p. 361 Apply the Skills
Thinking About the Book Review

1. Sample response: He thinks the starchy British English sounds absurd.
2. Sample response: The first translation does not sound like a typical American conversation. The second translation sounds more like an American conversation.

Reading Skill

3. Sample response: Kirsch's main purpose is to express an opinion about Schmidt's translation.
4. Some students may say that they believe Kirsch because he uses quotations from Schmidt, Tolstoy, and Chekov. Other students may say that Kirsch's knowledge of Chekov and his works adds to his credibility.

Play Hard; Play Together; Play Smart
from The Carolina Way
Dean Smith with John Kilgo

p. 364 Note-taking Guide
Sample response:
Attitude Toward Winning: a by-product of the process but not the goal; too many uncontrollable events, such as injuries or bad calls; win and lose as a team
How They Measured Success: whether players had fun and worked together; whether players did great things for people in all walks of life
Play Hard: maximum effort, including practices
Play Together: game that counts on togetherness, taking care of one another, being unselfish
Play Smart: drilled until skills became habits

p. 365 Activate Prior Knowledge
Students may say that playing a sport taught them that hard work and dedication could help them accomplish their goals in life.

p. 365 Themes in Literature
Students may say that Coach Smith's philosophy did surprise them because they think that winning would be the number one goal. Students may say that his philosophy stresses the strength of loyalty and the importance of heroism. Each player must be dedicated to the team by acting intelligently, unselfishly and with courage. Each player must also act in the best interest of the team and show effort on the court.

p. 365 Reading Check
Students should underline "Hard meant with effort, determination, and courage; together meant unselfishly, trusting your teammates, and doing everything possible not to let them down; smart meant with good execution and poise, treating each possession as if it were the only one in the game."

p. 366 Stop to Reflect
Students may point out that most of Coach Smith's principles can be applied to life. Working hard and accentuating the positive can apply to school, friendships, and many other parts of life.

p. 366 Themes in Literature
Students may react by saying that every player must do whatever it takes to help his teammates succeed. Other students may not like the idea of "punishing" the whole team because one person does not do what he or she is supposed to do.

p. 366 Reading Check
Students should underline "But each of them could control the effort with which he played."

p. 366 Themes in Literature
Some students may suggest that working together is a shared value because people in all walks of life need to work together to survive.

p. 367 Stop to Reflect
Students may suggest that developing good work habits is important in school or at a job.

p. 367 Themes in Literature
Students may suggest that the themes in Coach Smith's philosophy reflect the culture of the United States because he focuses on working hard and on achieving certain goals.

p. 367 Reading Check
Students should underline "Our former players are doing great things for people in all walks of life."

p. 367 Reader's Response
Students may say that they agree with Smith. They may think that good sportsmanship, hard work, and dedication are more important than winning a game. Even if they lose a game, the players have still acquired values that will lead them to success in life. Other students may say that winning is more important. They may think that values and a strong work ethic may not be so important if the end result is not favorable.

p. 368 Apply the Skills
1. Sample response: If each player plays hard, plays smart, and plays together, the team can work to better deal with the unexpected. If they cannot deal with it effectively, then at least they have given it their best shot.
2. Coach Smith probably feels that his career was successful because he was both a teacher and a coach. He believes that the two should be one and the same.

3. Graphic Organizer

Sample response:

Value: Play hard. Play together. Play smart.

Examples: Give maximum effort, including in practice. Admit to being tired, and take a break so that you do not slack off. / Put the team before yourself, and do everything possible not to let them down. Do not be selfish. Trust your teammates. / Learn the fundamentals, and practice them until they are perfected.

Application: Be the best you can be. Do not be ashamed to ask for help if you need it. / Workers in a company should put the company before themselves. With everyone working toward the same goal, everyone will benefit. / Treat each task you attempt as important and essential. Use every resource you have to accomplish your goals.

4. Students will probably agree that sports are an important part of the cultural context of the United States. They may explain that team playing and working hard are a part of the American work ethic.

from The Odyssey, Part 1, The Cyclops Homer

p. 370 Graphic Organizer

Sample response:

Historical/Cultural Detail: "We lit a fire, burnt an offering, / and took some cheese to eat . . ."

Background: Odysseus and his men offer a prayer of thanks to the gods and give a portion of their meal to the gods out of respect.

Analysis: Religion played an important role in ancient Greek culture. The gods appear in the *Odyssey*, often helping Odysseus or playing a part in his suffering. Ancient Greek beliefs and customs are reflected in Odysseus' offering.

p. 371 Reading/Writing Connection

Sample response: The journey involved an encounter with the local people. I had to interact with a new culture. The highlight of this experience was learning a new language.

p. 371 Note-taking Guide

Sample response:

Event 1: Odysseus and his men arrive at the land of the Cyclopes.

Event 2: Odysseus and his men are trapped in Polyphemus' cave.

Event 3: Odysseus finds an enormous club and turns it into a spike.

Event 4: Odysseus and his men blind Polyphemus with the spike.

Event 5: Odysseus hides his men under the Cyclops's sheep, and they escape.

Final Outcome: Odysseus and his men leave the land of the Cyclopes.

p. 372 Activate Prior Knowledge

Students may say that an adventure story needs a hero whom readers can admire and villains against whom the hero must struggle.

p. 372 Reading Skill

Students should underline lines 109–120. The Greeks valued a civilized society. They valued their laws and farming their land.

p. 372 Literary Analysis

Odysseus' investigation of the shore shows that he is brave, adventurous, and unafraid of challenges. He is also resourceful because he takes his twelve best warriors with him in case they come across danger.

p. 373 Reading Skill

Odysseus' detailed description of the wine shows that the Greeks valued gifts. They also believed in saving their best wine for their guests and treated their guests very well.

p. 373 Literary Analysis

Students should circle "Ah, / how sound that was!" and "it turned out."

p. 373 Reading Check

Students should circle "But Cyclops / had gone afield, to pasture his fat sheep."

p. 374 Literary Analysis

The Cyclops thinks Odysseus and company may be robbers. Students may underline "are you wandering rogues" and "ravage other folk by sea."

p. 374 Reading Skill

Odysseus expresses the Greek custom of offering hospitality to any guest—stranger or friend.

p. 374 Reading Check

Students should underline "We felt a pressure on our hearts, in dread / of that deep rumble and that mighty man."

p. 375 Stop to Reflect

Sample response: Odysseus suspects that the Cyclops may want to destroy his ship, so he avoids telling the giant where it is. Odysseus also does not tell the Cyclops about his other men, who have remained behind with the ship, because he does not want to put them in danger.

p. 375 Literary Analysis

If Odysseus were to kill the giant, he and his men would be trapped in the cave. They would be unable to move the slab blocking the cave's mouth and would eventually die. Students should underline ". . . if I killed him / we perished there as well, for we could never / move his ponderous doorway slab aside."

p. 375 Reading Skill

Odysseus would pray to Athena for the wisdom to overcome his situation because she is the goddess of wisdom and intellect.

p. 376 Literary Analysis

Sample response: Odysseus shows that he is resourceful, creative, and brave. He also joins his men in the most dangerous tasks and is apparently a good judge of his men's abilities and characters.

p. 376 Stop to Reflect

Sample response: Odysseus is bragging about his courage and his leadership abilities. He might also be exaggerating about events in the story to make himself seem to be a hero.

p. 376 Reading Skill

Sample response: Odysseus' comment tells that giving gifts in return for favors is important.

p. 376 Reading Check

Students should underline "four strong men, and I made five."

p. 377 Stop to Reflect

Students may say that in certain dangerous situations, lying is necessary for self-preservation or to prevent harm to others.

p. 377 Reading Skill

Sample response: The ancient Greeks valued the gods' assistance. They also believed that the gods controlled the fate of humans. Odysseus' comment contrasts him with the Cyclops because it shows that Odysseus

respects and believes in the gods, whereas the Cyclops does not seem to be religious.

p. 377 Reading Check

Students should underline "Nohbdy's my meat, then, after I eat his friends."

p. 378 Reading Skill

Sample response: The response of the other Cyclopes suggests that the Greeks believed that the gods had control over the health of each individual. Gods delivered pain.

p. 378 Literary Analysis

Sample response: Odysseus is proud of his cunning.

p. 378 Reading Check

Students should circle the sentence that begins, "Now Cyclops, wheezing as the pain came on him . . ."

p. 379 Literary Analysis

Sample response: Odysseus' plan shows him to be clever and resourceful in a tight situation.

p. 379 Stop to Reflect

Students may say that Odysseus is cleverer than Polyphemus because Polyphemus does not seem suspicious of his sheep's behavior. Students should underline lines 405–408.

p. 379 Reading Skill

Sample response: Stealing property may be considered revenge for evil intentions.

p. 380 Literary Analysis

Odysseus is taunting the Cyclops. Students may say that Odysseus is allowing his anger to get the best of him. He is acting in a boastful and vindictive manner.

p. 380 Reading Skill

Sample response: Odysseus' combination of weakness and strength suggest that the Greeks believed that even great men could be flawed. Their gods and heroes had human traits.

p. 380 Reading Check

Students should circle lines 448–454.

p. 381 Stop to Reflect

Sample response: The god will do as Polyphemus asks and Odysseus will never get home; or if he does, it will take him many years, and he will lose his men and his ship in the process.

p. 381 Reading Skill

Sample response: The Greeks believed that the gods played an active part in the lives of humans.

p. 381 Reading Check

Polyphemus is amazed that Odysseus, a "small, pitiful and twiggy" man, defeated him. Students should circle lines 468–471.

p. 382 Literary Analysis

Sample response: Odysseus shows a sense of fairness by dividing the sheep equally among the men.

p. 382 Reading Skill

Sample response: Odysseus' punishment shows that the Greeks did believe in justice. Not even heroes got away with their crimes or sins.

p. 382 Reading Check

Students should underline "destruction for my ships he had in store / and death for those who sailed them, my companions."

p. 382 Reader's Response

Students may find the scene in which Odysseus and his men blind the Cyclops the most exciting because the men are clever and escape from a troublesome situation.

p. 383 Apply the Skills

1. Some students will say that they would like to have Odysseus as a leader because he is brave, clever, and resourceful. He forms a strong bond with his men. Others will say that they would not like to have him as a leader because he is boastful and lets his anger get the best of him. His mistakes put the lives of his men in danger.

2. Students may say that the story endures because of its pace, adventures, and remarkable characters.

3. **Graphic Organizer**

Sample response:

Action: Odysseus tricks the Cyclops in order to escape his cave. He taunts the Cyclops and receives Poseidon's wrath. He urges his men not to lose heart in the rough sea.

Trait: cleverness; pride or boldness; fellowship

4. Sample response: Students may say that Odysseus would have benefited from a navigation system and a communication system.

from The Odyssey, Part 2
Homer

p. 385 Graphic Organizer

Sample response:

Detail in Text: Odysseus kills the suitors.
Meaning for Characters: The suitors had intruded on Odysseus' home and family. Trespassers deserved to die.
Meaning in My Culture: Killing is against the law. These murders were not committed in self-defense.

p. 386 Note-taking Guide

Sample response:

Conflict: Odysseus' home has been overrun by men who want to kill his son and marry his wife.
Exposition: The Greek hero Odysseus has just come home to Ithaca after twenty years and finds himself and his home in danger.
Event 3: Odysseus kills Antinous.
Climax: Odysseus removes his disguise.
Event 4: Odysseus, Telemachus, Athena, and the herdsmen kill the suitors.
Event 5: Penelope tests Odysseus.
Resolution: Odysseus and Penelope embrace.

p. 387 Activate Prior Knowledge

Students may say that the characteristics of a hero include courage, intelligence, cleverness, and willingness to sacrifice for others.

p. 387 Literary Analysis

The old beggar is comparing Penelope's name or reputation with the honor of a great king.

p. 387 Reading Skill

Sample response: In Penelope's culture, it is important to offer hospitality to others in need.

p. 387 Reading Check

Students should underline lines 1301–1305.

p. 388 Reading Skill

Sample response: People in modern times also do things to honor the dead; however, people today do not follow rituals as did the people in ancient Greece.

p. 388 Stop to Reflect

Sample response: Penelope's actions tell that she is clever and independent.

p. 388 Reading Check

Students should circle lines 1340–1344.

p. 389 Reading Skill

Sample response: The beggar's prediction shows that people of the time relied on the sun and moon to tell time. Today people would predict a coming event by naming the day, month, or year.

p. 389 Literary Analysis

Sample response: Students should underline "so the taut gut vibrating hummed and sang / a swallow's note." The simile describes Odysseus' skill with the bow and how easily he can string it.

p. 389 Reading Check

Students should underline "Penelope says she will marry the man who can string Odysseus' bow and shoot an arrow through twelve axhandle sockets."

p. 390 Stop to Reflect

Sample response: Penelope probably set this test because she knows that Odysseus is so skilled with the bow. Few can match his skill.

p. 390 Reading Skill

Odysseus' success shows that skill with weapons was considered a good trait in Greek culture.

p. 390 Reading Check

Students should underline "The hour has come to cook their lordships' mutton— / supper by daylight."

p. 391 Reading Skill

Some students may say that the fight is not fair because Antinous does not get a chance to fight back. Other students may say that Odysseus acts fairly because Antinous has insulted him and taken advantage of his family and their hospitality. Antinous tried to steal everything that was important to Odysseus.

p. 391 Literary Analysis

Students should circle lines 1421–1425. The description of Antinous' death is not an epic simile. The word *like* is used to describe just one image.

p. 391 Reading Check

Students should underline "For they imagined as they wished—that it was a wild shot, / an unintended killing."

p. 392 Reading Skill

Students may say that this behavior is not part of ancient Greek culture. Homer shows this by portraying Eurymachus as selfish and deceitful.

p. 392 Stop to Reflect

Students may say that the offer of repayment seems fair. However, the suitors cannot be trusted, and they will try to kill Odysseus their at first chance. Students may suggest that they would place the suitors in prison.

p. 392 Reading Check

Students should underline "wine and meat," "a tithe of twenty oxen," and "bronze and gold."

p. 393 Literary Analysis

The comparison is not an epic simile because it compares a sword to a razor. An epic simile is longer and sustains a comparison over many lines.

p. 393 Reading Check

Students should underline "But the kingly man let fly / an arrow at that instant, and the quivering feathered butt / sprang to the nipple of his breast as the barb stuck in his liver."

p. 393 Reading Skill

Sample response: Telemachus' joining the fight shows the importance of loyalty to the family. It also shows that a son should obey and support his father.

p. 394 Reading Skill

Sample response: The contrasting descriptions show that heroes battle courageously and that deceitful bullies behave fearfully under pressure.

p. 394 Literary Analysis

The comparison to gold and silver, the mention of craftsman, the mention of fine art, and the phrase "whose work moves to delight" all compare Odysseus' hair to artwork.

p. 394 Reading Check

Students should underline "Athena, Telemachus, Eumaeus, and other faithful herdsmen."

p. 395 Stop to Reflect

Students may say that they would test Odysseus because they would want to have the final sign that he is truly Odysseus.

p. 395 Reading Check
Students should underline lines 1554–1558.

p. 395 Literary Analysis
The comparison is not an epic simile because it is mentioned only once and does not include other details.

p. 396 Reading Skill
Sample response: Penelope has shown qualities of faithfulness to her husband, determination, and intelligence.

p. 396 Literary Analysis
Sample response: The epic simile shows how Odysseus has suffered and struggled to get home. It also shows his joy at finally arriving safely.

p. 396 Reading Check
Students should circle lines 1593–1596.

p. 396 Reader's Response
Sample response: Students may say that Odysseus is courageous and good to those who treat him fairly, but he is also boastful and violent. He may not be exactly what they would consider a hero. To them, a hero may never make mistakes or show any imperfections.

p. 397 Apply the Skills
1. Sample response: Odysseus faced many dangers, but Penelope suffered years of waiting, never knowing what had happened to Odysseus.
2. Her experience with the suitors has made Penelope act cautiously. She believes that she must be sure of his identity.
3. **Graphic Organizer**
Sample response:
Items Being Compared: Odysseus' longing for his wife is compared with a swimmer's longing for the shore.
Details of Epic Simile: "rough water," "Poseidon's blows," "gale winds and tons of sea," "big surf," "clotted with brine," "kindly beaches"
Purpose: to show the intensity of Odysseus' feelings as he returns to Penelope
4. Sample response: Many of Odysseus' values are universal. For instance, we still value hospitality and we can understand and sympathize with his longing for home. Many people may not share his belief that the gods participate and interfere in human affairs.

Reading Informational Materials: Applications

p. 402 Apply the Skills
Thinking About the Application
1. Sample response: The application asks for a personal essay so that the applicant can give more information about his or her reasons for applying. The applicant can also explain more about career plans and why he or she would be a good volunteer for this project.
2. Sample response: References can be more objective. References can also describe how well the applicant works with other people.

Reading Skill
3. Each volunteer is expected to take part in all excavation duties.
4. Applicants must list any archaeology and classics classes they have taken.

"Three Skeleton Key"
George G. Toudouze

"The Red-headed League"
Sir Arthur Conan Doyle

p. 403 Graphic Organizer
Sample response:
"Three Skeleton Key"
Protagonist: the narrator
Goals and Actions: He wants to get rid of the rats. He, Le Gleo, and Itchoua close all entrances to the lighthouse. They leave the lighthouse lantern unlit so that the outside world can see that they are in trouble.
Antagonist: the rats
Goals and Actions: The rats want to survive. They search for food. They take over a Dutch ship and eat the crew. Then, they overtake Three Skeleton Key and the lighthouse.
Conflict: The rats want to kill the men, and the men want to kill the rats.
Universal Motives or Struggles: the fight for survival

"The Red-headed League"
Protagonist: Sherlock Holmes
Goals and Actions: He wants to solve the mystery of the Red-headed League. He investigates the mystery.
Antagonist: John Clay
Goals and Actions: He plans to rob the bank. He digs a tunnel.
Conflict: Clay wants to rob the bank. Holmes wants to catch him.

Universal Motives or Struggles: the struggle of good against evil

p. 404 Reading/Writing Connection
Sample response: Lighthouse keepers often had more access to quiet simplicity. However, their duties often forced them to forgo social activities. Such isolation could induce loneliness.

p. 404 Note-taking Guide
Sample response:
Dangers at the Lighthouse: the sharks
Supporting Details: ". . . the waters about our island swarmed with huge sharks who kept an eternal patrol around the base of the light."
Dangers at the Lighthouse: the rats
Supporting Details: "fierce, bold animals"; ". . . brave . . . and vengeful. If you so much as harm one, his sharp cry will bring hordes of his fellows to swarm over you, tear you and not cease until your flesh has been stripped from the bones."

p. 405 Activate Prior Knowledge
Students may say that they are most frightened of snakes. If trapped and surrounded by snakes, they would probably panic and feel as though there were no escape.

p. 405 Literary Analysis
Some details that students may underline include: "My most terrifying experience," "When I was a young man," "I volunteered for service," and "I signed up, boarded ship."

p. 405 Reading Check
Students should underline "the waters about our island swarmed with huge sharks who kept an eternal patrol around the base of the light."

p. 406 Stop to Reflect
Some students may say that they would like such a job. The advantages might be the peace and quiet and having free time. Other students may say that they would not like such a job. The disadvantages would be the isolation and boredom.

p. 406 Reading Skill
The narrator points out that the head-keeper, Itchoua, is about a dozen, or twelve, years older than he and Le Gleo.

p. 406 Reading Check
Students should underline "Itchoua pointed, and following his finger, we saw a big three-master, with all sail set, heading straight for the light."

p. 407 Literary Analysis
Sample response: The details about the arrival of the abandoned ship, which looks like it may crash into the lighthouse and bring some harm to the protagonist, may interest students in what will happen to the protagonist.

p. 407 Reading Skill
Le Gleo seems most frightened. He is afraid that the ship may be a ghost ship.

p. 407 Reading Check
Students should circle "No doubt some freak of current and wind, of which our island was the center, kept her near us."

p. 408 Reading Skill
Both are excited at seeing the ship. Le Gleo is anxious to see the ship smashed. The narrator is sad that such a beautiful ship would be wrecked.

p. 408 Literary Analysis
Students should underline three of the following details: "They had been driven out by the rats," "fierce, bold animals," "Large, strong and intelligent, clannish and seawise," "they are brave, these rats, and vengeful," "swarm over you, tear you and not cease until your flesh has been stripped from the bones," and "In twenty-four hours they had been overwhelmed, killed, and eaten by the rats."

p. 408 Reading Skill
These rats are larger and smarter; they are fierce and "seawise."

p. 409 Stop to Reflect
Students may say that they would be scared and look for a way off the island.

p. 409 Literary Analysis
Students may note details such as the rats that attack and eat the crew and the starving army of rats approaching. The reader may be sympathetic because the protagonist may be attacked and killed by the rats.

p. 409 Reading Check
Students should circle "her small boats were all in place."

p. 410 Literary Analysis
They are in conflict with the rats.

p. 410 Reading Skill
Both the rats and the sharks are predators, quickly and savagely attacking and eating their prey.

p. 410 Stop to Reflect
Sample response: The narrator makes the actions of the rats seem believable. He gives details about what they do and how they act together.

p. 410 Reading Check
Students should underline "the turning beam completely maddened the beasts."

p. 411 Literary Analysis
Sample response: The men must have periods in which they are calm because they stop to watch the rats' behavior long enough to give the rats names.

p. 411 Stop to Reflect
Le Gleo sees skeletons dancing around him. Students should underline "in which he would see the three skeletons dancing around him, gleaming coldly, seeking to grasp him." Le Gleo's descriptions of the skeletons are so detailed and realistic that Itchoua and the narrator begin to see them as well.

p. 411 Literary Analysis
Sample response: The two characters feel loyal to Itchoua. They do not want to see him killed in such a horrible way.

p. 411 Reading Check
Students should underline "we decided not to light the lantern that night."

p. 412 Literary Analysis
Some students may say that the rats are intelligent and organized creatures. Students should underline "One of them, larger than the others, who seemed to lead them in their rushes against the glass," and "the door was eaten through and gave way." Other students may say that the rats are vicious, mindless animals. Students should underline "raging cries of the rats," and "horde of maddened rats which flowed through the gaping window."

p. 412 Reading Skill
Sample response: The narrator is stronger and in control of his feelings. Le Gleo allows his feelings to take control of him.

p. 412 Reading Check
Students should underline "the patrol was there to investigate the failure of our light."

p. 413 Stop to Reflect
Sample response: The narrator suggests that the rats have the power to reason and to communicate feelings such as ridicule or resentment.

p. 413 Literary Analysis
Sample response: The men are in danger of being killed by the rats. The struggle involves human beings trying to survive against the forces of nature.

p. 413 Reading Check
Students should underline "He lit it and, using a plank placed and withdrawn before the beam to form the dots and dashes, quickly sent out our story to those on the vessel."

p. 414 Literary Analysis
The rats were tough adversaries, and he respects their fighting spirit.

p. 414 Stop to Reflect
Students may say that human intelligence wins out in the conflict. The rescuers trick the rats into jumping on a huge barge where they are destroyed.

p. 414 Reading Skill
Sample response: Why has the narrator not changed much? Why are the rats so vicious?

p. 415 Apply the Skills
1. Sample response: Their arrival on a crewless ship gives the impression that the rats are dangerous and destructive. They have already brought down an entire crew of men and have taken over the ship.
2. Sample response: Itchoua's remark suggests that if the rats get into the lighthouse and kill them, three more skeletons could be added to the name of the island.
3. The conflict between the narrator and the rats represents the universal struggle for survival.
4. **Graphic Organizer**
Sample response:
Beginning Only: The narrator is young and inexperienced. He enjoys life on the island. He is not superstitious.

End Only: The narrator has nearly died from the rat attack, and he has lost two friends. He is wiser now.

Beginning and End: He still enjoys the island and working in the lighthouse. He still does not believe the superstitions.

p. 417 Reading/Writing Connection

Sample response: You might perceive that a pencil is round, but most pencils have six sides. If you observe pencil lead closely, you can see that it has a rough surface. One way to differentiate between a pen and a pencil is to note that pencils often weigh less than pens.

p. 417 Note-taking Guide

Sample response:

Box 2: Wilson loses his job.

Box 3: Wilson asks Sherlock Holmes for help.

Box 4: Holmes uncovers the crime.

p. 418 Apply the Skills

1. Holmes finds Wilson's story interesting because it is different from any Holmes has heard before.

2. Spaulding's trousers showed that he had been digging in the cellar. The bank's property bordered Wilson's shop.

3. The protagonist is Sherlock Holmes. His goal is to solve the mystery and catch the criminal behind it.

4. **Graphic Organizer**

Sample response:

Beginning Only: Holmes is curious about Wilson's story.

End Only: Holmes can take pride in capturing a known criminal.

Beginning and End: Holmes uses reasoning to solve crimes. He solves crimes to escape boredom. He waits for the next new crime.

Reading Informational Materials: Encyclopedia Entries

p. 423 Apply the Skills
Thinking About Encyclopedia Entries

1. Sample response: To "play fair" means that the author gives the reader the same information found by the detective. This information gives readers a fair chance to solve the mystery as they read.

2. The American style of mystery introduced in the 1920s focused on a tough detective as its hero. The mystery featured action and violence. It had a colorful narrative style.

Reading Skill

3. Sample response: to learn which writers are famous for writing detective stories

4. You would find this information in the section with the subhead "History."

"There Is a Longing"
Chief Dan George

"Glory and Hope"
Nelson Mandela

p. 424 Graphic Organizer
Sample response:

"There Is a Longing"

Philosophical Assumptions: The greatness of the Native American people is in the future as well as in the past. The road to greatness will be difficult but will be worth it.

Evaluation: His beliefs support his purpose because they empower Native Americans to improve their lives.

"Glory and Hope"

Philosophical Assumptions: Democracy is a form of government that is superior to apartheid.

Evaluation: This belief supports Mandela's purpose of bringing a message of hope and inspiration to the people of South Africa.

p. 425 Reading/Writing Connection

Sample response: Connecting with one's own heritage can reinforce a tolerance for other cultures. Contemporary culture does encourage the acceptance of other cultures. A blending of other cultures can produce a wide spectrum of beliefs and traditions.

p. 425 Note-taking Guide
Sample response:

The Speaker's Longings: for his people to live without welfare and take their place in a society that is "rightly" theirs; to take back the "courage of the olden Chiefs" so that he can lead his people; to accept the "new culture" of the white man, succeed in it, and move forward; to learn the skills of the white man so that he and his people can succeed in the white man's world; to see his people fill the roles of the most important and successful white men; to see his people fill government positions so that they, too, will lead this country and bring to it Native American values

p. 426 Activate Prior Knowledge
Students may say that people need qualities such as determination, flexibility, and compassion in order to succeed in today's society.

p. 426 Literary Analysis
Chief George's purpose for writing is to empower Native Americans so that they can reemerge as a proud and strong people. He assumes that his people wish to survive and prosper, that the greatness of his people is in the future as well as the past, and that the road will be difficult.

p. 426 Reading Skill
The new warriors will use ideas instead of weapons. Their training will be longer and more demanding.

p. 426 Reading Check
Students should circle "the only weapon left to me is speech."

p. 427 Apply the Skills
1. Sample response: He believes that young Native Americans need to be prepared so that they can seize opportunities rather than accept welfare from the government.
2. Sample response: He means that he must fight for the future of his people by speaking out for them. He will use reason and logic as his weapons to fight for their rights.
3. Sample response: His audience might have shared his faith and his belief in the potential of Native Americans. Students may support their answers with the following: "There is a longing among / the young of my nation to secure for themselves / and their people the skills that will / provide them with a sense of worth and / purpose."
4. **Graphic Organizer**
Sample response:
Past: His people were once great. They fought their wars with weapons. Training to be great warriors was easier in the past. The olden Chiefs had great courage.
Present: The people are filled with longing. They are faced with hard work, isolation, and studying. The Chief has only the power to make speeches.
Future: His people can be great again. They can be leaders. They can be educated. They can be free.

p. 429 Reading/Writing Connection
Sample response: A good speech from a leader can evoke emotions such as hope. People stand for the national anthem to signify their pride. The time people devote to learning about voting issues shows that they care.

p. 429 Note-taking Guide
Sample response:
Old South Africa: White people ran the government. Black people faced discrimination. The rest of the world looked down on South Africa. South Africa was a shameful country.
New South Africa: The government is a democracy. All citizens are equal and free. The world has a high opinion of South Africa. South Africa is a proud country.

p. 430 Apply the Skills
1. Students may cite such ideas as equality, dignity, and peace.
2. Sample response: Mandela believes that the present moment is glorious and that the future is hopeful.
3. Sample response: Mandela assumes that apartheid was wrong and that democracy is a good form of government. Also, Mandela believes that South Africa is a beautiful land with people who deserve freedom.
4. **Graphic Organizer**
Sample response:
Past: South Africa was oppressed by the apartheid system.
Present: South Africa is experiencing "newborn liberty."
Future: South Africa faces many challenges on its way to becoming a full-fledged democracy.

ANSWERS TO UNIT 1

from The Giant's House
Elizabeth McCracken

"Desiderata"
Elizabeth McCracken

p. 4 Note-taking Guide
Sample response:
What character thinks: He wants to find a cure for his condition. He is impatient with Peggy for playing dumb.
What others say about character: Giant describes him.

p. 5 Activate Prior Knowledge
Students may say that *gigantic, enormous, myth and folklore, Cyclops, Goliath, Hercules, Titan, Jack and the Beanstalk,* and *monstrous in strength and anger* come to mind.

p. 5 Read Fluently
Students should underline "Look in the big books on the table—see those books?"

p. 5 Fiction
Sample response: James has a problem with his height. He wants to find out more about people like him and what they do. Peggy has a problem figuring out what James really wants to know, not just what he says he wants to know.

p. 6 Fiction
Sample response: Peggy pays attention to the kinds of books library patrons check out; she wants people to learn to do their own research. Students should underline "After closing that evening, Peggy begins the search herself" and "As a librarian she feels the familiar urge to find information."

p. 6 Fiction
Students should circle "Giant described him."

p. 6 Reading Check
Students should underline "The books described weak stomachs and legs and bones. Sometimes what made them tall showed in their faces . . ."

p. 7 Fiction
Sample response: The narrator is not part of the other giants' lives. She only reads about them in her research.

p. 7 Stop to Reflect
Students may say that James will be sad that his height labels him as abnormal and a freak. Other students may say he will be happy to read about other people like him and discover that they lived happy lives.

p. 7 Reading Check
Students should underline "Abnormalities, human."

p. 8 Fiction
Sample response: James wants to stop growing. He is looking for a medical solution to his problem.

p. 8 Fiction
Students should circle "Medicine, or operations, or something;" "That was a lie, I knew we didn't;" "Really, you should ask your doctor;" "I've asked a lot of doctors."
Sample response: It is important to teenagers to be ordinary. No matter how adults try to protect them, young people have to learn to face reality.

p. 9 Note-taking Guide
Sample response:
To entertain: Martha's letters about serving The Dollies chicken are entertaining.
To persuade: Family papers are a useful part of a family's genealogy.
To reflect: Paper collections force a person to draw conclusions based on incomplete information.

p. 10 Activate Prior Knowledge
Students may say that a shopping list would tell them what people were eating or how much money they had. They might say that an old family letter would reveal information about a parent when he or she was younger.

p. 10 Read Fluently
Sample response: McCracken collects family letters, notes, and papers. She values these and keeps them to learn more about her family.

p. 10 Nonfiction
Students should underline "a family history," "stories," "poems," "letters," "diaries," and "laundry lists."

p. 11 Nonfiction
Students should underline "You might find out about family problems you would rather not know. You might learn that relatives could be mean-spirited. You might learn painful things as well."

p. 11 Nonfiction
Students should circle "attorney," "small business person," and "died at age 90 at home." Students should double underline "complex woman" and "worried and doubtful person."

p. 11 Reading Check
Students should underline "What is most frustrating, however, is how little you can learn about people through letters."

p. 12 Stop to Reflect
Sample response: The grocery list shows rather than tells the kinds of pieces the author has collected.

p. 12 Nonfiction
Students should underline "seeing good or bad luck in everything," "believed in fortune cookies," and "bought lottery tickets."

p. 12 Nonfiction
Sample response: She adds humor with this example, showing the competition between herself and her brother. This example is meant to entertain her readers. This example also shows the variety of the papers she collects.

p. 13 Nonfiction
Students should underline "I never imagined my grandfather, my quiet careful grandfather, was the sort of man who'd write any kind of love letter, never mind this kind" and "And my grandmother had saved it for over fifty years."

p. 13 Read Fluently
Sample response: The colon sets up the question that Elizabeth McCracken asks

about who found the letter more important. If she dropped the colon, the sentence would be hard to understand because there are two verbs in a row (is was).

p. 13 Reading Check
Student should circle "I've forgotten the exact words my grandfather used."

p. 14 Apply the Skills
1. Students may say that Peggy did help James because she got him as much information as she could. Other students might say that Peggy did not help him because she couldn't find the information he was looking for.
2. **Graphic Organizer**
Sample response:
Research questions: What is giantism? What role do genes play in the disease? What are the characteristics of the disease? What are the symptoms? How is it diagnosed? What is the most successful treatment?
Possible Source: dictionary and encyclopedia; science and medical books; Internet sites; expert interviews.
3. Sample response: James's problem is affected by the setting of the story because physical differences were not as accepted in 1955 as they are today. There were fewer medical treatment options. Little information was available in the small-town library.
4. Sample response: Some students might say that McCracken uses a combination of two purposes. In the process of reflecting on her relatives' interest in collecting family history, she informs her readers of the process and why it led her to write fiction. Others may say that they agree that her main purpose is to reflect and the other purposes are less important.

"The Washwoman"
Isaac Bashevis Singer

"New Directions"
Maya Angelou

p. 16 Graphic Organizer
Sample response:
"The Washwoman"
Detail: "That winter was a harsh one."
Question: Why does the author mention this detail?

Prediction: The bad weather will make it hard for the washwoman to do her job.
Verification: The prediction was accurate.

"New Directions"
Detail: "She placed stones in two large pails and walked three miles . . ."
Question: Why does the author mention this detail?
Prediction: She will carry food to the factories so that she can sell it.
Verification: The prediction was accurate.

p. 17 Reading/Writing Connection
Sample response: When people accomplish a difficult task, they may feel more confident. They want to demonstrate that they can finish the task. When people confront their problems, they will become stronger.

p. 17 Note-taking Guide
Sample response:
Circle 1: cares for son
Circle 3: is not bitter about her life
Circle 4: is hardworking and dedicated to her job

p. 18 Apply the Skills
1. Sample response: She is dedicated to her work. It is important for her to finish what she starts.
2. Sample response: The author says nothing about her family history or what she does besides laundry.
3. **Graphic Organizer**
Sample response:
The Washwoman: She is small, old, and wrinkled; she does her work well and gives people a good price; she is not angry with her son.
The Washwoman's Son: He is rich; his mother embarrasses him; he does not invite her to his wedding.
4. Sample response: Prediction: The washwoman will not survive her walk home in the cold weather. Details: The washwoman is in bad health. The weather is rough, and it will be hard for her to make it home.

p. 20 Reading/Writing Connection
Sample response: When people initiate a change, they must prepare for the unexpected. To transform their lives, they must be willing to take risks. Later, they can analyze the result in order to know how successful they were.

p. 20 Note-taking Guide
Sample response:
Circle 1: resourceful
Circle 3: determined
Circle 4: reliable

p. 21 Activate Prior Knowledge
Students may say that they worked through a problem by keeping a positive attitude and thinking of the future.

p. 21 Literary Analysis
Students should underline "Annie was left with two small sons, very little money, and little education." Sample response: Annie's need to support herself and her children, and the fact that she has very little opportunities and many obstacles, sets the story in motion.

p. 21 Reading Skill
Students may predict that Annie is preparing to carry heavy loads of her cooking and that she will have to work hard to make her plans happen. Students should underline "First, she placed stones in two large pails and walked three miles to the first factory," "she took some stones out of the pails, and then she walked another five miles," "There, she dumped out the stones and walked home," and "Then she knew she could carry heavy loads a long distance."

p. 22 Reading Skill
Sample response: Annie is determined to succeed. Her determination may lead a growing and successful business.

p. 22 Read Fluently
Students may say that "found a new path for herself" means she discovered a way to move forward and to become successful.

p. 22 Reading Check
Students should underline "In years that stall became a store where customers could buy cheese, meal, syrup, cookies, candy, writing tablets, pickles, canned goods, fresh fruit, soft drinks, coal, oil, and leather soles for worn-out shoes."

p. 23 Apply the Skills
1. Sample response: Annie is a smart businessperson. She knows how to plan ahead and how to attract customers.

2. Some students may say taking a new direction often can lead to a better life, so it is worth the risk of failure. Others may say that some new directions are too scary and not worth the risk.

3. **Graphic Organizer**

Sample response:

Annie Johnson: She is a good cook. She makes careful plans for her business.

Annie Johnson's Husband: He moves to Oklahoma. He takes the family's money when he leaves.

4. Sample response: Annie will make food and sell it to the factory workers. She will build a successful business.

Reading Informational Materials: Instructions: Recipes

p. 26 Reading Instructions: Recipes

Sample response: People need the ingredients ready before they can begin the steps in the recipe.

p. 26 Read Fluently

Students should circle "FILLING" and "PASTRY DOUGH." Sample response: The first column's ingredients are for the filling. The second column's ingredients are for the pastry dough.

p. 26 Reading Skill

Students should circle "chopped," "minced," "thawed," and "cooked." Sample response: These signal words tell readers what to do with the ingredients before combining them.

p. 27 Stop to Reflect

Sample response: Reading the recipe will help readers understand the amount of work the main character had to do.

p. 27 Reading Check

Students should underline "In a separate saucepan, melt the butter or margarine over medium heat."

p. 27 Reading Skill

Sample response: There are four steps.

p. 27 Reading Informational Materials

Sample response: Photographs and drawings of the steps would make it easier to follow. Numbering the steps would also make it easier to follow.

p. 28 Apply the Skills
Thinking About the Instruction: Recipe

1. The finished turnovers are a half-moon shape.

2. Dipping the fork in flour when crimping the edges will help keep the fork from sticking to the dough.

Reading Skill

3. You need three tablespoons of celery.

4. You should whisk the sauce continually.

5. The last thing you are supposed to do before baking the pies is cut a slit in the top of each turnover.

"Sonata for Harp and Bicycle"
Joan Aiken

"The Cask of Amontillado"
Edgar Allan Poe

p. 29 Graphic Organizer

Sample response:

"Sonata for Harp and Bicycle"
Prediction: Jason will sneak into the building after quitting time.
Outcome: He climbs the fire escape and gets in.
Analysis of Prediction: The prediction was accurate.

"The Cask of Amontillado"
Prediction: Fortunato's love of wine will lead him into danger.
Outcome: A cask of amontillado brings Fortunato to his destruction.
Analysis of Prediction: The prediction was accurate.

p. 30 Reading/Writing Connection

Sample response: A good detective must anticipate what a criminal will do. Detectives can expose criminals by setting traps. A detective will not eliminate anything that seems suspicious while searching for clues.

p. 30 Note-taking Guide

Sample response:

Circle 1: a fire escape
Circle 2: a bicycle bell
Circle 3: the echoing sound of music
Circle 5: two eyes carved out of air
Circle 6: Ashgrove's new hair color

p. 31 Activate Prior Knowledge

Students may suggest the adventures of Sherlock Holmes. The main character is a smart, daring person who solves the mystery. The main character often has a sidekick.

p. 31 Literary Analysis

Sample response: The first paragraph creates suspense by making readers wonder why no one is allowed in the building after 5 o'clock. The building clears out at exactly the same time every day and that makes readers wonder why the workers would do that.

p. 31 Reading Skill

Students may predict that the new assistant will enter the building after 5 o'clock to try to find out what goes on during the night. Students may underline "But why is it?" and "But I want to know now."

p. 32 Reading Skill

Students may predict that there will be a romance between Jason and Miss Golden. Students might circle "what she chiefly wanted was Mr. Jason Ashgrove, but he had not realized this yet."

p. 32 Stop to Reflect

Sample response: Jason is curious and wants to know more about the mystery. Miss Golden is frightened.

p. 32 Reading Check

Students should underline "He does, however, hear her say something about a bicycle and a harp."

p. 33 Literary Analysis

Sample response: Jason's actions add suspense to the story by making the reader wonder what will happen to him while he is in the Grimes Buildings.

p. 33 Reading Skill

Students may predict that Jason will encounter ghosts in the Grimes Buildings. Students might circle "everything is silent and empty," "quickly," "senses that it is dangerous," "small place to hide," and "heart tried to shake itself loose in his chest."

p. 33 Literary Analysis

Sample response: The passage is part of the rising action because it introduces the ghost, which is a part of the central conflict.

p. 34 Reading Skill

Students may say that their predictions were correct. Reading on provided them with more information to verify their predictions.

p. 34 Reading Check

Students should underline "His dark hair has turned white."

p. 34 Stop to Reflect

Students may say that Jason was very scared.

p. 35 Reading Skill

Students may suggest that the added information changed some of their predictions concerning the ghosts.

p. 35 Literary Analysis

Sample response: The new information sets up another conflict. Jason could be in danger. He is faced with the information that others who have met Heron's ghost have jumped off the fire escape.

p. 35 Reading Check

Students should underline "awakened by a device on her phone."

p. 36 Reading Check

Students may circle "harp music swelling out, sweet and triumphant," "'The room was too full of music,'" and "She saw that his eyes were shining."

p. 36 Read Fluently

Sample response: Jason and Berenice held hands outside of the door. They never spoke about what they saw. They were left with an image as clear as a painting of a harp, a bouquet, and a bottle of wine riding on a bicycle.

p. 36 Reading Skill

Students may say that their prediction that Jason and Berenice would start a relationship was proven correct. They might point to the fact that Jason and Berenice kiss and jump off the fire escape together as events that verify their predictions.

p. 37 Apply the Skills

1. Sample response: Miss Golden is more concerned. She believes that there is a curse that cannot be escaped. She is not aware of Jason's plan to try to break it.

2. Sample response: If Heron had not killed himself, he would have seen Miss Bell the next day. She would have explained about the alarm. Making quick decisions sometimes means you do not get the whole story.

3. **Graphic Organizer**
Sample response:

Rising Action: Jason asks questions about the strange behavior of the people in the office.

Climax: Jason puts the wine and the roses outside the door of room 492.

4. Students may have predicted that Jason would meet a ghost inside the building.

p. 39 Reading/Writing Connection
Sample response:
1. Reading a scary story lets people safely participate in scary or dangerous situations.
2. A scary setting helps contribute to the overall mood of a story.
3. A reader can interpret a scary story by analyzing the author's purpose.

p. 39 Note-taking Guide
Sample response:
Event 2: Fortunato goes with Montresor to his palace. They wander through caves filled with wine bottles and bones.
Event 3: Montresor gets Fortunato drunk as they walk deeper into the caves.
Event 4: Montresor chains Fortunato to the wall of a small room. He walls up the room and leaves him to die.

p. 40 Apply the Skills
1. Sample response: Fortunato is proud that he knows so much about wine. Because of this, he is very anxious to judge the wine. Montresor takes advantage of the fact that Fortunado is so vain.
2. Sample response: Montresor feels that Fortunato has insulted and injured him.

3. **Graphic Organizer**
Sample response:
Rising Action: Montresor invites Fortunato to the vaults to try his wine.
Climax: Montresor thrusts his torch into the crypt and hears only the jingling of the bells on Fortunato's costume.
Falling Action: Montresor replaces the bones to cover the crypt's entrance.
4. Students may have predicted that Montresor would use Fortunato's interest in wine to get his revenge.

from A White House Diary
Lady Bird Johnson

"My English"
Julia Alvarez

p. 42 Graphic Organizer
Sample response:
from **A White House Diary**
Text feature: title
Insight into Purpose: The title suggests a day-by-day or hour-by-hour account of personal experience.

"My English"
Text Feature: title
Insight About Purpose: The title suggests a personal relationship with the language.

p. 43 Reading/Writing Connection
Sample response: The words of Martin Luther King Jr. motivate me to seek justice in the world. The actions of Dr. King illustrate his philosophy of nonviolence. For me, these actions evoke feelings of courage and resolve.

p. 43 Note-taking Guide
Sample response:
Circle 2: fear
Circle 3: sympathy
Circle 4: sorrow
Circle 5: stress
Circle 6: anguish

p. 44 Activate Prior Knowledge
Students may say that many people keep diaries to record thoughts and feelings and reflect on the significance of events. A diary entry is a private place to express powerful emotions and personal thoughts.

p. 44 Reading Check
Students should circle "Dallas."

p. 44 Literary Analysis
Sample response: At the time of the assassination, the author could not consider that something so horrible could happen to the President. The events were happy and festive.

p. 45 Read Fluently
Sample response: These dashes set off extra information in the sentence. In the bracketed passage, it seems that Mrs. Johnson forgot to include this information earlier.

p. 45 Reading Skill

Sample response: The author included these names to suggest the closeness of those in the President's inner circle. It showed how the President's assassination affected those people.

p. 45 Reading Check

Students should circle "I think it was from Kenny's face that I first knew the truth and from Kenny's voice that I first heard the words 'The President is dead.'"

p. 46 Literary Analysis

Sample response: The repetition of "caked" and "blood" makes her sound disbelieving and horrified. Her use of the dash stresses the description of Mrs. Kennedy, a blending of beautiful and gruesome images.

p. 46 Reading Skill

Students should underline "Mrs. Kennedy's dress was stained with blood. One leg was almost entirely covered with it and her right glove was caked, it was caked with blood— her husband's blood" and "that immaculate woman exquisitely dressed, and caked in blood." Sample response: The details help to show Mrs. Kennedy's shock and grief. It also emphasizes the horror of what has happened.

p. 46 Reading Check

Students should circle "'I want them to see what they have done to Jack.'"

p. 47 Stop to Reflect

Sample response: Mrs. Johnson may have felt tired, sad, and deeply shaken. She had just witnessed the assassination and death of the President. Her husband has also become President in an unexpected way.

p. 48 Apply the Skills

1. Sample response: Mrs. Kennedy wants the nation to see evidence of the brutality of the assassination.
2. Sample response: It is a powerful comment. It makes Mrs. Kennedy's feelings clear.
3. **Graphic Organizer**
Sample response:
Attitude: "There had been such a gala air about the day that I thought the noise must come from firecrackers . . ."
Sentence structure: "And then with almost an element of fierceness—if a person that

gentle, that dignified, can be said to have such a quality—she said. . ."
4. Sample response: The general purpose is to inform readers about the assassination. She gives details about events, the setting, and people's feelings.

p. 50 Reading/Writing Connection

Sample response:
1. In a democracy, people may debate ideas about the government without worrying about being punished.
2. Demonstrating against the government is often against the law in a dictatorship.
3. In a dictatorship, people are deprived of the right to speak out about abuses of their freedoms.

p. 50 Note-taking Guide

Sample response:
Spanish
Negative Memory: "I grew insecure about Spanish. My native tongue was not quite as good as English . . ."
Spanglish
Positive Memory: "*Butter, butter, butter, butter.* All day, one English word . . . But would you be needing some butter on your bread?"
Negative Memory: "At school, a Spanish word would suddenly slide into my English . . . 'Do you mean a *swing*?'"
English
Positive Memory: "I learned not to hear it as English, but as sense . . . I relaxed in this second language."

p. 51 Apply the Skills

1. Sample response: The teacher at Carol Morgan School took a more technical approach. She focused on teaching vocabulary and grammar.
2. Sample response: Her parents spoke English when they did not want the children to understand them. English kept Alvarez out of the conversation.
3. **Graphic Organizer**
Sample response:
Word Choice: "another strange tongue emerged from my papi's mouth or my mami's lips."
Attitude: "Supposing, just supposing . . . My mind would take off, soaring into possibilities . . ."

Sentence Structure: "I thought about the snow. I saw how it might fall on the hills . . . on people out late walking on the streets . . ."
4. Sample response: Her general purpose was to inform and entertain. She wanted readers to know what it was like to learn English. She also wanted them to enjoy reading about her experience.

Reading Informational Materials: Spanish/English Dictionaries

p. 56 Apply the Skills
Thinking About the Spanish/English Dictionary
1. Sample response: You would look under the heading Vowels in the Key to Spanish Pronunciation.
2. Sample response: The Note on Spanish Gender would give you this information.
Reading Skill
3. Sample response: The masculine form of the noun means *boundary mark* or *landmark.* The feminine form means *headless nail* or *brad.* Therefore, using one for the other would completely change the meaning.
4. Sample response: First, find the entry by looking up the keyword. Then, read the entry to find the part of speech. The italicized letter or letters immediately following the keyword show you what the part of speech is.

"The Secret Life of Walter Mitty" James Thurber

"Uncle Marcos" Isabel Allende

p. 57 Graphic Organizer
Sample response:
"The Secret Life of Walter Mitty"
Story Event or Detail: Walter Mitty forgets what his wife wants him to purchase.
Possible Importance: Walter Mitty is so involved in his daydreams that he has trouble remembering details about his real life
Author's Purpose: to show that Walter Mitty is out of touch with real life

"Uncle Marcos"
Story Event of Detail: Uncle Marcos performs strange exercises at night. He sleeps during the day in a hammock.
Possible Importance: Uncle Marcos is an unusual person.

Author's Purpose: to reveal Uncle Marcos's unique character

p. 58 Reading/Writing Connection
Sample response: Daydreaming can enhance life by making it more interesting. A daydream might derive from real life events. Sometimes daydreams project my real-world experience into an imaginary world.

p. 58 Note-taking Guide
Sample response:
Daydream: Mitty is a surgeon saving a patient's life; Mitty is a criminal standing trial in a courtroom; Mitty is a pilot on a dangerous mission.
Reality: Mitty parks the car to buy overshoes; Mitty buys the biscuits and waits for his wife in a chair; Mrs. Mitty goes on another errand.

p. 59 Activate Prior Knowledge
Students may say they think about being a great athlete, singer, writer, actor, or mountaineer, or about becoming someone who is already famous.

p. 59 Literary Analysis
Students may say the Commander is a flat character because he is a typical hero. Students may underline "He wore his full-dress uniform, with the heavily braided white cap pulled down rakishly over one cold gray eye" and "brave Commander."

p. 59 Reading Check
Students should circle "'Not so fast! You're driving too fast!'" and "What are you driving so fast for?"

p. 60 Reading Skill
Sample response: The author's purpose is to show that sometimes Mitty's daydreams cause him to be scatterbrained or to not pay attention to what he is doing in his real life.

p. 60 Reading Check
Students should circle "Puppy biscuit."

p. 60 Stop to Reflect
Sample response: Mitty may imagine himself to be a shooting expert because it is dangerous and exciting. His real life is not dangerous or exciting.

p. 61 Read Fluently
Students should underline "I've been looking all over this hotel for you"; "Why did you have to hide in this old chair? How did you

expect me to find you?"; "What?"; "Did you get the what's-its-name? The puppy biscuit? What's in the box?"; "Couldn't you have put them on in the store?"; and "I'm going to take your temperature when I get home." Students should circle "Things close in"; "Overshoes"; "I was thinking"; and "Does it ever occur to you that I am sometimes thinking?" Sample response: Quotation marks mean that a character is talking and authors will often tell you which character said it.

p. 61 Reading Skill
Sample response: The author's purpose is to show the contrast between a man's exciting daydreams and his real life, which may seem boring. Thurber uses Mitty's daydreams to show the human desire for adventure and escape from everyday life.

p. 62 Apply the Skills
1. Sample response: In his imaginary life, Mitty is landing a plane, doing surgery, testifying in court, fighting a war, and facing a firing squad.
2. Sample response: The tasks of Mitty's daily life are boring and dull. The tasks of Mitty's fantasy life are exciting.
3. **Graphic Organizer**
Sample response:
Detail from Daydream:
2. "The other doctors are relieved that Walter can save the patient."
3. "Bravely, he stands ready to face his death."
Desired Character Trait:
2. Heroism
3. Fearlessness
4. Sample response: Thurber's purpose may have been to show the positive effects of imagination in the face of everyday troubles and defeats.

p. 64 Reading/Writing Connection
Sample response: One event that may evolve is my brother's skateboarding story. People might enhance the details of the story to make it seem more exciting. People might alter the reality of the event by exaggerating actual events.

p. 64 Note-taking Guide
Sample response:
Box 2: Marcos's flying machine carries him over the mountains.

Box 3: Marcos and Clara have great success telling fortunes.
Box 4: Marcos dies of an African plague during his travels.

p. 65 Apply the Skills
1. Sample response: Clara's reaction shows her faith and positive attitude. It may also suggest her innocence about death and her belief in her uncle's powers of magic.
2. Sample response: People can learn that their successes depend on their own attitudes. Be adventurous; be yourself; develop your sense of wonder; seek adventure; be unique.
3. **Graphic Organizer**
Sample response:
Project or Adventure: performs alchemy; takes trips around the world; builds flying machine
Character Traits: curiosity; adventurous; inventiveness
4. Sample response: Uncle Marcos never allows failure or the attitudes of others to discourage him. Allende's purpose may have been to encourage readers to be true to themselves.

"The Jade Peony"
Wayson Choy

p. 69 Note-taking Guide

Sample response:

Plot: Grandmama takes home remedies to treat her illness; Grandmama makes wind-chimes out of found objects; grandmother and Sek-Lung hide collections under her bed until rest of family is out; Sek-Lung has missed school because he has been sick; Grandmama works on her last windchime; Grandmama dies; Sek-Lung discovers that she has left him her prize possession, a peony carved out of jade.

Conflict: Grandmama's collection process embarrasses other members of family; Sek-Lung's fear and sorrow at losing Grandmama; the family's ties to its Chinese heritage versus its desire to be modern and Canadian; the other children's dislike of studying Mandarin

Characters: Grandmama: 83; artistic; treasures memories of the past, particularly of the juggler who gave her the jade peony; believes in signs. Sek-Lung: 8; illness has kept him at home; close ties with Grandmama. Two brothers, sister, father, and stepmother.

Setting: Vancouver, Canada; Grandmama dies in September

p. 70 Activate Prior Knowledge

Sample response: An older adult can play a supportive role for a young person. He or she could teach the young person skills or lessons about the past.

p. 70 Short Story

Students should circle "Vancouver, Canada" and "modern Canadians."

p. 70 Short Story

Sample response: Grandmama is decisive and old-fashioned. She believes in Chinese home remedies. She is tied to the past. She loves her grandson.

p. 71 Stop to Reflect

Sample response: Grandmama keeps the jade peony because it reminds her of the juggler. She can think of him and their time together every time she touches the pendant.

p. 71 Short Story

Sample response: She is important to them, and they love her. However, they are embarrassed about the way she acts.

p. 71 Reading Check

Students should underline "He promised to return to her one day."

p. 71 Short Story

Sample response: The older children are worried about what other people think of them. They are worried that their grandmother's garbage picking makes them look poor.

p. 72 Stop to Reflect

Sample response: They are sacred pieces because they are from a church. Also, Sek-Lung and his Grandmama had an abundance of beautiful pieces to choose from.

p. 72 Read Fluently

Sample response: We smelled like smoke and were covered in soot when we got home. We had a carton full of glass pieces with us. It was early, so we were able to sneak them into the house. We put them under Grandmama's bed.

p. 72 Reading Check

Students should circle "she tells him that the juggler she loved so much never came back."

p. 73 Stop to Reflect

Students may identify an object that they bought at a festival that reminds them of the event.

p. 73 Short Story

Grandmama says that her spirit will be drawn to the windchime after she dies. Then, she will be able to come back to the house and tell her family good-bye.

p. 73 Reading Check

Students should circle "She explains that it is because death is closing in on her."

p. 74 Short story

Sample response: It shows that he loved his grandmother very much because he devoted so much time to her.

p. 74 Stop to Reflect

Sample response: She will remain in his memory. Every time he looks at the wind-chimes, he will remember her and what she taught him.

p. 74 Reading Check
Students should circle "It was all white and had pink eyes like sacred fire."

p. 75 Short Story
Sample response: The white cat symbolizes the juggler from Grandmama's past. He had white hair and pink eyes, as well. Grandmama thinks he has finally come back to her.

p. 75 Short Story
Sample response: The theme of this story is that family and traditions are important. A person must blend the past and the present together in order to be a complete person. Young people should honor older people for what they can teach. Sample response: The theme is implied. Choy never says that people should honor and respect the past. However, his deep relationship with his grandmother helps him understand who he is and what life is all about.

p. 76 Apply the Skills
1. Sample response: Making windchimes was a recreation of Grandmama's past. Not only was she maintaining tradition in creating the chimes, but she was also using fragments from the past to make them.
2. Sample response: Sek-Lung supports and understands Grandmama's activities. He is happy to be included in the process. The rest of the family is embarrassed by her activities.
3. **Graphic Organizer**
Sample response:
What It Says: The family waits for a sign.
What It Means: Grandmama's rest is peaceful, and her family is safe.
Why It Is Important: These signs or omens signify the attachment to and belief in the past.
4. Sample response: The theme is that the past is important because it forms people's characters and a culture's shared understanding. Students should explain how the chart did or did not affect their understanding of the story's theme.

"American History"
Judith Ortiz Cofer

"The Most Dangerous Game"
Richard Connell

p. 78 Graphic Organizer
Sample response:
"American History"
Detail: The door was painted green, the color of hope.
Question: Why might a writer describe a door as having the color of an emotion?
Inference: The door stands for opportunity.

"The Most Dangerous Game"
Detail: The island that Rainsford swims to is described as forbidding.
Question: Why would an island be described this way?
Inference: This island must hold something evil.

p. 79 Reading/Writing Connection
Sample response:
1. A natural disaster can transform peoples' lives.
2. Bravery and kindness emerge when people go through a crisis.
3. People define themselves as survivors after living through a hurricane.

p. 79 Note-taking Guide
Sample response:
Story Detail 2: Even though she gets straight A's, the honors classes are not open to Elena.
Conflict 2: Elena is viewed as low class.
Story Detail 3: President Kennedy has just been killed, but Elena can't help but feel excited about the time she is going to spend with Eugene.
Conflict 3: Elena's mother thinks that Elena is disrespectful. She warns Elena that she is headed for heartbreak.
Story Detail 4: Eugene's mother asks Elena whether she lives "there" in the El Building.
Conflict 4: Eugene's mother does not want Elena spending time with her son.

p. 80 Apply the Skills
1. Sample response: Elena thinks her home is large and noisy. She thinks Eugene's home is quiet and comfortable.

2. Sample response: Elena's tears are just for herself because she feels her personal pain more than she feels the pain of the national tragedy.

3. **Graphic Organizer**
Sample response:

Elena vs. another person: Elena's conflict with her mother's expectations of her occurs when Elena chooses to go to Eugene's house instead of going to church.

4. Sample response: One inference is the love that people had for the president. This inference is based on their anguish.

p. 82 Reading/Writing Connection
Sample response:

1. I do not want to contemplate what could happen if a dangerous game became real.
2. Some people tried to simulate death and destruction.
3. Opponents might utilize real weapons to win the game.

p. 82 Note-taking Guide
Sample response:

Event 2: Rainsford meets Ivan and Zaroff on a nearby island.
Event 3: Rainsford refuses to hunt men and becomes the one who is hunted.
Final Event: Rainsford kills Zaroff.

p. 83 Activate Prior Knowledge
Students may suggest that playing a game with unfamiliar rules was confusing at first. They may say that they had to take time to learn how to play the game.

p. 83 Read Fluently
Students should underline "Don't talk rot, Whitney"; "Who cares how a jaguar feels?"; and "Bah! They've no understanding." Students should circle answer (c).

p. 83 Reading Check
Students should circle "the hunters and the huntees."

p. 84 Literary Analysis
Rainsford struggles for his life against the sea.

p. 84 Reading Skill
Students may infer that an animal is in trouble, perhaps fighting for its life.

p. 84 Reading Check
Students should underline "I've read your book about hunting snow leopards in Tibet, you see."

p. 85 Reading Skill
Students may infer that Zaroff's "new animal" is human.

p. 85 Literary Analysis
Conflict develops over hunting men for sport. Zaroff considers the game ideal; Rainsford knows that this game is murder.

p. 85 Read Fluently
Rainsford probably feels horrified and terrified because he realizes that Zaroff murders people.

p. 85 Reading Check
Students should underline "If he cannot find the man in three days, then the man wins."

p. 86 Literary Analysis
Sample response: Either decision—to hunt or to face Ivan—is deadly. The internal conflict would be choosing whether to die quickly by Ivan's hands or whether to prolong their death in the hopes of escape.

p. 86 Reading Skill
Students may infer that Zaroff will give Rainsford the option of the hunt or Ivan's torture, and Rainsford will choose the hunt.

p. 86 Stop to Reflect
Zaroff hunts human beings. Students will probably say Zaroff is a demented, horrible person.

p. 87 Reading Skill
Students may infer that Zaroff is an excellent hunter. He is extremely strong and clever. He is able to track Rainsford and escape his trap alive. He is also extremely determined. He will come back for Rainsford.

p. 87 Stop to Reflect
Sample response: Rainsford most likely feels tension and fear, then relief, followed by new tension and fear.

p. 87 Literary Analysis
Rainsford's decision to jump into the sea was an internal conflict. He had to choose between being caught by Zaroff and his hounds or jumping into the sea. Either choice is almost certain death.

p. 88 Reading Skill
Students may infer that Rainsford does not feel like he has yet won the game. He still feels he is "a beast at bay." He thinks that the only way to win is to kill Zaroff.

p. 88 Literary Analysis
The conflict is resolved through a hands-on fight between the two men. Rainsford wins.

p. 88 Reading Skill
Students may infer that Rainsford is at peace. He has successfully overcome his enemy and won the game.

p. 89 Apply the Skills
1. Students may like Rainsford's courage, intelligence, and self-control under pressure. They may not like his attitude about hunting.
2. Sample response: Zaroff forces Rainsford to be the prey of a hunt. If Rainsford hunts, he will certainly think about the prey's experience.
3. **Graphic Organizer**
Sample response:
Rainsford vs. himself: not panicking when thrown from boat; controlling anxiety during hunt
4. Sample response: Whitney's desire to relate to the animals shows that he is a more sensitive man than Rainsford.

Reading Informational Materials: Signs and Instructions

p. 92 Reading Signs and Instructions
Students should circle the small falling person in the sign and underline the words "CAN CAUSE SERIOUS INJURIES OR DROWNING."

p. 92 Reading Skill
Sample response: Students may say that the picture does give a clear message because they can clearly see that a person is sucked under by a huge wave. They may say that the words "WARNING" and "HIGH SURF" should be as big as they are because they attract attention and relay the main message quickly.

p. 92 Reading Check
Students should circle "twenty-five feet plus" and "fifteen feet plus."

p. 92 Read Fluently
Students should circle "life" and "depend." Sample response: These words are the most important because they tell exactly what could be at risk if someone ignores the sign.

p. 93 Reading Skill
Sample response: The sign is a little unclear. Someone might have to read the words to understand what the sign means.

p. 93 Reading Signs and Instructions
Students should circle "WARNING" and "STRONG CURRENT."
Warning; Strong Current

p. 93 Reading Check
Students should underline "YOU COULD BE SWEPT AWAY FROM SHORE AND COULD DROWN."

p. 93 Reading Informational Materials
Sample response: Signs and instructions should be easy to understand because everyone needs to be able to read the message. Some people cannot read difficult text. Some people will not take the time to read a sign with too many words.

p. 94 Apply the Skills
Thinking About the Sign and Instruction
1. Sample response: The simple pictures suggest danger without need for words.
2. Sample response: People who are very good surfers and who are familiar with big waves might be safe.

Reading Skill
3. Sample response: Large, powerful waves are the danger shown in the first sign.
4. Sample response: A "strong current" is water that is moving so quickly that it can overpower people who are trying to walk or swim against it. It is dangerous because people can be swept into deep water, and then they could drown or be seriously injured.

"The Gift of the Magi"
O. Henry

"The Interlopers"
Saki

p. 95 Graphic Organizer
Sample response:
"The Gift of the Magi"
Detail: Jim is shocked when he sees Della's hair.
My Experience: People are often speechless when something happens that they do not expect.
Inference: Jim was not expecting Della to cut her hair, so his gift may be something that she can use in her hair.

"The Interlopers"
Detail: The two men are alone when they get caught under the tree.

My Experience: It would take time to find people in a large forest. It would take even longer if you did not suspect that something was wrong.

Inference: The two men will not be rescued.

p. 96 Reading/Writing Connection
Sample response:
1. Some people might adjust the amount they spend on gifts.
2. A person can embody love simply by doing a special favor for a loved one.
3. Someone can emphasize love by giving a family member a treasured possession.

p. 96 Note-taking Guide
Sample response:
Della Action: Della sells her hair to buy the chain.
Unexpected Result: Della receives combs for hair she no longer has.
Jim Christmas Gift Idea: hair combs
Action: Jim sells his watch to buy the combs.
Unexpected Result: Jim receives a watch chain for a watch he no longer has.

p. 97 Activate Prior Knowledge
Students may list several types of sacrifices. For example, they may have sacrificed free time by taking a job to be able to afford something they wanted. They may have given up something they were accustomed to, such as new clothes or video games.

p. 97 Literary Analysis
Della only will be able to afford an inexpensive present for Jim. Students may underline "small amount of money she has managed to save" or "she had only $1.87 with which to buy Jim a present."

p. 97 Reading Check
Students should circle one of the following: "She is crying because it is so little"; "Tomorrow would be Christmas day, and she had only $1.87 with which to buy Jim a present"; "Only $1.87 to buy a present for Jim."

p. 98 Read Fluently
Sample response: She let her hair down.

p. 98 Stop to Reflect
Students may say that people give expensive gifts because they think it shows how much they care. Others may say that people want to give expensive gifts because they want to show off.

p. 98 Reading Skill
Sample response: Jim will probably not mind how long or short her hair is. He loves her.

p. 98 Reading Check
Students should circle " 'Twenty dollars,' said Madame, lifting the mass with a practiced hand."

p. 99 Literary Analysis
Jim's gift is ironic because Della cannot use the combs on her short hair.

p. 99 Reading Skill
Sample response: He sees that what has happened is humorous. He appreciates how much she loves him.

p. 99 Literary Analysis
The ending is a surprise because neither Della nor the reader knows that Jim has sacrificed something, too.

p. 99 Reading Check
Students should circle "They gave up what they treasured most, out of love for each other."

p. 100 Apply the Skills
1. Della's action shows that she is generous and self-sacrificing.
2. Sample response: Wisdom is the understanding that some things, such as love and kindness, are more important than money or expensive things.
3. Sample response: This situational irony conveys the idea that life is not predictable. It also shows that gifts are not the best way for showing someone you love them.
4. Students may be familiar with characters who were in love from books, television, or movies. These characters were willing to sacrifice for each other, as well.

p. 102 Reading/Writing Connection
Sample response:
1. To end a feud, the groups involved could participate in a peace conference.
2. A court could verify which of the feuding parties owns the land.
3. Participants could focus more on ending rather than fighting the feud.

p. 102 Note-taking Guide

Sample response:

Detail: The two families have hated each other for three generations.

What the Reader Expects: Ulrich and Georg will never be able to resolve their conflict.

What Actually Happens: They resolve their conflict.

Detail: Ulrich offers to end the feud.

What the Reader Expects: Georg will refuse Ulrich's offer.

What Actually Happens: Georg agrees to end the feud. They decide to become friends.

Detail: Nine or ten figures respond to their cries for help.

What the Reader Expects: The men will be rescued. They will surprise everyone when they announce that they are friends.

What Actually Happens: The figures are wolves.

p. 103 Apply the Skills

1. Georg does not accept the court's decision.
2. Sample response: Their present situation makes the two men realize that their dispute is a waste of time.
3. Sample response: One message is that people should resolve their differences while they have the opportunity.
4. Sample response: Saki probably intended readers to infer that the men are proud and stubborn. He may have also wanted readers to infer that the unexpected situation makes the men see how good their lives could have been without the feud.

"The Necklace"
Guy de Maupassant

"Rules of the Game"
Amy Tan

p. 105 Graphic Organizer

Sample response:

"The Necklace"

Narrator's comments: "She would weep for whole days at a time from sorrow, regret, despair, and distress."

What They Show About the Character: Madame Loisel is unhappy with being poor.

Character's thoughts and words: ". . . there's nothing more humiliating than to look poverty-stricken among a lot of rich women."

What They Show About the Character: She is very sensitive about her appearance and social status.

Character's actions: "She does all the hated household chores."

What They Show About the Character: She works hard to repay debts.

Character's appearance: "Disheveled, her skirts askew, with reddened hands, she spoke in a loud voice . . ."

What They Show About the Character: The hard work and poverty she endures have made her indifferent to her appearance.

What Others Say or Think about the Character: "Oh, my poor, poor Mathilde!"

What They Show About the Character: She really has changed.

"Rules of the Game"

Narrator's comments: " . . . she asked without a trace of knowing how wicked I was being"

What They Show About the Character: The narrator's comments reveal that Waverly is being sarcastic.

Character's thoughts and words: "I read the rules and looked up all the big words in a dictionary . . . I studied each chess piece, trying to absorb the power each contained." "By my ninth birthday, I was a national chess champion."

What They Show About the Character: Waverly's thoughts and words reveal her intelligence.

Character's actions: "I raced down the street, dashing between people, not looking back as my mother screamed shrilly, 'Meimei! Meimei!'"

What They Show About the Character: Waverly's actions show how Waverly argues with her mother.

Character's appearance: "In my crisp pink-and-white dress with scratchy lace at the neck, one of two my mother had sewn for these special occasions . . . "

What They Show About the Character: Waverly's special dresses for tournaments show her mother's involvement in her life.

What Others Say or Think about the Character: "Is shame you fall down nobody push you.'"

What They Show About the Character:
Waverly's mother thinks that Waverly is talented enough to play in competitions.

p. 106 Reading/Writing Connection
Sample response:
1. Some people think expensive things identify them as having a successful and happy life.
2. Buying expensive items may cause some people to exceed their financial limits.
3. Many people think that expensive possessions will help them obtain admiration from others.

p. 106 Note-taking Guide
Sample response:
Box 2: She goes to the party and loses the necklace.
Box 3: The Loisels replace the necklace and work ten years to pay for it.
Final Event: Madame Loisel learns the secret of the necklace.

p. 107 Activate Prior Knowledge
Students may describe feeling upset, panicked, and regretful.

p. 107 Literary Analysis
Students should underline "She is bitter and unhappy about not being rich. She feels that she deserves a gracious, luxurious life and hates her old, plain home and life of poverty."

p. 107 Reading Skill
Madame Loisel is unhappy because she is not rich.

p. 107 Reading Check
Students should circle the passage that begins with "She had a rich friend . . . " and ends with " . . . regret, despair, and distress."

p. 108 Literary Analysis
Madame Loisel's words show that she is concerned with her appearance and social class.

p. 108 Read Fluently
Students should underline "Wait—you silly thing!" and "She danced enraptured—carried away . . . to the heart of a woman."

p. 108 Reading Check
Students should circle "Why don't you go and see Madame Forestier and ask her to lend you some jewelry."

p. 109 Reading Skill
The stress of losing the necklace causes Monsieur Loisel to age five years.

p. 109 Literary Analysis
Sample response: This statement shows that Monsieur Loisel is honest and responsible.

p. 109 Stop to Reflect
Students may suggest that it will buy the Loisels more time to make decisions. Other students may say that the Loisels are too embarrassed to tell the truth. The Loisels may believe that the necklace still can be found.

p. 109 Read Fluently
Students should circle *old, strong, hard, coarse, disheveled, askew, reddened,* and *loud.*

p. 110 Literary Analysis
Sample response: Madame Loisel longs to be beautiful and admired again. This passage contains indirect characterization.

p. 110 Reading Skill
Madame Forestier is surprised by how much Mathilde has changed.

p. 110 Stop to Reflect
Sample response: Madame Forestier should sell the diamond necklace and repay Madame Loisel. Madame Loisel and her husband deserve to live comfortably after ten years of unnecessary work.

p. 110 Reading Check
Students should circle the passage beginning with "'You remember the diamond necklace . . . '" and ending with "'Anyway, I'm glad it's over and done with.'"

p. 111 Apply the Skills
1. Sample response: Monsieur Loisel is much less selfish and much more loving than his wife is.
2. Sample response: Madame Loisel loses her charm and beauty. She becomes old before her time. She also learns to work hard.
3. Sample response: Madame Loisel is interested in material possessions and appearances. An example of indirect characterization is her depression after she visits her rich friend.
4. **Graphic Organizer**
Sample response:
Causes: She is invited to a party.
Effects: She looks beautiful at the party.

p. 113 Reading/Writing Connection

Sample response: Games can induce feelings such as satisfaction, anger, or happiness. These feelings may initiate friendships that cross age or culture barriers. Games can also evoke conflicts that divide friends or family members.

p. 113 Note-taking Guide

Sample response:

Event 2: Waverly learns to play chess.

Event 3: Waverly wins many tournaments.

Climax: Waverly runs away when she and her mother quarrel.

Resolution: She thinks about her next move in this mother-daughter conflict.

p. 114 Apply the Skills

1. Sample response: She pretends to be weaker than she is.

2. Sample response: Waverly will win the game of doing what she wants to do. She has learned from her mother.

3. The conversation is an example of indirect characterization. Waverly's mother does not realize that Waverly is being wicked. Her mother tells her that the Chinese do the best torture. These remarks show the cultural and generational differences between the two people.

4. **Graphic Organizer**

Sample response:

Causes: One cause for her success is her intelligence.

Effects: One effect of her success is that her self-confidence has increased.

"Blues Ain't No Mockin Bird" Toni Cade Bambara

"The Invalid's Story" Mark Twain

p. 116 Graphic Organizer

Sample response:

"Blues Ain't No Mockin Bird"

Cause: The twins ask whether the man in the story jumped.

Mental Picture: Granny stares at the twins.

Effect: Granny gets angry about the twins' responses to her story.

"The Invalid's Story"

Cause: The smell in the train becomes overwhelming.

Mental Picture: Thompson's face is buried in a handkerchief. The narrator's face has no color.

Effect: The men smoke cigars to try to cover up the smell.

p. 117 Reading/Writing Connection

Sample response: I would intervene if I saw someone abusing an animal. Laws should oblige people to respect animal rights. I write letters to a newspaper to promote the protection of endangered animals.

p. 117 Note-taking Guide

Sample response:

Beginning Event: The two men offend Granny.

Box 2: Granddaddy arrives.

Box 3: Granddaddy brings down the hawk.

Box 4: Granddaddy disables the camera.

Box 5: The cameramen back off.

Final Event: Granny goes back to making cakes.

p. 118 Activate Prior Knowledge

Students may describe a disapproving scowl or a glare that the older person has.

p. 118 Literary Analysis

The use of the words *ain't* and *no* and the dropping of the final *g* in words show that this story is written in dialect.

p. 118 Reading Check

Students should underline "The other man explains that they are making a film for the county food-stamp program."

p. 119 Literary Analysis

No, the twins do not understand the lesson that Granny is trying to teach them. They are asking whether the man jumped. Instead, Granny wants them to think about why the photographer's actions were wrong.

p. 119 Read Fluently

Students have a choice of several words written in dialect. Students could underline "lookin," "Thanksgivin," and "visitin."

p. 119 Reading Skill

Students should underline "people wouldn't pay her for things like they said they would," "Mr. Judson bringin us boxes of old clothes and raggedy magazines," and "Mrs. Cooper comin in our kitchen and touchin everything and sayin how clean it all was."

p. 120 Stop to Reflect

Students may say that they would not like people taking pictures of them without permission. It would be an invasion of privacy.

p. 120 Reading Skill

Students should underline "Cathy say it's because he's so tall and quiet and like a king. And people just can't stand it."

p. 120 Reading Check

Students should circle "So he nails the bird to the toolshed door, the hammerin crackin through the eardrums."

p. 121 Reading Skill

Granddaddy stands straight and watches the hawk. Granddaddy does not appear to be afraid.

p. 121 Stop to Reflect

Students should look at "'Good day, gentlemen'" and circle "Like he'd invited them . . . it was time to go." Sample response: Granddaddy's greeting confuses the men because, although he is being calm and polite, he is still asking them to leave.

p. 121 Reading Skill

Sample response: By visualizing the scene, one can see the men trying to gather the spilled film as they back away. The men's reaction shows that Granddaddy's opening of the camera has made them nervous and afraid.

p. 122 Apply the Skills

1. Some students may choose Granddaddy because he is tall and dignified. Other students may choose the narrator because she sees things as they are.

2. **Graphic Organizer**
Sample response:

Hawks and Granddaddy: Granddaddy is threatening. He tries to protect his mate and drive away the threatening men.

What the Hawks Represent: The hawks represent Granny and Granddaddy. The intruders have walked onto Granny's property (as into a hawk's territory). Granddaddy, her mate, is trying to protect her.

3. The grammar shows dialect by the phrase "always got," instead of "have," and "teaches steady," instead of "steadily." The spelling shows dialect with the *g* dropped from "somethin."

4. Sample response: The men have taken motion pictures of his family.

p. 124 Reading/Writing Connection

Sample response: Seeing how characters analyze a problem might help readers deal with real-life situations. A reader might focus on how the characters find a solution. Finding humor in these stories can verify the importance of keeping a sense of humor.

p. 124 Note-taking Guide

Sample response:
2: The coffin is switched with a box of guns and a block of cheese.
3: The narrator and Thompson stand on the platform to avoid the smell.

p. 125 Apply the Skills

1. Thompson says that the corpse "wants to travel alone" because it is creating the bad smell.

2. The contrast between a serious and a harmless source of the odor is humorous.

3. **Graphic Organizer**
Sample response:

Humorous Details: The narrator and Thompson mistake the cheese odor for the smell of a dead body. Thompson gasps over the box near the cheese.

Evaluation: The story is funny because of all of the confusion and drama a simple cargo mix-up causes.

4. Students might say that the dialect makes the speaker come alive. The dialect makes the characters and setting more vivid because it makes them seem more realistic.

5. The smell makes the men leave the car.

Reading Informational Materials: Brochures

p. 128 Reading Skill

Students should circle the map and the hours and admission information. Sample response: They are located next to each other to help people easily find the information needed to visit the museum.

p. 128 Stop to Reflect

Brochures often are meant to persuade people to come to a place. The maps help people get to the place.

p. 128 Read Fluently
Students should circle the colons after Oct. 31 and Mar. 31. Students should underline the semicolon after 5 P.M.

p. 129 Reading Skill
Students should write "A" next to "The Museum." Students may write "B" next to "Barber Junction," "The Robert Julian Roundhouse," or "Historic Spencer Shops." Students may write "C" next to "Spencer Shops' mission was . . ." or "Southern Railway was one of the first U.S. rail systems . . . "

p. 129 Reading Check
Students should underline "While the museum is young—founded in 1977—the story of the Spencer Shops reaches back more than one hundred years."

p. 129 Reading Brochures
Sample response: The man in the picture seems happy. His happiness could make the museum seem like a fun place to visit.

p. 129 Reading Informational Materials
Sample response: This brochure shows the reader the different activities that they could choose from when visiting the museum.

p. 130 Apply the Skills
Thinking About the Brochure
1. Sample response: Placing learning opportunities earlier would leave the reader wondering what there was to learn about.
2. Sample response: This building was chosen so that people could both learn history about trains and see train repairs taking place.

Reading Skill
3. Sample response: It is a good idea to put the map on the front page because it is easily and quickly seen there. The map is more useful to the reader on the first page.
4. You would look under the heading "Learning Opportunities."

ANSWERS TO UNIT 3

"Before Hip-Hop Was Hip-Hop"
Rebecca Walker

p. 133 Note-taking Guide
Sample response:

Circle 1: Hip-hop helped bridge the gap between different cultures.

Circle 2: The revolution of hip-hop affected music, fashion, and dance.

Circle 3: Hip-hop created new words and slang.

Circle 4: Hip-hop taught her creativity, community, and self-confidence.

p. 134 Activate Prior Knowledge
Students may say that Ronald Reagan was President followed by George Bush. They may say that they think of slap bracelets, neon-colored clothing, home video and cable television, *Sixteen Candles* and *The Breakfast Club*, MTV, moonwalking, the Phillies winning their first World Series, the Rubik's Cube, video games, designer jeans, Smurfs, or Cabbage Patch dolls. Some of the music from the era includes Bruce Springsteen, Devo, Duran Duran, and Madonna.

p. 134 Nonfiction
Students should underline "EO," "ATL," "can't," "latest 'steelo,'" "cocked," "old school," and "sodas." Sample response: Walker may have chosen informal English because it seems more personal and fits better with the ideas of the story. It also reflects the language of hip-hop culture.

p. 134 Reading Check
Students should underline "The vast empire of hip-hop amazes me because I knew hip-hop before it was hip-hop. I was there when it all began."

p. 135 Nonfiction
Sample response: She wants readers to see how accepting and diverse hip-hop was when it began and also how flexible.

p. 135 Read Fluently
Students may underline "45s" as the unfamiliar word. Some may figure out by context that the word has something to do with music. Context clue definition: "Small records with two songs on them."

p. 135 Stop to Reflect
Students may say that they like many different kinds of music, just as Walker does. Students may say that they like country music because that is what they listen to at home. Some students may say that they like rap music because it is fast and they like to dance to it.

p. 136 Read Fluently
Students may underline "cliques" and "vicious." Sample response: "Cliques" are "small groups of people that stick together and remain aloof from others." "Vicious" means "spiteful" or "malicious."

p. 136 Nonfiction
Sample response: Both examples show the unexpectedness of what the author found in hip-hop culture. The author did not expect the reserved Asian American girl to sneak a bright red sweatsuit under her coat. In the same way, she did not expect the preppy boy to support all religions.

p. 136 Reading Check
Students should underline "how they talked and used words"; "how they used their hands while talking"; "how they walked and joked and what they wore."

p. 137 Nonfiction
Sample response: She uses expository, narrative, and descriptive writing. She wants to explain and inform about hip-hop culture. She also wants to tell the story of how after-school and weekend activities led to its development. She describes the dancers so that readers will be able to "see" the dancers even if they have never seen breakdancing.

p. 137 Stop to Reflect
Students may agree with Walker and say that they do not like hip-hop music because it is sometimes violent and sometimes contains foul language. Students may describe hip-hop as a series of fast beats that repeat underneath one or more voices that are speaking very quickly and often in rhyme.

p. 137 Reading Check
Students should underline "special ways of walking, talking, and dancing"; "clothing accessories."

p. 138 Stop to Reflect

Sample response: People need something to bridge the differences in groups, and art can do this. Hip-hop was a kind of art because it came from many different places and brought people together.

p. 138 Nonfiction

Students may underline "art could bring people together and make them forget their differences"; "I could express myself and communicate with others through what I wore and how I walked and what music I liked"; "loyalty, community, self-confidence, and creativity"; "She wants kids of today to know that when hip-hop started, it was not about expensive cars and clothes"; "It was created by kids that were doing what felt good to them"; "hopes kids today will do the same"; "She wants them to be honest and think how they can create their own exciting new culture." Sample response: Walker wants to inspire her young readers to create something like hip-hop in their own lives.

p. 138 Reading Check

Students should underline "Walker lived in the Bronx for only one year."

p. 139 Apply the Skills

1. Sample response: Hip-hop bridged the gap by giving Walker and her friends common interests.
2. Sample response: It was important for Walker and her friends to express themselves in this way because it taught them how to bring people together and how to communicate with others.
3. Sample response: The tone is personal, passionate, joyous, and nostalgic. Her tone comes through when she states that she was there when hip-hop began. It also comes through in her descriptions of the wonderful times she and her friends shared.
4. Sample response: Walker has an informal, direct, and friendly style.

Graphic Organizer

Sample response:

Level of Formality: talks about kids not knowing the impact of their ideas

Word Choice: slang, contractions; brand names; musical groups and their recordings; uses "I"

Sentence Patterns: direct, short sentences; tendency to provide multiple examples in one sentence; asks and answers her own questions

"A Celebration of Grandfathers" Rudolfo A. Anaya

"On Summer" Lorraine Hansberry

p. 141 Graphic Organizer

Sample response:

"A Celebration of Grandfathers"

Question: What does Anaya feel about old people?

Detail/Answer: Old people have much to teach us.

Main Idea? We should respect old people.

"On Summer"

Question: How do Hansberry's feelings about summer change as she grows older?

Detail/Answer: She begins to see the beauty of summer's gentle sunsets and long days.

Main Idea? Summer is "the noblest of seasons."

p. 142 Reading/Writing Connection

Sample response:

1. Older people can help people <u>appreciate</u> the values of the past.
2. Talking to older people can help people <u>clarify</u> their own values.
3. Older people often <u>demonstrate</u> a respect for the land.

p. 142 Note-taking Guide

Sample response:

What was the author's grandfather like? Wise, spoke to the point, actively involved in life

Why are elders valuable? They work hard, are connected to the earth, have faith and inner strength, teach us valuable lessons

How are elders viewed now? They are supposed to look and act like young people.

p. 143 Activate Prior Knowledge

Students may say that a grandparent or older person has affected their lives by teaching them a respect for hard work and effort. Because life was not so easy in the past, a grandparent or older person may have taught them never to take life for granted or take for granted opportunities that have been presented to them.

p. 143 Literary Analysis
Students may say that the author creates a tone of admiration and respect for his elders.

p. 143 Reading Check
Students should underline "Buenos días le de Dios, abuelo."

p. 144 Read Fluently
Students should underline "Know where you stand." Sample response: The grandfather means that the boy should know where he is and what is happening around him.

p. 144 Stop to Reflect
Students may say that the advice could apply to them when they are faced with a difficult decision. It would help them make a choice to look at the circumstances surrounding them before coming to a decision.

p. 144 Reading Skill
Sample response: The main idea is that prayers are a meaningful action and wishing is not. When confronted with a problem, the grandfather wants Anaya to do meaningful things instead of wishing.

p. 145 Literary Analysis
Sample response: The repetition of the phrase "We need" puts the readers and Anaya into one group. His use of "need" means that the readers and Anaya must take certain actions.

p. 145 Reading Skill
Sample response: Some details are "the leaves falling from the tree"; "vision blurs, health wanes"; "the act of walking carries with it the painful reminder of the autumn of life."

p. 145 Reading Check
Students could circle "American society celebrates youth, but not old age. TV ads show older people as healthy and lively, but that is not the way it is for many of the elderly."

p. 145 Stop to Reflect
Students may say that they admire Anaya's grandfather's wisdom, gentleness, and respect for the land.

p. 146 Apply the Skills
1. Sample response: The old ones are strong, wise, and independent. Modern mass media show images of old people who appear youthful, lively, and healthy.
2. Sample response: Anaya believes that old people should be treated with patience and care because growing old can be painful and damaging.
3. **Graphic Organizer**
Sample response:
Diction: Buenos días le de Dios, abuelo; process of life; natural cycle of growth and change; transformation
Tone: admiration, respect, affection
Style: serious, thoughtful, informal
4. Sample response: Young people should respect old people because the elders are strong and wise and have something important to share.

p. 148 Reading/Writing Connection
Sample response:
1. The older members of my family embody stories from the past.
2. The pictures of our celebrations signify happy memories.
3. I react with pride when I see my family together.

p. 148 Note-taking Guide
Sample response:
As a Child: It is a mistake. It is excessive. It is an overstatement. It is too stark.
As an Adult: It is noble. It is life at its apex. It has the gentlest nights and the longest days. It is beauty. She has respect for it.

p. 149 Apply the Skills
1. Sample response: It is a memory of a specific summer. Hansberry's memories of her grandmother provide a contrast to her description of the woman in Maine.
2. Sample response: She considers summer noble because it represents life in its most complete form.
3. **Graphic Organizer**
Sample response:
Diction: "life at the apex," "gentlest nights," "noblest of the seasons"
Tone: respectful, admiring, affectionate
Style: thoughtful, solemn, formal
4. Sample response: Hansberry did not like summer as a young person, but she learned to appreciate it as an adult.

"The News"
Neil Postman

"Single Room, Earth View"
Sally Ride

p. 151 Graphic Organizer
Sample response:
"The News"
Details 1: Dramatic video is often shown to keep viewers' attention.
Details 2: The news anchor is chosen because he or she "looks" the part.
Main Idea: Television news cannot cover all of the news adequately because of its nature as entertainment.

"Single Room, Earth View"
Details 1: One moment she could see fires in Africa, and then she could see ice flowing in the Antarctic.
Details 2: The eddies and spirals in Earth's water eventually become visible.
Main Idea: Seeing the world from the space shuttle creates a new perspective on Earth.

p. 152 Reading/Writing Connection
Sample response: I rely on news Web sites to find out about current events. These sources clarify details and help me understand what is happening in the world. These sources also indicate how events will affect me in the future.

p. 152 Note-taking Guide
Sample response:
Newspapers: show many articles at the same time
Television News: shows stories in sequence
Both: supply news of the world

p. 153 Apply the Skills
1. Students may suggest that the comparison reveals that the news broadcast is an artificial order imposed on the real world. Real events appear "dramatized" on television news. This makes television news seem like a play.
2. Sample response: Time limits prevent the day's news from being covered sufficiently. The viewer gets only a series of impressions.
3. **Graphic Organizer**
Sample response:
Cause and Effect:
Example: The need for television news stories to keep all viewers results in brief stories that have widespread appeal.

Effect: This example illustrates why it is impossible for television news to cover news stories adequately.
4. Sample response: The main idea of "The News" is that television news has time limitations and must appeal to a wide audience. As a result, it gives a false impression of the world.

p. 155 Reading/Writing Connection
Sample response:
1. I had to alter my feelings about the city when I saw it from the Empire State Building.
2. Looking at something up close can emphasize how complex it is.
3. The sight of the moon seems to contradict what I thought the moon's surface looked like.

p. 155 Note-taking Guide
Sample response:
Geographical Sites: Ganges River, Sahara
Human-Made Structures: cities
Natural Occurrences: typhoons forming; volcanoes smoldering
Environmental Problems: oil spills, air pollution, destruction of forests.

p. 156 Activate Prior Knowledge
Students may say that Earth is very blue because most of its surface is water. They may say that because they can see the land-masses, it looks just like a globe. They may also point out weather patterns such as hurricanes.

p. 156 Reading Skill
Sample response: The space traveler is a giant step farther away. A space traveler can see typhoons forming, volcanoes smoking, and meteors streaking through the atmosphere. An astronaut can see Africa and Antarctica in the same moment.

p. 156 Reading Check
Students should underline "During her space trip, Ride circled the Earth every 90 minutes."

p. 157 Stop to Reflect
Some students may say that seeing the Caribbean from space would be the most interesting. They may like to watch hurricanes form and move across the ocean.

p. 157 Literary Analysis

Sample response: She describes the effects of pollution. She is using the sense of sight to help readers realize the damage that pollution is doing to Earth.

p. 157 Reading Check

Students should circle "Then I realized they were obscured by a huge dust storm, a cloud of sand that enveloped the continent from Morocco to the Sudan."

p. 158 Read Fluently

Students may say that they have an image of the ocean, covered with swirls and mixing colors.

p. 158 Literary Analysis

Students should circle "It looks like bursting balls of light, like a fireworks show." Students should underline "Blue and orange bands would streak along the horizon." Sample response: The description appeals to the sense of sight.

p. 158 Reading Check

Students should circle "eddies" and "spirals."

p. 159 Apply the Skills

1. Sample response: Ride thought that she could almost see geological forces working in the way the theories say they work.
2. Students may say that the way they think about Earth is very different. The essay may have given them a new sense of the unity and fragility of the planet Earth.
3. **Graphic Organizer**
Sample response:
Comparison/Contrast: comparison of the appearance of Earth from space in 1973 with the view in 1983
Effect: The example emphasizes the changes that have taken place on Earth.
Cause and Effect: the effects of pollution on the Earth's environment
Effect: The example illustrates the various types of damage that have been done to the environment.
4. Sample response: The main idea is that space travel offers an amazing view of the world.

Reading Informational Materials: Technical Documents

p. 161 Graphic Organizer

Sample response:
Narrative text
Information Provided:
basic facts
Diagrams
Information Provided: names and locations of parts as well as an overall view of the shuttle
Lists or statistics
Examples: the *Shuttle Statistics* list

p. 162 Reading Technical Documents

Students should write the following:
1. Length; 2. Height; 3. Wingspan; 4. Weight; 5. Maximum cargo to orbit; 6. SRB separation; 7. External Tank Separation; 8. Orbit.

p. 162 Reading Skill

Sample response: At the end of a mission, the space shuttle weighs 104,326 kilograms (230,000 pounds).

p. 162 Stop to Reflect

Sample response: A technical document might start with history and background to help familiarize readers with the topic.

p. 162 Reading Check

Students may underline "The space shuttle is the world's first reusable spacecraft"; "The shuttle launches like a rocket"; "Each of the three space shuttle orbiters now in operation—Discovery, Atlantis and Endeavour—is designed to fly at least 100 missions."

p. 163 Reading Skill

Sample response: The *Endeavour* was delivered in May 1991.

p. 163 Reading Technical Documents

Students may underline "Endeavour was built as a replacement following the Challenger accident" and "the Enterprise, never flew in space."

p. 163 Read Fluently
Students should circle "The space shuttle consists of three major components." Students should underline "the orbiter which houses the crew"; "a large external fuel tank that holds fuel for the main engines"; "and two solid rocket boosters which provide most of the shuttle's lift during the first two minutes of flight."

p. 163 Reading Check
Students should circle "The longest the shuttle has stayed in orbit on any single mission is 17.5 days on mission STS-80 in November 1996."

p. 164 Reading Technical Documents
Sample response: By looking at the diagrams, one can tell that the space shuttle is made up of at least four separate large pieces.

p. 164 Reading Skill
Sample response: NASA has made engine system improvements that have increased the safety of the shuttle.

p. 164 Reading Informational Materials
Sample response: NASA has been doing very well with this goal. Although two shuttles have exploded and resulted in loss of life, most of the people who have traveled in space shuttles have returned safely.

p. 165 Apply the Skills
Thinking About the Technical Document
1. Sample response: The author probably discusses the shuttle's launch record because he or she previously mentioned accidents. The launch record shows that the space shuttle is largely a successful design. The author then mentions design improvements to show the progress being made to improve the shuttle.
2. Sample response: The text and the diagram give the reader different kinds of information about the shuttle parts. The text tells what the functions of the parts are. The diagram shows the reader where the parts are located.

Reading Skill
3. Sample response: *Discovery*, *Atlantis*, and *Endeavour* are now in use.
4. Sample response: The shuttle's wingspan is 23.79 meters (78.06 feet).

"Carry Your Own Skis"
Lian Dolan

"Libraries Face Sad Chapter"
Pete Hamill

p. 166 Graphic Organizer
Sample response:
"Carry Your Own Skis"
Claim: Be responsible for yourself and your stuff, or you miss out.
Logical? yes
Evaluation: The author shows how being responsible leads to a fuller life.

"Libraries Face Sad Chapter"
Claim: Reading is not an assignment, it is a pleasure.
Logical? no
Evaluation: The author shows how losing library services would deprive children of access to information found in books.

p. 167 Reading/Writing Connection
Sample response: Activities that involve hardship would frustrate people who expect life to be easy. Some people, however, love the challenge of pushing themselves to extremes. They like to display their courage and their ability to face life's hardships.

p. 167 Note-taking Guide
Sample response:
Those Who Carry Their Own Skis: are liked by others; are asked to participate in other activities; are responsible; are not afraid to work hard
Those Who Do Not Carry Their Own Skis: are not always liked by others; are not always asked to participate in other activities; are not responsible; do not like to work hard

p. 168 Activate Prior Knowledge
Students may say that learning to write in cursive was difficult for them. They may say that they are glad now that they learned to do it because it looks nicer when they write.

p. 168 Reading Skill
Sample response: The details show that skiers used gear that did not keep them "dry and warm" and wooden skis that were "heavy" and "bulky." Lodges had no luxuries. The words Dolan uses show that skiing was uncomfortable and tiring.

p. 168 Literary Analysis

Students may point out the details "cold, wet, and tired" and "on our own." These details are so unpleasant that they make skiing seem like something a person would not want to do.

p. 169 Reading Skill

Sample response: Dolan gives examples of girls who did not help out with chores on camping trips.

p. 169 Read Fluently

Students should underline "provide food or do all the cleanup." Students may list CD or DVD as abbreviations they know.

p. 169 Reading Check

Students should circle "Be responsible for yourself and your stuff or you miss out."

p. 170 Literary Analysis

Sample response: Her motive might be to persuade other people to be responsible for themselves or to "carry their own skis." She might also be trying to tell people that those who do not take responsibility make life difficult for others.

p. 170 Reading Skill

Sample response: She shows how being forced to be responsible for her skis, even though she did not like it, taught her that she had to be responsible for other things in life. She would have to be responsible if she wanted to fully enjoy life.

p. 170 Stop to Reflect

Students may say that people who do not take responsibility for themselves annoy them. When others are not responsible, they make more work for responsible people.

p. 171 Apply the Skills

1. Sample response: This lesson guided her in getting a job and then working hard for the company that was providing her paycheck.
2. Some students may agree that taking personal responsibility leads to a fuller life because others are more likely to accept a person who does so. Other students may disagree, saying that avoiding responsibility may affect a person positively because others will do things for that person.

3. Graphic Organizer

Sample response:

Passage: Section beginning "The lesson was simple, really. Be responsible for yourself and your stuff or you miss out."

Reason or Emotion: She appeals to reason by explaining in a logical way why it was important to "carry your own skis."

4. Sample response: The author was convincing because she gave specific examples of people who do accept responsibility and people who do not accept responsibility.

p. 173 Reading/Writing Connection

Sample response: My first library visit did reveal that there are books on every topic. Seeing so many books helped me perceive that the world is a very big place. I knew then that I wanted to dedicate my life to reading books.

p. 173 Note-taking Guide

Sample response:

Circle 2: to check out books

Circle 3: to learn about jobs

Circle 5: to study to become a U.S. citizen

p. 174 Apply the Skills

1. Some students may say they share Hamill's feelings because they had many happy experiences in a library as a child. Other students may not share Hamill's feelings, saying that people can get information by television, online, or by purchasing books.
2. Sample response: He believes that books feed the mind and imagination.

3. Graphic Organizer

Sample response:

Passage: paragraph beginning "We passed into that library . . ."; paragraph beginning "We could live in the South Seas . . ."

Reason or Emotion: He appeals to emotion by remembering how important libraries were to him as a child. He appeals to emotion by explaining how he liked to learn about history.

4. Students may say that Hamill's arguments are well reasoned and logical. He gives facts about how important libraries are to immigrants. He explains how the city government may be forced to cut services. He explains the importance of libraries today with the cost of books and the lack of good shows on television.

"I Have a Dream"
Martin Luther King, Jr.

"First Inaugural Address"
Franklin D. Roosevelt

p. 176 Graphic Organizer
Sample response:
"I Have a Dream"
Technique: restatement of "let freedom ring"
Purpose: to energize the audience and make them feel patriotic
Effect: makes listeners believe that there is support for them

"First Inaugural Address"
Technique: repetition of "stricken" in ". . . a stricken nation in the midst of a stricken world . . ."
Purpose: to show that it is not just this country that is having a problem
Effect: People will believe that they are not alone in the world.

p. 177 Reading/Writing Connection
Sample response:
1. When it comes to fairness, Americans embody the meaning of good sportsmanship.
2. Freedom and justice comprise two of the most important American ideals.
3. Most Americans define tolerance as the acceptance of other people and ideas.

p. 177 Note-taking Guide
Sample response:
Whom will it affect? everyone, regardless of race or religion
What will it take? faith in the cause of equality
What will it be like? Inequality will disappear; descendants of slaves and slave owners will be equal; people will be judged by their character, not by their skin color; all people will be truly free.

p. 178 Activate Prior Knowledge
Students may say that the United States celebrates the holiday because King was a great civil rights leader and national figure. Some students will be aware of his role in leading the Montgomery Bus Boycott, the protests in Selma, and the March on Washington. Some may be familiar with his philosophy of nonviolence and the fact that he was assassinated.

p. 178 Reading Skill
Students may say that they feel angry that people have been judged by the color of their skin. They may also say that they feel hopeful for the future because this is something that can be changed.

p. 178 Reading Check
Students should underline "sons of slaves" and "sons of slaveholders."

p. 179 Literary Analysis
Students should underline "Let freedom ring." Sample response: This parallelism emphasizes King's ideas that America is a nation of freedom and should live up to its ideals in every state.

p. 179 Read Fluently
Sample response: King wants freedom and equality for all Americans. King finishes his speech by saying that all people will be free when the sound of freedom is everywhere.

p. 179 Stop to Reflect
Students may suggest that Dr. King's dreams did come true because many laws have been passed to make sure that people are not judged by their race or religion. Others may believe that some of his dream was accomplished, but that there is still more work that needs to be done.

p. 180 Apply the Skills
1. Sample response: He reminds everyone that the country was founded on a promise of liberty.
2. Sample response: The mention of these places ties in with his message of equality for everyone across the country.
3. **Graphic Organizer**
Sample response:
Example: "let freedom ring"
Effect: This emphasizes the hope that one day everyone will be free.
4. Students may say that King is effective because the rhetorical devices and emotion-charged language emphasize his ideas.

p. 182 Reading/Writing Connection
Sample response: A speaker's true excitement can evoke excitement in those who are listening. When I hear a person project his or her ideas, I think about what the ideas mean to me. Good ideas stimulate me to make changes.

p. 182 Note-taking Guide

Sample response:

Who is giving this speech? Franklin Delano Roosevelt, the thirty-second president of the United States

Why is he giving this speech? It is his first speech as president. All new presidents give a speech at the inauguration, or swearing-in.

In what year is he giving this speech? 1932

What is the greatest problem for the country at this time? Many people are unemployed and do not have any money to make a living.

What is the main promise that is made in the speech? Roosevelt wants to help people find jobs.

p. 183 Apply the Skills

1. Sample response: He sends the message that the people have been misled and cheated.

2. Sample response: His listeners probably felt encouraged.

3. **Graphic Organizer**

Sample response:

Repetition

Example: He repeats that he will perform his "duty."

Effect: The repetition helps give listeners a sense that he will do what they expect of a leader.

Parallelism

Example: "on honesty, on honor, on the sacredness of obligations, on faithful protection, on unselfish performance..."

Effect: This listing of virtues gives readers a sense of momentum, or forward motion.

Analogy

Example: He compares the state of the nation today with its state in other dark times in the country's history, when good leadership and support of the people pulled the country through.

Effect: This analogy helps give listeners a sense that the country will pull through this tough time, as it has in the past.

4. Sample response: Roosevelt plays to people's feelings when he says, "We are stricken by no plague of locusts. Compared with the perils which our forefathers conquered because they believed and were not afraid, we have still much to be thankful for."

Reading Informational Materials: Historical Research Study

p. 185 Graphic Organizer

Sample response:

Statement: "Only a foolish optimist can deny the dark realities of the moment."

Provable: no

Fact or Opinion: opinion

Statement: *Defending Your Life* was a 1991 movie written and directed by its star, Albert Brooks.

Provable: yes

Fact or Opinion: fact

p. 186 Reading Historical Research Studies

Sample response: This study begins with a quotation to capture the reader's attention. It reminds the readers that the study is about a speech. It includes the famous line, "The only thing we have to fear is fear itself."

p. 186 Stop to Reflect

Sample response: Axelrod starts the article with a description of a popular movie to catch the reader's attention.

p. 186 Reading Skill

Sample response: This statement is an opinion. It is not something that can be proved.

p. 186 Reading Check

Students should underline "First inaugural address, March 4, 1933."

p. 187 Reading Skill

Students may underline "In 1921 polio threatened first to kill him and then paralyzed him. . . ." Students may circle "He did not blink at the odds."

p. 187 Reading Historical Research Studies

Sample response: President Roosevelt is in a wheelchair and looks like he likes dogs. He also likes reaching out to people.

p. 187 Stop to Reflect

Sample response: Axelrod repeats the words "fog of fear" to tie ideas in the study together.

p. 188 Reading Historical Research Studies

Sample response: Axelrod used this quotation to show that Roosevelt did not lie to the nation. He wants to show how straight forward Roosevelt was and how determined he was to conquer the challenge of the high unemployment rate.

p. 188 Stop to Reflect
Students may say that Americans probably felt inspired by Roosevelt's attitude and as though they were moving toward ending the Depression.

p. 188 Reading Skill
Sample response: This statement is an opinion. It cannot be proved true.

p. 188 Reading Check
Students should underline "Lift the fog of fear and you could see that the Great Depression was not of natural, supernatural, or inevitable origin."

p. 189 Reading Historical Research Studies
Sample response: Axelrod is offering an explanation of the quote above.

p. 189 Reading Check
Students should underline "their efforts have been cast in the pattern of an outworn tradition."

p. 189 Reading Skill
Students should underline the word "always." Sample response: This word warns that the sentence might be a generalization because it cannot be proved that Roosevelt "always" navigated between the new and the age-old.

p. 190 Read Fluently
Sample response: I want to buy those sneakers, and yet I do not have enough money.

p. 190 Reading Skill
Students may underline "Happiness lies not in the mere possession of money; it lies in the joy of achievement, in the thrill of creative effort." Sample response: Roosevelt is stating an opinion. No one can prove what causes happiness.

p. 190 Reading Check
Students should underline "The measure of the restoration lies in the extent to which we apply social values more noble than mere monetary profit."

p. 191 Stop to Reflect
Students may point out the microphones for CBS and NBC on the edge of the podium. Roosevelt's words were reaching the people over the radio.

p. 191 Reading Historical Research Studies
Sample response: Axelrod is summarizing Roosevelt's speech and his comments on it.

p. 191 Reading Skill
Sample response: The phrase tells readers that the statement is an opinion. It cannot be proved true.

p. 191 Reading Informational Materials
Sample response: Axelrod did a good job of supporting his thesis with examples. He included many quotations from the speech. He tied those quotations to events in time.

p. 192 Apply the Skills
Thinking About the Historical Research Study
1. Sample response: Axelrod means that people can pay too much attention to their fear. Then, they do not face the problem. Focusing on fear can cause people to think less clearly about possible solutions.
2. Sample response: Axelrod points out how Roosevelt shows his radically new ideas. He connects these new ideas to Roosevelt's plans for the "New Deal." He also points out Roosevelt's age-old and unchanging beliefs with references to the Bible.

Reading Skill
3. Sample response: "Our kind has conquered worse in the past."
4. Sample response: "He began by asking the American people to sweep aside the 'nameless, unreasoning, unjustified terror.'"

"Uncoiling"
Pat Mora

"A Voice"
Pat Mora

p. 195 Note-taking Guide
Sample response:
What is the main image of the poem?
giving a speech in front of people
What details support this image? "roars / and rivers leap," "howling / leaves off trees"; "lights on the stage unrelenting," "the only Mexican in the auditorium," "you wanted to hide from those strange faces"

p. 196 Activate Prior Knowledge
Students may compare a storm to an animal, a machine out of control, or an angry person. They might say that the storm might be cold if it were a machine and hot if it were an angry person.

p. 196 Poetry
Students should underline "scratches," "tosses her dark hair," "snares," "sighs," "spooks," and "spins."

p. 196 Reading Check
Students should circle "lightning," "cholla," "hawks," and "butterfly swarms."

p. 197 Poetry
Students should underline "the lights on the stage unrelenting / as the desert sun."

p. 197 Poetry
Five stanzas are on the page. Each stanza has 4 lines.

p. 197 Poetry
Students should underline "You like," "You liked," "You liked," "all the," "all those," "How did I do it?" and "How did I do it." Sample response: Mora emphasizes that her mother has strong motivations and desires to speak in public. However, she still feels nervous about speaking in public.

p. 198 Stop to Reflect
Sample response: Mora means that families like to find similarities in their members, particularly over generations. By doing so, they preserve family characteristics, or blood.

p. 198 Read Fluently
For the stanzas that run from lines 29–36, students should bracket "You, who are never . . . like an ice cube."

p. 198 Reading Check
Students should underline "You, who are never at a loss / for words, felt your breath stick in your throat / like an ice cube. 'I can't,' you whispered. / 'I can't.'"

p. 199 Apply the Skills
1. The speaker is describing a desert storm.
2. Sample response: That day's failure taught Mora's mother that it was important to teach her children to use their voices.
3. Sample response: The storm is wild, powerful, and destructive. The women are frightened and timid but also protective.
4. **Graphic Organizer**
Sample response:
What It Says: The mother's breath sticks in her throat.
What It Means: The mother cannot make herself speak.
Effect: The image conveys a feeling of fright and helplessness.

Poetry Collection 1

Poetry Collection 2

p. 201 Graphic Organizer
Sample response:
Poetry Collection 1
Example: "Does it dry up / like a raisin in the sun?"
Type: simile
Meaning or Effect: The simile stresses that when dreams are pushed away, they may lose their power and importance.

Poetry Collection 2
Example: "where mammals and computers / live together in mutually / programming harmony / like pure water / touching clear sky"
Type: simile
Meaning or Effect: The simile stresses how effortlessly the author wants mammals and computers to live together.

p. 202 Reading/Writing Connection
Sample response:
1. Dreams help people achieve their goals.
2. People can benefit from their dreams by taking steps to make them come true.

3. People who believe in dreams can <u>maintain</u> a positive attitude.

p. 202 Note-taking Guide
Sample response:
Dreams: to show that dreams should be followed
I Wandered Lonely as a Cloud: to lovingly recall an inspiring scene of nature
Meciendo: to compare rocking one's son to God's rocking of nature
Sonnet on Love XIII: to compare the poet's love to the idea of an inventor from long ago

p. 203 Activate Prior Knowledge
Sample response: Nature is a source of inspiration because of its beauty. Nature provides imagery to which most people can relate.

p. 203 Reading Check
Students should circle "What happens to a dream deferred?"; "Does it dry up / like a raisin in the sun?"; "Or fester like a sore— / And then run?"; "Does it stink like rotten meat?"; "Or crust and sugar over— / like a syrupy sweet?"; "Or does it explode?"

p. 203 Reading Skill
The first stanza contains one sentence.

p. 203 Literary Analysis
Sample response: One metaphor is "Life is a broken-winged bird / That cannot fly."

p. 204 Literary Analysis
The speaker compares the daffodils to stars in the Milky Way.

p. 204 Reading Skill
The reader should stop reading after "breeze," "dance," and "daffodils."

p. 204 Stop To Reflect: Students may circle "tossing their heads in sprightly dance."
Sample response: This figurative language makes the reader think about little dancers tossing their heads around in happiness. The figurative language paints a vivid picture for the reader.

p. 205 Reading Skill
This translation contains seven sentences.

p. 205 Literary Analysis
The wind is "wandering" and "loving," and it "rocks the wheat."

p. 205 Reading Check
Students should underline "I rock my son."

p. 206 Literary Analysis
A paradox appears in the first stanza.

p. 206 Reading Skill
Sample response: Reading in sentences helps readers understand the poem because it keeps related ideas together, which makes the meaning clearer. It also keeps the rhythm natural.

p. 206 Reading Check
Students should underline "'Give me a place to stand,' Archimedes said, / 'and I can move the world.'"

p. 207 Read Fluently
Students should underline "from which to move a world out of joint." Sample response: I could tell that something was out of joint when my brother volunteered to clean the living room.

p. 207 Stop to Reflect
Sample response: The author connects his love with Archimedes' discovery because it is a strong and powerful love. Archimedes' lever could move the world, and the author is saying that his love could do the same.

p. 208 Apply the Skills
1. Sample response: Cherish your dreams. Life is meaningless without dreams.
2. Sample response: The sights and sounds fill the speakers with delight and comfort.
3. Sample response: One example is in "I Wandered Lonely as a Cloud": "A host, of golden daffodils . . . Fluttering and dancing in the breeze."
4. **Graphic Organizer**
Sample response:
Stanza: "The wind wandering by night / rocks the wheat. / Hearing the loving wind, / I rock my son."
Paragraph: The wind wandering by night rocks the wheat. Hearing the loving wind, I rock my son.

p. 210 Reading/Writing Connection
Sample response:
1. Computers <u>minimize</u> problems by helping people get organized.
2. E-mail allows us to <u>accelerate</u> communication.
3. Some choose to <u>interact</u> with computers instead of people.

p. 210 Note-taking Guide
Sample response:
"Hope" is the thing with feathers—: the characteristics of hope
Much Madness is divinest Sense—: the nature of sanity
The War Against the Trees: how progress destroys nature

p. 211 Apply the Skills
1. Sample response: The comparison suggests that the speaker feels comfortable and safe with computers.
2. Sample response: The image of war shows that the speaker feels that the trees are victims being unfairly attacked.
3. Sample response: The trees in "The War Against the Trees" are described as "great-grandfathers."
4. **Graphic Organizer**
Sample response:
Stanza: "I saw the ghosts of children at their games / Racing beyond their childhood in the shade, / And while the green world turned its death-foxed page / And a red wagon wheeled, / I watched them disappear / Into the suburbs of their grievous age."
Paragraph: I saw the ghosts of children at their games racing beyond their childhood in the shade, and while the green world turned its death-foxed page and a red wagon wheeled, I watched them disappear into the suburbs of their grievous age.

Reading Informational Materials: Case Studies

p. 213 Graphic Organizer
Sample response:
Details: Matt wants to study computer science and then become a professor; Gil wants to study robotics and explore other areas of robotics.
Generalization: Even people who have similar jobs at one point in their lives can go on to do different things in their futures.

p. 214 Reading Case Studies
Sample response: Readers learn that this case study examines the different paths that can be taken to a career in robotics.

p. 214 Reading Skill
Sample response: Matt, like other boys his age, needs to be motivated by a subject matter to be able to excel in it.

p. 214 Read Fluently
Students should circle "says Matt." Sample response: "I want to go to the movies," she said.

p. 214 Reading Check
Students should circle "Think you'll never use high school math? Think again . . ."

p. 215 Reading Check
Students should underline "physics, math, science, engineering, communications, and others."

p. 215 Reading Case Studies
Sample response: 1. He went to college to study political science. 2. He took an artificial intelligence class. 3. He took part in robotics competitions.

p. 215 Stop to Reflect
Sample response: It was worth it to give up their summers because they gained experience that helped them get jobs.

p. 216 Reading Case Studies
Sample response: Internships can often present opportunities for jobs.

p. 216 Reading Skill
Sample response: One detail that supports this generalization is "Often internships are the first step through the door."

p. 216 Reading Informational Materials
Students may say that this case study made them appreciate math class. Others may say that it had no effect on their feelings about math.

p. 216 Reading Check
Students should underline "variety" and "you usually get to learn something big and new every few weeks."

p. 217 Apply the Skills
Thinking About the Case Study
1. Sample response: Gil started working hard in high school. Matt did not start working hard until college.
2. Sample response: Yes; this case study's advice about pursuing a robotics career applies to other fields as well.

Reading Skill

3. Sample response: Matt took classes in psychology, philosophy, and anthropology.

4. Sample response: Matt did not do well in high school. But when he got to college and found a subject that he was interested in, he began to do well in school.

Poetry Collection 1
Poetry Collection 2

p. 218 Graphic Organizer
Sample response:

Poetry Collection 1: "Summer"
Sight: "old men sleeping"
Hearing: "bugs buzzin"
Smell: "daisies"
Taste: "juices dripping"
Touch: "hot"

Poetry Collection 2: "The Bells"
Sight: "twinkle"
Hearing: "tinkle, tinkle, tinkle"
Smell: none
Taste: "rust within their throats"
Touch: "balmy"

p. 219 Reading/Writing Connection
Sample response:
1. I anticipate summer because I love to go swimming.
2. During the fall, we are blessed with a display of colorful leaves.
3. When spring arrives, I can participate in baseball.

p. 219 Note-taking Guide
Sample response:
Summer
Two events: Bugs fly through the air. Old men sleep.
The Eagle
The topic of the poem: a look at an eagle
Two events: An eagle stands on a mountain.
Analysis of Baseball
The topic of the poem: the basics of baseball
Two events: The ball bounces. The fans cheer.

p. 220 Activate Prior Knowledge
Some students may say that winter is their favorite season because they love skiing. Other students may say that summer is their favorite season because they like swimming.

p. 220 Reading Skill
Sample response: "Summer" appeals to all five senses. "Juices dripping" appeals to the sense of taste. "Old men sleeping" appeals to the sense of sight. "Bugs buzzin" appeals to the sense of sound. "Daisies" appeals to the sense of smell. "Hot" appeals to the sense of touch.

p. 220 Literary Analysis
Students should circle "clasps," "crag," "crooked," "close," "lonely," and "lands."

p. 221 Literary Analysis
Students should circle "about," "bat," "mitt," "hits," "bat," "it," "hits," "mitt," "Bat," "doesn't," "hit," "bat," "meets," "it," bat," "it," "fits," and "mitt."

p. 221 Read Fluently
The stanza contains four sentences.

p. 221 Reading Check
Students should underline "to take bat's / bait."

p. 222 Literary Analysis
Students should circle "pow."

p. 222 Reading Skill
The words "40,000 fans" appeal to the sense of sight because there are so many people. "Exploded" appeals to the sense of sound because the crowd sounds like an explosion.

p. 222 Stop to Reflect
Students may say that it is not necessary to know the rules of baseball in order to enjoy the poem. The sound devices and imagery make the poem enjoyable.

p. 222 Reading Check
Students should circle "It's about / the ball, / the bat, / the mitt, / the bases / and the fans" and "It's about / home, and it's / about run."

p. 223 Apply the Skills
1. Sweat or nectar may be dripping.
2. The eagle is probably watching for something to eat.
3. **Graphic Organizer**
Sample response:
Alliteration
Effect: makes the poem more rhythmic
Consonance
Effect: strengthens the feeling of wetness

Assonance
Example: "Summer": "daisies lay"
Effect: makes the daisies seem relaxed
4. Sample response: Fluent reading helps readers appreciate the musical quality that the sound devices give the poems.

p. 225 Reading/Writing Connection
Sample response: The buzz of my alarm clock is a trigger that gets me up and moving. It makes me appreciate my daily routine. My alarm clock helps me contemplate how valuable time is.

p. 225 Note-taking Guide
Sample response:
The Bells: different bells
Jabberwocky: the Jabberwock

p. 226 Apply the Skills
1. The ball dropping through the net makes the sound described.
2. Students may say that the poem is at least mocking stories of heroism.
3. **Graphic Organizer**
Sample response:
Alliteration
Effect: gives the poem a rhythmic quality
Consonance
Example: Slam, Dunk, & Hook: "but a hot"
Effect: quickens the reading pace
Assonance
Example: Jabberwocky: "left it dead"
Effect: makes this line sound depressing
4. Sample response: Fluent reading helps readers appreciate the musical qualities of the poems.

Poetry Collection 1

Poetry Collection 2

p. 228 Graphic Organizer
Sample response:
Poetry Collection 1
Lines of Poetry: "It looked extremely rocky for the Mudville nine that day; / The score stood two to four, with but an inning left to play."
Details in Lines of Poetry: The team is losing with one inning left to play.
Paraphrase: The Mudville team is losing by two runs. Only one inning remains in the game.

Poetry Collection 2
Lines of Poetry: "Ah, distinctly I remember it was in the bleak December, / And each separate dying ember wrought its ghost upon the floor."
Details in Lines of Poetry: The speaker clearly remembers a December night next to his fire.
Paraphrase: I remember a specific December evening when the fire was casting shadows on the floor.

p. 229 Reading/Writing Connection
Sample response:
1. Some events that evoke happiness are birthdays and graduations.
2. People respond to sad news by trying to stay positive.
3. People can reinforce happiness in others by being a giving person.

p. 229 Note-taking Guide
Sample response:
Casey at the Bat
What Happens Next: Casey gets two strikes.
Final Event: Casey strikes out.
Fifteen
What Happens Next: The boy imagines riding the motorcycle.
What Happens Next: Teenager finds the driver of the bike.
Final Event: The driver rides away.
Twister Hits Houston
Beginning Event: A bad storm is coming.
What Happens Next: The father and mother don't take shelter.
What Happens Next: The tornado rips through the yard.
Final Event: The family survives.

p. 230 Activate Prior Knowledge
Students may say that pressure improved their performance because it sharpened their ability to focus and got their adrenaline flowing. Others may say that they would have performed better without the added pressure.

p. 230 Reading Skill
Sample response: Some people get up to leave the game. But the ones who stayed were hopeful. They thought that if only Casey would get a chance to play, Mudville could still win the game.

p. 230 Reading Check
Students should underline "There was Blakey safe at second and Flynn a-huggin' third."

p. 231 Literary Analysis
Sample response: The poem's mood is optimistic, confident, and excited.

p. 231 Reading Skill
Students should underline "eyes were on him," "tongues applauded," and "pitcher ground the ball into his hip."

p. 231 Read Fluently
Sample response: Unheeded, the ball sped close by the sturdy batsman.

p. 232 Reading Skill
Sample response: Casey smiled a look of generosity. He quieted the crowd, and the game continued. The pitcher threw the ball again, and Casey didn't try to hit it. The umpire called, "Strike two."

p. 232 Literary Analysis
Sample response: The mood goes from optimistic to determined and tense. Casey is getting serious and wants to make sure that he gets the hit.

p. 232 Reading Check
Students should circle "And it's likely they'd have killed him had not Casey raised his hand" and "He stilled the rising tumult."

p. 233 Reading Skill
Sample response: Somewhere in the world everyone is happy. However, everyone in Mudville is sad because Casey struck out.

p. 233 Stop to Reflect
Sample response: Casey shows that he is a confident player when he lets the first two balls go by without swinging at them. Also, he calms the crowd and doesn't seem upset at the umpire for calling strikes.

p. 234 Stop to Reflect
Students may say that a poem is an effective way to tell a story because poets normally include only the most important and vivid details. Other students may say that the poetry doesn't allow the author to give enough details and description.

p. 234 Reading Skill
Sample response: The speaker means that he could ride the bike toward the horizon.

p. 234 Literary Analysis
The characters are the speaker and the owner of the motorcycle.

p. 234 Reading Check
Students should underline "South of the bridge on Seventeenth / I found back of the willows one summer / day a motorcycle with engine running."

p. 235 Literary Analysis
The poem takes place in a house in Houston. A tornado hits the house. The speaker is the son or daughter of the parents caught in the tornado.

p. 235 Reading Skill
Sample response: The tornado banged against the door like an angry cat.

p. 235 Stop to Reflect
Students may describe the ferocity of specific storms. They may say that they stayed in their houses and away from the windows during the storms.

p. 235 Reading Check
Students should underline "Papa was on the front porch. / Mama was in the kitchen."

p. 236 Apply the Skills
1. Sample response: He may have been overly confident. He let two pitches go by without swinging. He believes that he can get a hit when he wants.
2. Sample response: No, his behavior is not appropriate. A tornado is very dangerous. One would not sit calmly on the porch and watch it. One would take cover.
3. **Graphic Organizer**
Sample response:
Casey at the Bat
Plot: The ballgame is in the ninth inning. The opposing team is winning by two runs. Casey comes to bat. He strikes out.
Fifteen
Setting: the side of a road
Characters: a fifteen-year-old boy, a motorcycle rider
Plot: A fifteen-year-old boy finds an overturned motorcycle on the roadside. He pushes it back on the road. He imagines what it would be like to ride away on it. Instead, he helps the owner get back to his cycle.

Twister Hits Houston
Setting: a family home in Houston
Characters: Mama, Papa, the speaker
Plot: A speaker is retelling the story of a tornado that strikes the speaker's home. Papa sits on the front porch. Mama is in the kitchen. The storm uproots a big tree. It also drops a car in the yard and bangs the screen door.
4. Sample response: The baseball came flying, but Casey ignored it. He said that it wasn't his style. The umpire called strike one.

p. 238 Reading/Writing Connection
Sample response: Things in my life that evoke happy feelings include my family and friends. I respond to these feelings by spending more time with these people. When I am in a bad mood, I react by not talking.

p. 238 Note-taking Guide
Sample response:
The Horses
Event: The horses come.
Effect: The people are filled with hope.
The Writer
Event: The speaker hears his daughter typing.
Effect: The father stops in the hallway and thinks about his daughter and her life.

p. 239 Apply the Skills
1. Students might describe the speaker's state of mind as horrified or despairing.
2. Sample response: The sounds of his daughter's typing, trying to set her imagination free, remind him of the starling trying to gain its freedom.
3. **Graphic Organizer**
Sample response:
The Raven
Characters: the speaker and the raven
Plot: The speaker misses his lost love, Lenore. He grows more and more upset by a visiting raven. He asks the raven questions. The raven always answers "Nevermore."
The Horses
Characters: people living in the world and horses
Plot: After a war nearly destroys the world, a community abandons its tractors. The people farm with oxen and plows. Then, one day a herd of horses appears and gives the people hope of a new world.

The Writer
Characters: a girl, her father, a bird
Plot: A speaker is listening to his daughter struggle to type a story. He is reminded of when a starling was trapped in her room, struggling to find freedom through an open window.
4. Sample response: One gloomy night, while I tiredly pored over some old books . . .

Reading Informational Materials: Web Sites

p. 244 Apply the Skills
Thinking About the Web Site
1. The link "Nature's Most Violent Storms" provides information about measures schools can take to ensure the safety of students and teachers. The "You are in school" link on the "Weather Safety for Kids" page may also provide safety measures for schools.
2. Category F5 tornadoes have wind speeds greater than 260 mph and cause tremendous damage, such as houses lifted from their foundation and objects as large as cars thrown over 100 meters.

Reading Skill
3. The link "Storm Reports" has information on current storms.
4. It is a government-sponsored weather Web site.

Poetry Collection 1

Poetry Collection 2

p. 246 Graphic Organizer
Sample response:
Poetry Collection 1
Original Lines: "Two roads diverged in a yellow wood, / And sorry I could not travel both / And be one traveler, long I stood / And looked down one as far as I could / To where it bent in the undergrowth;"
Lines in Smaller Sentences: Two roads diverged in a yellow wood. I was sorry that I could not travel both. I was one traveler. I stood a long time. I looked down one as far as I could. I looked to where it bent in the undergrowth.
Paraphrase: There were two roads in the woods. I could not go down both roads. I stood and looked down one of the roads. I looked to where it curved into the bushes.

Poetry Collection 2
Original Lines: "But if I had to perish twice, / I think I know enough of hate / To say that for destruction ice / Is also great / And would suffice."
Lines in Smaller Sentences: But if I had to perish twice, I think I know enough of hate. For destruction ice is also great. It would suffice.
Paraphrase: If I had to die again, I know that hatred can be just as destructive.

p. 247 Reading/Writing Connection
Sample response:
1. People who challenge themselves can achieve great things.
2. Some people refuse to conform because they want to be different.
3. People like to distinguish themselves from those around them.

p. 247 Note-taking Guide
Sample response:
We never know how high we are: rising above fears to achieve wonderful things
Macavity: The Mystery Cat: a cat named Macavity who lives a life of crime

p. 248 Activate Prior Knowledge
Students may say that they like images the most in their favorite poems because they like vivid description. Other students may say that they like poems about subjects they are interested in.

p. 248 Literary Analysis
Students may underline "rise" and "skies."

p. 248 Reading Check
Students should circle "For fear to be a King—."

p. 249 Reading Skill
Sample response: The speaker takes the other path because it is just as pleasant and a little less worn.

p. 249 Literary Analysis
The rhyme scheme is *abaab*.

p. 249 Read Fluently
Students may circle "sigh," "ages and ages," "less traveled by," and "difference." Sample response: These words are the most important because they show the speaker's main idea.

p. 250 Literary Analysis
Students should underline "Paw" and "Law" or "despair" and "there."

p. 250 Reading Skill
Sample response: You may seek him in the basement. You may look up in the air. But I tell you once and once again, Macavity's not there.

p. 250 Reading Check
Students should underline "He's broken every human law, he breaks the law of gravity / His powers of levitation would make a fakir stare."

p. 251 Reading Skill
Sample response: Macavity is unlike any other cat. He's a monster who happens to look like a cat. You might see him on the street. However, he is never at a crime scene.

p. 251 Literary Analysis
"Glass" and "past" are an example of both slant and internal rhyme. They both end with an "s" sound, and they are in the middle of the line instead of at the end of the line.

p. 251 Reading Check
Students should circle "ginger," "tall," "thin," "sunken," "lined," "domed," "dusty," and "uncombed."

p. 252 Reading Skill
Sample response: Breaking down long sentences makes the text easier to read and gives the reader a better understanding of the subject matter.

p. 252 Stop to Reflect
Some students may say that their favorite animal is a dog. They may imagine a dog getting into an adventure near a lake because many dogs like to swim.

p. 252 Reading Check
Students should underline "Napoleon of Crime."

p. 253 Apply the Skills
1. **Graphic Organizer**
Sample response:
What Does It Mean? This choice might represent a choice of colleges to attend or a career to follow.
2. Sample response: Cats are mischievous and curious. They get into things, and they can move silently and quickly disappear.

3. Sample response: "We never know how high we are" has a more regular meter. Every other line has the same meter.

4. Sample response: Two roads diverged in a yellow wood. I was sorry I could not travel both and be one traveler. Long I stood and looked down one as far as I could. I saw where it bent in the undergrowth.

p. 255 Reading/Writing Connection
Sample response:
1. Childhood experiences help an individual acquire qualities such as patience.
2. As children grow older, they may alter their views and opinions.
3. Young adulthood is a time when most people cease to depend upon their parents.

p. 255 Note-taking Guide
Sample response:
maggie and milly and molly and may: to describe the characters' self-discovery

The Seven Ages of Man: to describe a person's journey through life

p. 256 Apply the Skills
1. **Graphic Organizer**
Sample response:
What Does It Mean? Fire works as a metaphor for desire because desire "burns." Ice is fitting for hate because hate is a "cold" emotion.
2. Sample response: Each character is drawn to something that reflects her inner likes or fears.
3. Sample response: The words "severe" and "beard" show both slant rhyme and internal rhyme.
4. Sample response: Maggie found a shell that sang so sweetly she couldn't remember her troubles. Milly befriended a stranded star. Its rays were five languid fingers.

from The Shakespeare Stealer
Gary Blackwood

p. 260 Note-taking Guide
Sample response:
Box 1: Dr. Bright discovers that Widge was caught stealing a sermon.
Box 2: Falconer buys Widge from Dr. Bright and takes him to Bass's house.

p. 261 Activate Prior Knowledge
Some students may not think copying music is a crime because music is available on the radio. Other students may give examples of when stealing seems acceptable—such as when a father steals diapers for a baby or a mother steals food to feed her children. Other students may say that in the past, perhaps there were reasons to steal. However, today, there is no reason to steal.

p. 261 Drama
Students should circle "Among these are the apothecary, or drug store, in the first scene. It also will represent Widge's living space and Simon Bass's home."

p. 261 Read Fluently
Students should circle "a florid, overweight man in his forties or fifties." Sample response: The details are important because they describe Dr. Bright.

p. 262 Drama
Sample response: The stage directions help the actor playing Widge know what actions to take in reaction to Dr. Bright's angry comments. The stage directions help readers of the play imagine what is happening on stage.

p. 262 Read Fluently
Sample response: The dots suggest a pause in which an upset and frustrated Dr. Bright is trying to think of names to call Widge. The dashes suggest that Widge is stuttering because he is so upset.

p. 262 Drama
Sample response: The dialogue shows the conflict between the two characters and how the characters feel about each other. Students may underline "clod-pated drivel," "simpleton," and "Have you let a hint drop to anyone of what you were up to?"

p. 263 Drama
Sample response: Widge is an orphan. Dr. Bright took him in and educated him. Widge is unhappy working for Dr. Bright.

p. 263 Drama
Sample response: Widge makes these comments to the audience so that Dr. Bright does not hear. The comments are probably funny to the audience but they would make Dr. Bright angrier.

p. 263 Reading Check
Students should circle "It is a book on charactery, or swift writing."

p. 264 Stop to Reflect
Sample response: Falconer is interested in Widge's skills. He wants to use them for his own purposes.

p. 264 Drama
Students may suggest dimming the lights, raising and lowering the curtain, having some of the action go on in front of the lowered curtain, or using a revolving set.

p. 264 Drama
Sample response: It is possible that Falconer and Bass are the same person. Bass may pretend to be Falconer so that he can conduct business in secret.

p. 265 Drama
Sample response: Bass has an interest in theater and is not concerned about the possible issues involved with taking ideas from other people.

p. 265 Reading Check
Students should underline "Widge says he has only seen plays at church, and they were not worth 'stealing.'"

p. 265 Drama
Sample response: Bass tells Widge that it is business. They are borrowing the work completely to make sure that it is something that the original author can be proud of.

p. 266 Stop to Reflect
Sample response: Dr. Bright used the copied sermons because he was too lazy to write his own. Bass admits that his reason is to make money.

p. 266 Drama

Sample response: Widge will copy the play and run into difficulty. Perhaps Shakespeare will catch him. Falconer will be there to protect him. Widge may learn about the negative consequence of swift writing.

p. 267 Apply the Skills

1. Sample response: Widge has an excellent memory and excellent writing skills. He was able to recall the sermon. He was able to produce a version good enough that Dr. Bright did not know about the incident until he received a letter from the bishop.

2. Sample response: Falconer does not trust Dr. Bright. He wants to see for himself whether the system works and whether Widge can do the job.

3. Sample response: Dr. Bright uses words such as "clod-pated drivel," and "halfwitted hoddypeak."

4. Graphic Organizer

Sample response:

Prop: Dr. Bright uses a walking stick.

How It Is Used: He uses it to scare Widge.

What It Shows: Dr. Bright likes to control others, but he yells more often than he hits with his stick.

Prop: Widge uses a notebook and pencil.

How It Is Used: He uses these to carry out tasks assigned by Dr. Bright, Falconer, and Samuel Bass.

What It Shows: These props represent his skill and his confidence in himself.

The Tragedy of Romeo and Juliet, Act I
William Shakespeare

p. 269 Graphic Organizer

Sample response:

Scene: one

Summary of Action: A fight breaks out between servants and relatives of the two families. The prince breaks up the fight. Benvolio finds out that Romeo is sad about a lost love.

p. 270 Reading/Writing Connection

Sample response:

1. Sad events inspire artists to illustrate people's tragic flaws.

2. To contrast perfection and reality, writers give readers detailed descriptions.

3. Composers can emphasize the pain of lost love by making their music sound dreary.

p. 270 Note-taking Guide

Sample response:

Box 2: Romeo and Benvolio attend the Capulets' feast.

Box 3: Romeo and Juliet meet and fall in love.

Final Outcome: Romeo and Juliet discover that their families are enemies.

p. 271 Apply the Skills

1. Sample response: Romeo is moody and romantic. Juliet is an obedient girl. Before meeting Romeo, she has not given much thought to love. They both fall in love easily.

2. Some students may say that Romeo's passion for Rosaline shows the deep feelings teenagers can have. Other students may say the fact that he forgets about Rosaline after meeting Juliet shows that teens' feelings can change quickly. Other students may say that Romeo is too violent in his passions and does not accurately portray teenagers in love.

3. Graphic Organizer

Sample response:

Character: Juliet

Dialogue: lines 97–99

Reveals: Juliet is an obedient daughter.

Character: Lady Capulet

Dialogue: lines 69–74

Reveals: Lady Capulet believes Juliet is not too young to marry.

4. Sample response: "Leave him alone. Who's in charge here, me or you? If you don't leave him alone, my guests will riot. But you want to act macho. Someday that's going to hurt you. Now, settle down!"

The Tragedy of Romeo and Juliet, Act II, Scene ii
William Shakespeare

p. 273 Graphic Organizer

Sample response:

Character: Juliet

Character's Speech: Formal

Character's Actions: Juliet wants to protect Romeo from her family.

Character's Rank: Important; Aristocrat

p. 274 Note-taking Guide
Sample response:
Effect/Cause: Romeo promises to send word about his plans to marry Juliet.
Effect/Cause: Romeo goes to ask the Friar for help.

p. 275 Activate Prior Knowledge
Students may say that they know that Romeo and Juliet are young lovers. Some may know their tragic end.

p. 275 Literary Analysis
Students should circle "thou," "maid," "far," "fair," and "she."

p. 275 Reading Skill
Students should circle "Deny" and "Capulet."

p. 275 Reading Check
Students should underline "In Act II, Scene ii, Romeo stands in the orchard outside Juliet's home. She appears at her balcony window above him."

p. 276 Stop to Reflect
Sample response: They care for each other more than they care for their own families.

p. 276 Literary Analysis
Sample response: The stressed syllables draw attention to the words "I," "written," "I," "tear," and "word." These words strengthen Romeo's message that he hates his name.

p. 276 Reading Skill
Sample response: Romeo swears his love by the moon, but Juliet thinks that the changing moon is not a good choice. She suggests that he swear by his own self.

p. 276 Reading Check
Students should circle "My name, dear saint, is hateful to myself / Because it is an enemy to thee."

p. 277 Literary Analysis
Students should underline "words," "Rom-," "and" "night," "-deed," "that," "bent," "love," "hon-," "-able," "pur-," "marr-," "send," "word," "-mor-," "one," "I'll," "-cure," "come," "thee," "and," "time," "wilt," "-form," "rite," "all," "for-," "at," "foot," "lay," "fol-," "thee," "lord," "-out," and "world."

p. 277 Read Fluently
Students should circle "Where and what time thou wilt perform the rite."

p. 277 Reading Skill
Sample response: It is almost daytime. I want you to leave. But I do not want to let you go. I am like a child that has a string tied to a bird. I let you go a little and then pull you back.

p. 278 Literary Analysis
Sample response: The splitting of the syllables between two characters shows that they are connected. This suggests that Romeo and Juliet are in a close relationship.

p. 278 Reading Check
Students should circle "Then he leaves to tell his priest about Juliet. He plans to ask the priest for help."

p. 279 Apply the Skills
1. Sample response: The darkness hides Romeo from Juliet's relatives. It makes the lovers feel as if they are alone and can reveal their true feelings.
2. Students may say that the romantic words and images, the vivid descriptions, and the expressions of devotion make the audience share the characters' emotions.
3. **Graphic Organizer**
Sample response:
Blank Verse Pattern: Stressed syllables are "words," "Rom-," "and," "night," "-deed." Unstressed syllables are "Three," "dear," "-eo," "good," and "in-".
Key Words: words, Romeo, night
Why are the stressed words important ones? They emphasize Juliet's request.
4. Students should say that there are four sentences.

The Tragedy of Romeo and Juliet, Act III
William Shakespeare

p. 281 Graphic Organizer
Sample response:
Allusion: "Gallop apace, you fiery-footed steeds, / Towards Phoebus' lodging!"
Refers to: the horses that pulled the sun chariot of the god of the sun, Phoebus
Purpose: refers to the sun moving more quickly across the sky; time moving more quickly

p. 282 Note-taking Guide

Sample response:

Effect/Cause: Romeo kills Tybalt.

Effect: Romeo is not allowed to come back to Verona.

p. 283 Apply the Skills

1. Graphic Organizer

Sample response:

What Does It Mean? Mercutio means the statement as a curse. He blames both sides for the fight.

2. Sample response: Romeo means that he is a victim of fate.

3. Sample response: Juliet is impatient for the night to arrive so she can be with Romeo.

4. Sample response: Banishment is torture, not mercy. Heaven is where Juliet lives. While every little creature may look upon Juliet, I cannot. I must go. Even flies have it better than I. They can hear Juliet speak. But I cannot hear Juliet's voice because I am banished. You say that exile is not death, but it is. The damned howl the word *banished* in hell. How can you torture me with the word *banished*?

The Tragedy of Romeo and Juliet, Act IV
William Shakespeare

p. 285 Graphic Organizer

Sample response:

Line of Dialogue: "I met the youthful lord at Lawrence' cell / And gave him what becomèd love I might, / Not stepping o'er the bounds of modesty."

Lines in Smaller Sentences: "I met the youthful lord at Lawrence' cell. I gave him what becomèd love I might. I did not step o'er the bounds of modesty."

Summary of Line: Juliet is telling her father that she met Paris and showed him appropriate affection.

p. 286 Note-taking Guide

Sample response:

What character does: Juliet takes a potion to escape marriage to Paris.

What character thinks: Juliet is sad because of Romeo is gone and because she is being forced to marry Paris.

What others say about character: "A peevish self-willed harlotry it is." "How now, my headstrong?"

p. 287 Apply the Skills

1. Some students may find the advice risky and tricky and say that Romeo and Juliet should have admitted their marriage. Other students may say that, at the time, the plan seemed to be the only option.

2. Sample response: The soliloquy reveals that Juliet is fully aware of the great risks she is taking. However, she is still willing to take them.

3. Graphic Organizer

Sample response:

What Character Thinks: Capulet thinks Juliet is in her bed asleep.

What Audience Knows: The audience knows that Juliet is in a comatose state and cannot be awakened.

4. Sample response: Juliet tells Friar Lawrence that she will kill herself if he cannot help her. He must tell her something immediately or she will die.

The Tragedy of Romeo and Juliet, Act V
William Shakespeare

p. 289 Graphic Organizer

Sample response:

Cause: Friar John is unable to deliver the message to Romeo.

Effect/Cause: Romeo believes that Juliet is truly dead.

Effect: Romeo wants to kill himself.

p. 290 Note-taking Guide

Sample response:

Event 1: Romeo buys poison.

Event 2: Romeo goes to Juliet's grave in Verona.

Event 3: Romeo kills Paris.

Event 4: Romeo poisons himself.

Event 5: Juliet wakes to see Romeo.

Event 6: Juliet stabs herself.

Final Event: The Montagues and Capulets agree to stop fighting.

p. 291 Apply the Skills

1. Students may be surprised that Romeo kills Paris because it seems so sudden. Some students may be surprised that Lady Montague dies of grief because Romeo was not dead, he was only banished.

2. Some students will say it is not a fair exchange. The lovers might have stopped the

fighting through their marriage. Others may say that two lives may save many more in the future.

3. **Graphic Organizer**
Sample response:
Fate or Chance: the accidental meeting of the two lovers; Tybalt's misunderstanding of Romeo's presence at the Capulets; the Friar's plan goes wrong
Other Causes: the feud between the Montagues and the Capulets
4. Sample response: Romeo hurries to Juliet's tomb and meets and kills Paris. Romeo kills himself because he believes Juliet is dead. Juliet awakens to find Romeo dead. She stabs herself. Families, servants, lawmen, and the Prince gather at the tomb. The Friar explains everything. The Prince, Capulet, and Montague meet at the tomb and the two families end their feud.

Reading Informational Materials: Atlases

p. 296 Apply the Skills
Thinking about the Atlas
1. Sample response: Palermo is the largest city in Sicily. No other city in Sicily uses a symbol that shows greater population.
2. Sample response: Sixteen percent of Italy's exports travel by sea.
Reading Skill
1. Students may list Rome, Florence, Venice, or Padova.
2. Sample response: Illegal immigration became a major issue in the 1993 election.

The Inspector-General
Anton Chekhov
Adapted by Michael Frayn

p. 297 Graphic Organizer
Sample response:
Information Provided: Traveler wants to talk about himself.
Conclusion: He thinks he is an important man.

p. 298 Reading/Writing Connection
Sample response: It can be difficult to interpret what others say. The person cannot respond because the person's identity is secret. If he or she chooses to ignore the conversation, he or she might miss something.

p. 298 Note-taking Guide
Sample response:
What character says: "Wheezes? That's not wheezing! That's the way he talks!" "He's never touched a drop!"
What character does: tries to sneak up on the towns; drinks vodka; wheezes when he talks; orders the driver to turn around when he realizes the town knows he is coming
What others say about the character: "We know everything about all of them up there!" The driver calls the new inspector-general good compared to the last one. The driver says the new inspector-general creeps into town trying to be sneaky. "He drinks, mind!" "Oh, like a hole in the ground. Famous for it." The driver says the new inspector-general hides his drinking. The driver explains that the people are more afraid of the inspector-general's housekeeper than of the inspector-general.

p. 299 Activate Prior Knowledge
Students may suggest feelings of anger or resentment. If they are doing what they should be doing, they might resent someone's distrusting them.

p. 299 Literary Analysis
Sample response: The inspector-general tries to take a town by surprise by hiding his identity. This is humorous because the town already knows who he is.

p. 299 Reading Skill
Sample response: The inspector-general thinks he is clever. He thinks he will trick the townspeople by surprising them.

p. 300 Reading Skill
Students may underline "new inspector makes his visits very quietly" and "He travels in disguise." Sample response: The driver knows the traveler is the inspector-general.

p. 300 Literary Analysis
Sample response: The traveler is the inspector-general. This knowledge makes the scene humorous because the driver is insulting the inspector-general but the inspector-general cannot defend himself.

p. 300 Reading Check
Students should underline "The driver tells the traveler that the people tell many funny stories about the inspector-general."

p. 301 Reading Skill

Students should underline "The traveler discreetly pushes the traveling bag out of the driver's sight." Sample response: The traveler does not want the driver to see his traveling bag. It probably holds a bottle of vodka.

p. 301 Read Fluently

Students should underline "The driver says," "The driver says," and "the driver explains."

p. 301 Literary Analysis

Sample response: The traveler is trying to hide who he really is. The driver is pretending not to know that the traveler is the inspector-general.

p. 302 Reading Skill

Sample response: The inspector-general knows that his disguise has not fooled anyone.

p. 302 Literary Analysis

Students may underline "Don't want to go running into the Inspector-General, is that it?" Sample response: This sentence shows that the driver is still pretending not to know who the traveler really is. Students may underline: "Though if I know the old devil, he's like as not turned around and gone home again himself." Sample response: It is comic because the driver says he is describing a supposed situation. He is really saying exactly what is happening.

p. 303 Apply the Skills

1. Sample response: His identity is known and the people already know that he is coming. He is embarrassed to realize that he is not so clever after all.

2. **Graphic Organizer**
Sample response:
Questions: Who sent the anonymous letter?
Details: People in town seem to know that he is coming. Perhaps someone from the town sent the letter.
Understanding of the Play: Students' understanding may change because they understand why someone would want to contact the inspector-general.
Questions: Will the inspector-general ever visit the town again?
Details: The driver and everyone else in the town seem to know who he is and how he operates. The traveler turns around when he realizes that all the people know he is coming.

Understanding of the Play: Students' understanding may change because they understand why the driver might want to convince the inspector-general that he is expected.
Questions: Why does the driver not tell the traveler immediately that he knows who the traveler is?
Details: The traveler thinks he is being sneaky. The driver appears to enjoy the joke.
Understanding of the Play: Students' understanding may change because they realize that the driver could not have affected the traveler so strongly if the driver had been honest.

3. Sample response: The play ends happily because it's humorous that the only harm done is to the inspector-general's pride. The driver's dialogue is witty when he insults the inspector-general to his face and the inspector-general is forced to sit quietly because the inspector-general wants to protect his identity. The situation is comic because the inspector-general tries to sneak into the town but everyone knows who he is.

4. Sample response: The driver is clever and has a sense of humor. He outsmarts the traveler and he is happy without letting the traveler know that he has been discovered.

Reading Informational Materials: Book Review

p. 305 Graphic Organizer
Sample response:
Intent or reasons for writing: to discuss the new translation of Chekov's plays
Bias toward the subject: The writer likes the plays of Chekov. The writer also thinks that many of the translations are unreadable by Americans.
Thorough support for opinions: He uses excerpts from the other translations and the new translation to support his opinion that the new translation makes Chekov more accessible for American audiences.

p. 306 Reading Book Reviews
Sample response: He gives background and identifies a controversy.

p. 306 Read Fluently
Students should circle "Tolstoy voiced a common feeling. . . ."

p. 306 Reading Check
Students should circle "Uncle Vanya" and "Three Sisters."

p. 307 Reading Skill
Student may underline "But Chekhov's emphasis on tone and mood, and his faithful re-creation of ordinary conversation with all its hesitations, references, and silences. . . ."

p. 307 Stop to Reflect
Sample response: Including quotes is a good way to support his opinion that Schmidt's translation makes sense.

p. 307 Reading Book Reviews
Students may underline "The result is a sur-prisingly lively Chekov, colloquial and clear, which will come as a revelation to those who know the playwright through the widely read but rather stiff British translations of Constance Garnett and Elisaveta Fen." "The plays that emerge are funnier and more muscular than one might have expected."

p. 308 Stop to Reflect
Sample response: Yes, it is easier to under-stand. Americans would never say, "Who was it talking here just now?" But, Americans would say, "What's going on out there?"

p. 308 Reading Book Reviews
Sample response: Kirsch thinks it is a great translation. Americans should use this translation instead of older ones.

p. 308 Reading Informational Materials
Sample response: Chekhov's plays were first written in Russian. Chekhov's plays have been translated into British English.

p. 309 Apply the Skills
Thinking About the Book Review
1. Sample response: He thinks the starchy British English sounds awkward to Americans.
2. Sample response: The first translation does not sound like a typical American conversation. The second translation sounds more like an American conversation.

Reading Skill
3. Sample response: Kirsch's main purpose is to express an opinion about Schmidt's translation.

4. Some students may say that they believe Kirsch because he uses quotations from Schmidt, Tolstoy, and Chekov. Other students may that Kirsch's knowledge of Chekov and his works adds to his credibility.

**Play Hard; Play Together;
Play Smart**

from **the Carolina Way
Dean Smith with John Kilgo**

p. 312 Note-taking Guide
Sample response:
Attitude Toward Winning: making winning
the main goal of a sport is a poor way to
teach; many things happen that cannot be
controlled, such as injuries or bad calls
How They Measure Success: by the things
that players can control; whether players
had fun and worked together
Play Hard: playing with the greatest effort,
including practices
Play Together: game that counts on
togetherness, playing unselfishly and
sharing the ball
Play Smart: practicing the basics until they
become automatic

p. 313 Activate Prior Knowledge
Students may say that playing a sport taught
them that hard work and dedication could
help them accomplish their goals in life.

p. 313 Themes in Literature
Students may say that Coach Smith's philosophy did surprise them because they think
that winning would be the number one goal.
Students may say that his philosophy stress-
ing the strength of loyalty and the importance
of heroism. Each player must be dedicated to
the team by acting intelligently, unselfishly,
and with courage. Each player must also act
in the best interest of the team and show
effort on the court.

p. 313 Reading Check
Students should underline "Hard meant with
effort, determination, and courage."

p. 314 Read Fluently
Students should circle "that" and "was."
Sample response: That was out of his control
in the course of any given game.

p. 314 Themes in Literature
Some students may react by saying that every
player must do whatever it takes to help his
teammates succeed. Other students may not
like the idea of punishing the whole team

because one person does not do what he or
she is supposed to do.

p. 314 Stop to Reflect
Students may point out that all of his
principles could apply to most things in
life. Doing your best, working together, and
behaving as though every task were the
most important one would probably ensure
success at most tasks.

p. 315 Stop to Reflect
Students may suggest that developing good
work habits is important in school or at a job.

p. 315 Reading Check
Students should underline "Smith worked on
helping his players form good habits."

p. 316 Apply the Skills
1. Sample response: If each player plays
hard, plays smart, and plays together, they
as a team should be able to deal with the
unexpected. If they cannot deal with it
effectively, then at least they have given
it their best shot.
2. Sample response: Coach Smith probably
feels that his career was successful because
he was both a teacher and a coach. He
believes that the two should be one and the
same.
3. **Graphic Organizer**
Sample response:
Value: Play hard. Play together. Play smart.
Examples: Give your best effort, including
in practice. Admit to being tired, and take a
break. / Put the team before yourself, and
do everything possible not to let them down.
Do not be selfish. Trust your teammates. /
Learn the basics, and practice them until they
become automatic.
Application: Be the best you can be. Do not
be ashamed to ask for help if you need it. /
Workers in a company should put the company before themselves. With everyone
working toward the same goal, everyone will
benefit. / Treat each task you attempt as
important and essential. Use every resource
you have to accomplish your goals.
4. Students will probably agree that sports
are an important part of the cultural context
of the United States. They may explain that
team playing and working hard are a part of
the American work ethic.

from The Odyssey, Part 1,
The Cyclops
Homer

p. 318 Graphic Organizer
Sample response:
Historical/Cultural Detail: "We lit a fire, burnt an offering, / and took some cheese to eat . . ."
Background: Odysseus and his men offer a prayer of thanks to the gods and give a portion of their meal to the gods out of respect.
Analysis: Religion played an important role in ancient Greek culture. The gods appear in the *Odyssey*, often helping Odysseus or playing a part in his suffering. Ancient Greek beliefs and customs are reflected in Odysseus' offering.

p. 319 Reading/Writing Connection
Sample response: The journey involved an encounter with the local people. I had to interact with a new culture. The highlight of this experience was learning a new language.

p. 319 Note-taking Guide
Sample response:
Event 1: Odysseus and his men arrive at the land of the Cyclopes.
Event 2: Odysseus and his men are trapped in Polyphemus' cave.
Event 3: Odysseus finds an enormous club and turns it into a spike.
Event 4: Odysseus and his men blind Polyphemus with the spike.
Event 5: Odysseus hides his men under the Cyclops's sheep, and they escape.

p. 320 Activate Prior Knowledge
Students may say that an adventure story needs a hero whom readers can admire and villains against whom the hero must struggle.

p. 320 Reading Skill
Sample response: The Greeks valued a civilized society. They valued their laws and farming their land.

p. 320 Reading Check
Students should circle "the island of the Cyclopes."

p. 321 Stop to Reflect
Sample response: It was a bad decision for the men to stay in the cave. They were not invited, and they had no idea how the Cyclops would react to their presence.

p. 321 Literary Analysis
The Cyclops seals the opening of the cave with a huge rock. The men are now trapped and are at the mercy of the Cyclops.

p. 321 Literary Analysis
Sample response: If he kills the giant right away, they will all be trapped in the cave.

p. 321 Reading Check
Students should circle "beat their brains out."

p. 322 Read Fluently
Students should circle "Eyelid and lash were seared; the pierced ball / hissed broiling, and the roots popped." Both parts describe what happens to the eye.

p. 322 Reading Skill
Sample response: This passage shows that the Greeks believed that the gods did what they wanted to do. A god had to correct what another god had done.

p. 322 Reading Check
Students should underline "Odysseus heats up the pole in the fire. He and his men jam the sharp end into the Cyclops' eye."

p. 323 Literary Analysis
Sample response: Odysseus is proud of how clever he is. He does not always act wisely.

p. 323 Reading Check
Students should underline "He ties the Cyclops' sheep together in groups of three. Then he ties his men to the bellies of the sheep."

p. 323 Literary Analysis
In the bracketed passage, Odysseus is taunting the giant. Students may say that Odysseus is allowing his anger to get the best of him. He is also acting boastfully in victory.

p. 324 Reading Skill
The ancient Greeks believed that the gods could be called to act on events in the mortal world. They might act for or against the people that call on them.

p. 324 Literary Analysis
The flashback allows the reader a more complete picture of Odysseus because all of his life experiences influence the stories he recounts.

p. 324 Reading Check

Students should circle "I slew him / by the seaside and burnt his long thighbones / to Zeus."

p. 325 Apply the Skills

1. Some students will say that they would like to have Odysseus as a leader because he is brave, clever, and resourceful. Others will say that they would not like to have him as a leader because he is boastful and lets his anger get the best of him. His mistakes often put his men in danger.

2. Students may say that the story is popular because of its adventures and remarkable characters.

3. **Graphic Organizer**

Sample response:

Action: Odysseus tricks the Cyclops in order to escape his cave. Odysseus taunts the Cyclops and receives Poseidon's wrath.

Trait: cleverness; pride or boldness

4. Sample response: Students may say that Odysseus would have benefited from a navigation system and a communication system.

from The Odyssey, Part 2
Homer

p. 327 Graphic Organizer

Sample response:

Detail in Text: Odysseus kills the suitors.

Meaning for Characters: The suitors had intruded on Odysseus' home and family. Trespassers deserved to die.

Meaning in My Culture: Killing is against the law. These murders were not committed in self-defense.

p. 328 Note-taking Guide

Sample response:

Conflict: Odysseus' home has been overrun by men who want to kill his son and marry his wife.

Exposition: The Greek hero Odysseus has just come home to Ithaca after twenty years and finds himself and his home in danger.

Event 3: Odysseus kills Antinous.

Climax: Odysseus removes his disguise.

Event 4: Odysseus, Telemachus, Athena, and the herdsmen kill the suitors.

Event 5: Penelope tests Odysseus.

Resolution: Odysseus and Penelope embrace.

p. 329 Activate Prior Knowledge

Students may say that a hero should be courageous, smart, and willing to sacrifice for others.

p. 329 Literary Analysis

The beggar is comparing Penelope with a good king.

p. 329 Reading Skill

Sample response: Her culture probably prizes kindness toward strangers.

p. 329 Reading Check

Students should underline "He is sad. He does not want to cry in her home. She may think he has had too many cups of wine."

p. 330 Reading Skill

Sample response: Greeks considered it important to honor the dead. They wove shrouds for them. Today it is still important to honor the dead. People hold memorial services to honor the dead.

p. 330 Stop to Reflect

Sample response: Penelope's actions show that she is brave and clever. She also does not wish to marry.

p. 330 Reading Check

Students should underline "Her parents want her to marry. Her son does not want the suitors to use up all the property he should inherit."

p. 331 Literary Analysis

Sample response: This epic simile shows Odysseus' skill with the bow and his grace in using it.

p. 331 Stop to Reflect

Sample response: The success with the bow and arrow signals that the old beggar is really Odysseus. Penelope probably set this test for her suitors because her husband was the only man she thought could pass the test.

p. 331 Reading Check

Students should underline "He draws an arrow and aims it at Antinous."

p. 332 Reading Skill

Sample response: Odysseus' explanation shows that a man's respect for the gods and his reputation are very important. It reveals the importance of property and marriage and how one man should respect what belongs to another man.

p. 332 Stop to Reflect
Students may say that the offer of repayment seems fair. However, the suitors cannot be trusted, and they will try to kill Odysseus their at first chance. Students may suggest that they would place the suitors in prison.

p. 332 Reading Check
Students should circle "He explains that Antinous led the suitors."

p. 333 Reading Skill
Sample response: Telemachus' joining the fight shows the importance of loyalty to the family. It also shows that a son should obey and support his father.

p. 333 Literary Analysis
The simile emphasizes the cold, twitching appearance of the dead men. They look like dead fish.

p. 333 Reading Check
Students should underline "Aided by Athena, Odysseus, Telemachus, Eumaeus, and other faithful herdsmen kill all of the suitors."

p. 334 Literary Analysis
Students may include details such as "gold infused / on silver by a craftsman, whose fine art / Hephaestus taught him, or Athena: one / whose work moves to delight."

p. 334 Stop to Reflect
Some students may point out that Odysseus has been gone for a long time and someone with great skill may be pretending to be him. They would also test him. Other students may say that they would have been satisfied with the arrow test and his actions in the house. They would not feel the need to test him further.

p. 334 Reading Check
Students should underline "He describes the way he had built the bed."

p. 335 Read Fluently
Students should circle "in joy, in joy." Sample response: The repeated phrase lets the reader know that the feeling is deep and powerful.

p. 355 Reading Skill
Students may say that the epic ends the way that they expected. They may expect happy endings in stories. Others may not expect the ending. They may have expected Odysseus to

experience punishment for the deaths of the suitors.

p. 336 Apply the Skills
1. Sample response: Odysseus faced many dangers, but Penelope suffered years of waiting, never knowing what had happened to Odysseus.
2. Her experience with the suitors has made Penelope act cautiously. She believes that she must be sure of his identity.
3. **Graphic Organizer**
Sample response:
Items Being Compared: Odysseus' longing for his wife is compared with a swimmer's longing for the shore.
Details of Epic Simile: "big surf," "clotted with brine," "kindly beaches," "knowing the abyss behind"
Purpose: to show the intensity of Odysseus' feelings as he returns to Penelope
4. Sample response: Many of Odysseus' values are universal. For instance, we still value hospitality and we can understand and sympathize with his longing for home. Many people may not share his belief that the gods participate and interfere in human affairs.

Reading Informational Materials: Applications

p. 341 Apply the Skills
Thinking About the Application
1. Sample response: The application asks for a personal essay so that the applicant can give more information about his or her reasons for applying. The applicant can also explain more about career plans and why he or she would be a good volunteer for this project.
2. Sample response: References can be more objective. References can also describe how well the applicant works with other people.

Reading Skill
3. Each volunteer is expected to take part in all excavation duties.
4. Applicants must list any archaeology and classics classes they have taken.

"Three Skeleton Key"
George G. Toudouze

"The Red-headed League"
Sir Arthur Conan Doyle

p. 342 Graphic Organizer
Sample response:
"Three Skeleton Key"
Protagonist: the narrator
Goals and Actions: He wants to get rid of the rats. He, Le Gleo, and Itchoua close all entrances to the lighthouse. They leave the lighthouse lantern unlit so that the outside world can see that they are in trouble.
Antagonist: the rats
Goals and Actions: The rats want to survive. They search for food. They take over a Dutch ship and eat the crew. Then, they overtake Three Skeleton Key and the lighthouse.
Conflict: The rats want to kill the men, and the men want to kill the rats.
Universal Motives or Struggles: the fight for survival

"The Red-headed League"
Protagonist: Sherlock Holmes
Goals and Actions: He wants to solve the mystery of the Red-headed League. He investigates the mystery.
Antagonist: John Clay
Goals and Actions: He plans to rob the bank. He digs a tunnel.
Conflict: Clay wants to rob the bank. Holmes wants to catch him.
Universal Motives or Struggles: the struggle of good against evil

p. 343 Reading/Writing Connection
Sample response: Lighthouse keepers often had more access to quiet simplicity. However, their duties often forced them to forgo social activities. Such isolation could induce loneliness.

p. 343 Note-taking Guide
Sample response:
Dangers at the Lighthouse: the sharks
Supporting Details: "the sea, which is patrolled by sharks"
Dangers at the Lighthouse: the rats
Supporting Details: "large, ferocious, and smart," "They also stick together," "If one is attacked, the others rush to defend it."

p. 344 Activate Prior Knowledge
Students may say that they are most frightened of snakes. If trapped and surrounded by snakes, they would probably panic and feel as though there were no escape.

p. 344 Literary Analysis
Students may underline "My most terrifying experience," "When I was a young man," and "I volunteered."

p. 344 Reading Check
Students should circle "The rocks are very slippery, so it is easy to slip and fall into the sea, which is patrolled by sharks."

p. 345 Stop to Reflect
Sample response: The ship is probably in trouble. The crew may be sick or dead. The boat might be abandoned.

p. 345 Reading Skill
Le Gleo seems most frightened. He is afraid that the ship is a ghost ship.

p. 345 Reading Check
Students should underline "Are you saying that she's the Flying Dutchman?"

p. 346 Read Fluently
Students may describe the vision of a ship in the distance. In their vision, they see the ship crossing back and forth across the water, the wind filling the sails and then the sails dropping each time the wind dies. Each time the ship changes direction, it comes closer to the lighthouse.

p. 346 Literary Analysis
Sample response: The details about the arrival of the abandoned ship, which looks as though it may crash into the lighthouse and bring some harm to the protagonist, may interest students in what will happen to the protagonist. The students may also be interested in the rats and how they drove out the crew of the ship. Students may want to know how the rats drove out the crew.

p. 346 Reading Check
Students should underline "They had been driven out by the rats."

p. 347 Stop to Reflect
Students may say that they would feel frightened or amazed. They may think that the sight of so many large, hungry rats would be intimidating.

p. 347 Literary Analysis

The protagonist and two other men are now in conflict with the rats. The rats want to eat them, and the men do not want to be eaten.

p. 347 Reading Check

Students should underline "The rats leap into the sea and swim strongly to the island."

p. 348 Literary Analysis

The rats are struggling to survive by trying to kill the men for food. The men struggle to stay alive by protecting themselves from the rats.

p. 348 Literary Analysis

Students should underline "without food or drink." The new antagonist is starvation or dehydration.

p. 348 Reading Check

Students should underline "They decide to signal for help by not lighting the lantern."

p. 349 Reading Skill

Le Gleo is more easily frightened. He begins to go crazy. The other two men stay mostly in control of themselves.

p. 349 Stop to Reflect

Students may say that they would bait the rats to another area with food and then set the rats on fire. This strategy would enable them to rescue the men.

p. 349 Reading Check

Students should underline "Using the dots and dashes . . ."

p. 350 Literary Analysis

Sample response: Readers are interested in what happens to the protagonist because they feel sympathy for the protagonist. They would not want to be attacked by rats. They can understand his need to fight for survival.

p. 350 Stop to Reflect

Some students may say that human intelligence won out because the rats were destroyed and the men escaped the island. Others may think that the humans did not win completely because one man dies and another loses his mind.

p. 350 Reading Check

Students should underline "the barge was filled with meat" or "the barge reeking with the scent of freshly cut meat."

p. 351 Apply the Skills

1. Sample response: The rats are dangerous and desperate. They did not give up and drown in the sea. They will probably not give up if they attack the men.
2. Sample response: Itchoua means that if the rats get into the lighthouse, the men will die. Then, three more skeletons could be added to the name of the island.
3. The conflict between the narrator and the rats represents the universal struggle for survival.
4. **Graphic Organizer**
Sample response:
End Only: The narrator has nearly died from the rat attack, and he has lost two friends. He is wiser now.
Beginning and End: He still enjoys the island and working in the lighthouse. He still does not believe the superstitions.

p. 353 Reading/Writing Connection

Sample response: You might perceive that a pencil is round, but most pencils have six sides. If you observe pencil lead closely, you can see that it has a rough surface. One way to differentiate between a pen and a pencil is to note that pencils often weigh less than pens.

p. 354 Note-taking Guide

Sample response:
Box 2: Wilson loses his job.
Box 3: Wilson asks Sherlock Holmes for help.
Box 4: Holmes uncovers the crime.

p. 354 Apply the Skills

1. Holmes finds Wilson's story interesting because it is different from any Holmes has heard before.
2. Spaulding's trousers showed that he had been digging in the cellar. The bank's property bordered Wilson's shop.
3. The protagonist is Sherlock Holmes. His goal is to solve the mystery and catch the criminal behind it.
4. **Graphic Organizer**
Sample response:
End Only: Holmes can take pride in capturing a known criminal.
Beginning and End: Holmes uses reasoning to solve crimes. He solves crimes to escape boredom. He waits for the next new crime.

Reading Informational Materials: Encyclopedia Entries

p. 359 Apply the Skills
Thinking About Encyclopedia Entry
1. Sample response: To "play fair" means that the author gives the reader the same information found by the detective. This information gives readers a fair chance to solve the mystery as they read.
2. The American style of mystery introduced in the 1920s focused on a tough detective as its hero. The mystery featured action and violence. It had a colorful narrative style.

Reading Skill
3. Sample response: to learn which writers are famous for writing detective stories
4. You would find this information in the section with the subhead "History."

"There Is a Longing"
Chief Dan George

"Glory and Hope"
Nelson Mandela

p. 360 Graphic Organizer
Sample response:
"There Is a Longing"
Philosophical Assumptions: The greatness of the Native American people is in the future as well as in the past. The road to greatness will be difficult but will be worth it.
Evaluation: His beliefs support his purpose because they give Native Americans the power to improve their lives.
"Glory and Hope"
Philosophical Assumption: Democracy is a form of government that is better than apartheid.
Evaluation: This belief supports Mandela's purpose of bringing a message of hope and inspiration to the people of South Africa.

p. 361 Reading/Writing Connection
Sample response: Connecting with one's own heritage can reinforce a tolerance for other cultures. Contemporary culture does encourage the acceptance of other cultures. A blending of other cultures can produce a wide spectrum of beliefs and traditions.

p. 361 Note-taking Guide
Sample response:
The Speaker's Longings: for the young to become warriors in today's society; for his people to live without welfare and take their place in a society that is "rightly" theirs; for courage; for the ability to accept the "white man's" culture; to live in harmony with the new society, succeed in it, and move forward; to learn the skills of the white man so that he and his people can succeed in the white man's world; to see his people fill government positions so that they can rule themselves and change society

p. 362 Activate Prior Knowledge
Students may say that people need qualities such as determination, flexibility, and compassion in order to succeed in today's society.

p. 362 Reading Skill
Sample response: New warriors must learn different skills. They must go to school to learn these skills. The training will be more difficult than in the past.

p. 362 Reading Check
Students should circle "His words are his only weapons now."

p. 363 Read Fluently
Sample response: When young warriors and leaders have better education and new skills, they will be in a position to make changes. Students should indicate pauses where commas are used.

p. 363 Literary Analysis
Sample response: He wants to guide other Native Americans. He wants to give them the power to become a great and proud people once again.

p. 364 Apply the Skills
1. Sample response: He thinks this training is necessary for his people to be able to work in law and in government. With this training, his people will be able to rule themselves and change society.
2. Sample response: He means that he must fight for the future of his people by speaking out for them. He will use reason and logic as his weapons to fight for their rights.
3. Students may say that his audience shared his faith and his belief in the potential of Native Americans. Students may support

their answer with the following: "The young want to have a purpose in life. They want to be valuable to society."

4. **Graphic Organizer**

Sample response:

Past: Training to be great warriors was easier in the past. The olden Chiefs had power to make war.

Present: The people are filled with longing. They are faced with hard work and studying. The Chief has only the power to make speeches.

Future: His people can be great again. They can be leaders. They can be educated. They can rule themselves and be free. They can change society.

p. 366 Reading/Writing Connection

Sample response: A good speech from a leader can evoke emotions such as hope. People stand for the national anthem to signify their pride. The time people devote to learning about voting issues shows that they care.

p. 366 Note-taking Guide

Sample response:

Old South Africa: White people ran the government. Black people faced discrimination. The rest of the world looked down on South Africa. South Africa was a shameful country.

New South Africa: The government is a democracy. All citizens are equal and free. The world has a high opinion of South Africa. South Africa is a proud country.

p. 367 Apply the Skills

1. Students may point out such ideas as equality, dignity, and peace.

2. Sample response: Mandela believes that the present moment is glorious and that the future is hopeful.

3. Sample response: Mandela assumes that apartheid was wrong and that democracy is a good form of government. Also, Mandela believes that South Africa is a beautiful land with people who deserve freedom.

4. **Graphic Organizer**

Sample response:

Present: South Africa is experiencing "new-born liberty."

Future: South Africa faces many challenges on its way to becoming a democracy.

ANSWERS TO UNIT 1

from The Giant's House
Elizabeth McCracken

"Desiderata"
Elizabeth McCracken

p. 4 Note-taking Guide
Sample response:
What Character Thinks: He wants to find a cure for his condition. He is impatient with Peggy for playing dumb.
What Others Say about Character: Giant describes him.

p. 5 Activate Prior Knowledge
Students may say that the words *gigantic, enormous, myth and folklore, Cyclops, Goliath, Hercules, Titan, Jack and the Beanstalk*, and *monstrous in strength and anger* come to mind.

p. 5 Read Fluently
Students should underline "Look in the big books on the table—see those books?"

p. 5 Fiction
Sample response: James has a problem with his height. He wants to find out more about people like him and what they do. Peggy has a problem figuring out what James really wants to know, not just what he says he wants to know.

p. 6 Fiction
Sample response: Peggy pays attention to the kinds of books library patrons check out; she wants people to learn to do their own research. Students should underline "After closing that evening, Peggy begins the search herself;" "As a librarian she feels the familiar urge to find information."

p. 6 Fiction
Students should circle "Giant described him."

p. 6 Build English Skills
Sample response: *-s:* encyclopedias, catalogs; *-es:* indexes, circuses.

p. 7 Fiction
Sample response: The narrator is not part of the other giants' lives. She only reads about them in her research.

p. 7 Reading Check
Students should underline "Abnormalities, human."

p. 8 Fiction
Sample response: James wants to stop growing. He is looking for a medical solution to his problem.

p. 8 Fiction
Students should circle "Medicine, or operations, or something;" "That was a lie, I knew we didn't;" "Really, you should ask your doctor;" "I've asked a lot of doctors." Sample response: It is important to teenagers to be ordinary. No matter how adults try to protect them, young people have to learn to face reality.

p. 8 Vocabulary and Pronunciation
Students should circle "I could not lie to her."

p. 9 Note-taking Guide
Sample response:
To Entertain: Martha's letters about serving The Dollies chicken are entertaining.
To Persuade: Family papers are a useful part of a family's genealogy.
To Reflect: Paper collections force a person to draw conclusions based on incomplete information.

p. 10 Activate Prior Knowledge
Students may say that a shopping list would tell them what people were eating or how much money they had. They might say that an old family letter would reveal information about a parent when he or she was younger.

p. 10 Read Fluently
Sample response: McCracken collects family letters, notes, and papers. She values these and keeps them to learn more about her family.

p. 10 Nonfiction

Students should underline "a family history," "stories," "poems," "letters," "diaries," and "laundry lists."

p. 11 Nonfiction

Students should underline "You might find out about family problems you would rather not know. You might learn that relatives could be mean-spirited. You might learn painful things as well."

p. 11 Build English Skills

Students should circle "mean-spirited," "grandmother," and "great-aunts."

p. 11 Nonfiction

Students should circle "attorney," "small business person," and "died at age 90 at home." Students should double underline "complex woman" and "worried and doubtful person."

p. 11 Reading Check

Students should underline "What is most frustrating, however, is how little you can learn about people through letters."

p. 12 Stop to Reflect

Sample response: The grocery list shows rather than tells the kinds of pieces the author has collected.

p. 12 Nonfiction

Students should underline "seeing good or bad luck in everything," "believed in fortune cookies," and "bought lottery tickets."

p. 12 Nonfiction

Sample response: She adds humor with this example, showing the competition between herself and her brother. This example is meant to entertain her readers. This example also shows the variety of the papers she collects.

p. 12 Culture Note

A student from Greece may mention the "Evil Eye," a blue glass bead resembling an eyeball that is worn to ward off jealousy.

p. 13 Nonfiction

Students should underline "I never imagined my grandfather, my quiet careful grandfather, was the sort of man who'd write any kind of love letter, never mind this kind" and "And my grandmother had saved it for over fifty years."

p. 13 Read Fluently

Sample response: The colon sets up the question that Elizabeth McCracken asks about who found the letter more important. If she dropped the colon, the sentence would be hard to understand because there are two verbs in a row (is was).

p. 13 Vocabulary and Pronunciation

"Regret" is used as a verb in the underlined sentence.

p. 13 Reading Check

Student should circle "I've forgotten the exact words my grandfather used."

p. 14 Apply the Skills

1. Students may say that Peggy did help James because she got him as much information as she could. Other students may say that Peggy did not help him because she couldn't find the information he was looking for.

2. **Graphic Organizer**
Sample response:
Research Questions: What is giantism? What role do genes play in the disease? What are the characteristics of the disease? What are the symptoms? How is it diagnosed? What is the most successful treatment?
Possible Source: dictionary and encyclopedia; science and medical books; Internet sites; expert interviews.

3. Sample response: James's problem is affected by the setting of the story because physical differences were not as accepted in 1955 as they are today. There were fewer medical treatment options. Little information was available in the small-town library.

4. Sample response: Some Students may say that McCracken uses a combination of two purposes. In the process of reflecting on her relatives' interest in collecting family history, she informs her readers of the process and why it led her to write fiction. Others may say that they agree that her main purpose is to reflect and the other purposes are less important.

"The Washwoman"
Isaac Bashevis Singer

"New Directions"
Maya Angelou

p. 16 Graphic Organizer
Sample response:
"The Washwoman"
Detail: "That winter was a harsh one."

Question: Why does the author mention this detail?

Prediction: The bad weather will make it hard for the washwoman to do her job.

Verification: The prediction was accurate.

"New Directions"

Detail: "She placed stones in two large pails and walked three miles . . ."

Question: Why does the author mention this detail?

Prediction: She will carry food to the factories so that she can sell it.

Verification: The prediction was accurate.

p. 17 Reading/Writing Connection

Sample response: When people <u>accomplish</u> a difficult task, they may feel more confident. They want to <u>demonstrate</u> that they can finish the task. When people <u>confront</u> their problems, they will become stronger.

p. 17 Note-taking Guide

Sample response:

Circle 1: cares for son

Circle 3: is not bitter about her life

Circle 4: is hardworking and dedicated to her job

p. 18 Apply the Skills

1. Sample response: She is dedicated to her work. It is important for her to finish what she starts.

2. Sample response: The author says nothing about her family history or what she does besides laundry.

3. **Graphic Organizer**

Sample response:

The Washwoman: She is small, old, and wrinkled; she does her work well and gives people a good price; she is not angry with her son.

The Washwoman's Son: He is rich; his mother embarrasses him; he does not invite her to his wedding.

4. Sample response: Prediction: The washwoman will not survive her walk home in the cold weather. Details: The washwoman is in bad health. The weather is rough, and it will be hard for her to make it home.

p. 20 Reading/Writing Connection

Sample response: When people <u>initiate</u> a change, they must prepare for the unexpected. To <u>transform</u> their lives, they must be willing to take risks. Later, they can <u>analyze</u>

the result in order to know how successful they were.

p. 20 Note-taking Guide

Sample response:

Circle 1: resourceful

Circle 3: determined

Circle 4: reliable

p. 21 Activate Prior Knowledge

Students may say that they worked through a problem by keeping a positive attitude and thinking of the future.

p. 21 Literary Analysis

Students should underline "Annie was left with two small sons, very little money, and little education." Sample response: Annie's need to support herself and her children, and the fact that she has very little opportunities and many obstacles, sets the story in motion.

p. 21 Reading Skill

Students may predict that Annie is preparing to carry heavy loads of her cooking and that she will have to work hard to make her plans happen. Students should underline "First, she placed stones in two large pails and walked three miles to the first factory," "she took some stones out of the pails, and then she walked another five miles," "There, she dumped out the stones and walked home," and "Then she knew she could carry heavy loads a long distance."

p. 22 Vocabulary and Pronunciation

Sample response: The word "determined" is used as an adjective in the underlined sentence.

p. 22 Build English Skills

Students should circle "brought," "became," and "built."

p. 22 Read Fluently

Students may say that "found a new path for herself" means she discovered a way to move forward and to become successful.

p. 22 Reading Check

Students should underline "In years that stall became a store where customers could buy cheese, meal, syrup, cookies, candy, writing tablets, pickles, canned goods, fresh fruit, soft drinks, coal, oil, and leather soles for worn-out shoes."

p. 23 Apply the Skills

1. Sample response: Annie is a smart businessperson. She knows how to plan ahead and how to attract customers.
2. Some students may say taking a new direction often can lead to a better life, so it is worth the risk of failure. Others may say that some new directions are too scary and not worth the risk.
3. **Graphic Organizer**
Sample response:
Annie Johnson: She is a good cook. She makes careful plans for her business.
Annie Johnson's Husband: He moves to Oklahoma. He takes the family's money when he leaves.
4. Sample response: Annie will make food and sell it to the factory workers. She will build a successful business.

Reading Informational Materials: Recipe

p. 26 Reading Instructions: Recipes
Sample response: People need the ingredients ready before they can begin the steps in the recipe.

p. 26 Read Fluently
Students should circle "FILLING" and "PASTRY DOUGH." Sample response: The first column's ingredients are for the filling. The second column's ingredients are for the pastry dough.

p. 26 Reading Skill
Students should circle "chopped," "minced," "thawed," and "cooked." Sample response: These signal words tell readers what to do with the ingredients before combining them.

p. 27 Culture Note
A student from Bosnia may say that lokum makes them think of home. Lokum, also known as Turkish Delight, is a type of candy made from sugar and starch.

p. 27 Reading Check
Students should underline "In a separate saucepan, melt the butter or margarine over medium heat."

p. 27 Reading Skill
Sample response: There are four steps.

p. 27 Reading Informational Materials
Sample response: Photographs and drawings of the steps would make it easier to follow.

Numbering the steps would also make it easier to follow.

p. 28 Apply the Skills
Thinking About the Instruction: Recipe
1. The finished turnovers are a half-moon shape.
2. Dipping the fork in flour when crimping the edges will help keep the fork from sticking to the dough.

Reading Skill
3. You need three tablespoons of celery.
4. You should whisk the sauce continually.
5. The last thing you are supposed to do before baking the pies is cut a slit in the top of each turnover.

"Sonata for Harp and Bicycle" Joan Aiken

"The Cask of Amontillado" Edgar Allan Poe

p. 29 Graphic Organizer
Sample response:
"Sonata for Harp and Bicycle"
Prediction: Jason will sneak into the building after quitting time.
Outcome: He climbs the fire escape and gets in.
Analysis of Prediction: The prediction was accurate.

"The Cask of Amontillado"
Prediction: Fortunato's love of wine will lead him into danger.
Outcome: A cask of amontillado brings Fortunato to his destruction.
Analysis of Prediction: The prediction was accurate.

p. 30 Reading/Writing Connection
Sample response: A good detective must anticipate what a criminal will do. Detectives can expose criminals by setting traps. A detective will not eliminate anything that seems suspicious while searching for clues.

p. 30 Note-taking Guide
Sample response:
Circle 1: a fire escape
Circle 2: a bicycle bell
Circle 3: the echoing sound of music
Circle 5: two eyes carved out of air
Circle 6: Ashgrove's new hair color

p. 31 Activate Prior Knowledge
Students may suggest the adventures of Sherlock Holmes. The main character is a smart, daring person who solves the mystery. The main character often has a sidekick.

p. 31 Literary Analysis
Sample response: The first paragraph creates suspense by making readers wonder why no one is allowed in the building after 5 o'clock. The building clears out at exactly the same time every day and that makes readers wonder why the workers would do that.

p. 31 Reading Skill
Students may predict that the new assistant will enter the building after 5 o'clock to try to find out what goes on during the night. Students may underline "But why is it?" and "But I want to know now."

p. 32 Reading Skill
Students may predict that there will be a romance between Jason and Miss Golden. Students might circle "what she chiefly wanted was Mr. Jason Ashgrove, but he had not realized this yet."

p. 32 Stop to Reflect
Sample response: Jason is curious and wants to know more about the mystery. Miss Golden is frightened.

p. 32 Reading Check
Students should underline "He does, however, hear her say something about a bicycle and a harp."

p. 33 Literary Analysis
Sample response: Jason's actions add suspense to the story by making the reader wonder what will happen to him while he is in the Grimes Buildings.

p. 33 Reading Skill
Students may predict that Jason will encounter ghosts in the Grimes Buildings. Students might circle "everything is silent and empty," "quickly," "senses that it is dangerous," "small place to hide," and "heart tried to shake itself loose in his chest."

p. 33 Literary Analysis
Sample response: The passage is part of the rising action because it introduces the ghost, which is a part of the central conflict.

p. 34 Reading Skill
Students may say that their predictions were correct. Reading on provided them with more information to verify their predictions.

p. 34 Build English Skills
Students should circle the quotation marks before "How," "How," and "You."

p. 34 Reading Check
Students should underline "His dark hair has turned white."

p. 35 Reading Skill
Students may suggest that the added information changed some of their predictions concerning the ghosts.

p. 35 Vocabulary and Pronunciation
Sample response: The word "knight" is a homonym of "night." It means a "military servant of a king or queen."

p. 35 Literary Analysis
Sample response: The new information sets up another conflict. Jason could be in danger. He is faced with the information that others who have met Heron's ghost have jumped off the fire escape.

p. 35 Reading Check
Students should underline "awakened by a device on her phone."

p. 36 Reading Check
Students may circle "harp music swelling out, sweet and triumphant," " 'The room was too full of music,' " and "She saw that his eyes were shining."

p. 36 Read Fluently
Sample response: Jason and Berenice held hands outside of the door. They never spoke about what they saw. They were left with an image as clear as a painting of a harp, a bouquet, and a bottle of wine riding on a bicycle.

p. 36 Reading Skill
Students may say that their prediction that Jason and Berenice would start a relationship was proven correct. They might point to the fact that Jason and Berenice kiss and jump off the fire escape together as events that verify their predictions.

p. 37 Apply the Skills

1. Sample response: Miss Golden is more concerned. She believes that there is a curse that cannot be escaped. She is not aware of Jason's plan to try to break it.

2. Sample response: If Heron had not killed himself, he would have seen Miss Bell the next day. She would have explained about the alarm. Making quick decisions sometimes means you do not get the whole story.

3. **Graphic Organizer**
Sample response:
Rising Action: Jason asks questions about the strange behavior of the people in the office.
Climax: Jason puts the wine and the roses outside the door of room 492.

4. Students may have predicted that Jason would meet a ghost inside the building.

p. 39 Reading/Writing Connection

Sample response:
1. Reading a scary story lets people safely participate in scary or dangerous situations.
2. A scary setting helps contribute to the overall mood of a story.
3. A reader can interpret a scary story by analyzing the author's purpose.

p. 39 Note-taking Guide

Sample response:
Event 2: Fortunato goes with Montresor to his palace. They wander through caves filled with wine bottles and bones.
Event 3: Montresor gets Fortunato drunk as they walk deeper into the caves.
Event 4: Montresor chains Fortunato to the wall of a small room. He walls up the room and leaves him to die.

p. 40 Apply the Skills

1. Sample response: Fortunato is proud that he knows so much about wine. Because of this, he is very anxious to judge the wine. Montresor takes advantage of the fact that Fortunado is so vain.

2. Sample response: Montresor feels that Fortunato has insulted and injured him.

3. **Graphic Organizer**
Sample response:
Rising Action: Montresor invites Fortunato to the vaults to try his wine.

Climax: Montresor thrusts his torch into the crypt and hears only the jingling of the bells on Fortunato's costume.
Falling Action: Montresor replaces the bones to cover the crypt's entrance.

4. Reading Skill: Students may have predicted that Montresor would use Fortunato's interest in wine to get his revenge.

from A White House Diary
Lady Bird Johnson

"My English"
Julia Alvarez

p. 42 Graphic Organizer

Sample response:
from A White House Diary
Text feature: title
Insight into Purpose: The title suggests a day-by-day or hour-by-hour account of personal experience.

"My English"
Text Feature: title
Insight About Purpose: The title suggests a personal relationship with the language.

p. 43 Reading/Writing Connection

Sample response: The words of Martin Luther King Jr. motivate me to seek justice in the world. The actions of Dr. King illustrate his philosophy of nonviolence. For me, these actions evoke feelings of courage and resolve.

p. 43 Note-taking Guide

Sample response:
Circle 2: fear
Circle 3: sympathy
Circle 4: sorrow
Circle 5: stress
Circle 6: anguish

p. 44 Activate Prior Knowledge

Students may say that many people keep diaries to record thoughts and feelings and reflect on the significance of events. A diary entry is a private place to express powerful emotions and personal thoughts.

p. 44 Vocabulary and Pronunciation

Sample response: The word *shot* is used as a verb meaning "firing of a gun."

p. 44 Literary Analysis

Sample response: At the time of the assassination, the author could not consider that something so horrible could happen to the President. The events were happy and festive.

p. 45 Read Fluently

Sample response: These dashes set off extra information in the sentence. In the bracketed passage, it seems that Mrs. Johnson forgot to include this information earlier.

p. 45 Reading Skill

Sample response: The author included these names to suggest the closeness of those in the President's inner circle. It showed how the President's assassination affected those people.

p. 45 Reading Check

Students should circle "I think it was from Kenny's face that I first knew the truth and from Kenny's voice that I first heard the words 'The President is dead.'"

p. 46 Literary Analysis

Sample response: The repetition of "caked" and "blood" makes her sound disbelieving and horrified. Her use of the dash stresses the description of Mrs. Kennedy, a blending of beautiful and gruesome images.

p. 46 Reading Skill

Students should underline "Mrs. Kennedy's dress was stained with blood. One leg was almost entirely covered with it and her right glove was caked, it was caked with blood— her husband's blood" and "that immaculate woman exquisitely dressed, and caked in blood." Sample response: The details help to show Mrs. Kennedy's shock and grief. It also emphasizes the horror of what has happened.

p. 46 Build English Skills

Sample response: The word *change* is used as a verb meaning, "make different." The context clues show that Mrs. Johnson is talking about making Mrs. Kennedy's clothing different.

p. 47 Stop to Reflect

Sample response: Mrs. Johnson may have felt tired, sad, and deeply shaken. She had just witnessed the assassination and death of the President. Her husband has also become President in an unexpected way.

p. Reading Check

Students should underline "his first concerns back at the hospital was for his children."

p. 48 Apply the Skills

1. Sample response: Mrs. Kennedy wants the nation to see evidence of the brutality of the assassination.
2. Sample response: It is a powerful comment. It makes Mrs. Kennedy's feelings clear.
3. **Graphic Organizer**
Sample response:
Attitude: "There had been such a gala air about the day that I thought the noise must come from firecrackers. . ."
Sentence Structure: "And then with almost an element of fierceness–if a person that gentle, that dignified, can be said to have such a quality–she said. . ."
4. Sample response: The general purpose is to inform readers about the assassination. She gives details about events, the setting, and people's feelings.

p. 50 Reading/Writing Connection

Sample response:
1. In a democracy, people may debate ideas about the government without worrying about being punished.
2. Demonstrating against the government is often against the law in a dictatorship.
3. In a dictatorship, people are deprived of the right to speak out about abuses of their freedoms.

p. 50 Note-taking Guide

Sample response:
Spanish
Negative Memory: "I grew insecure about Spanish. My native tongue was not quite as good as English . . ."
Spanglish
Positive Memory: "*Butter, butter, butter, butter.* All day, one English word . . . But would you be needing some butter on your bread?"
Negative Memory: "At school, a Spanish word would suddenly slide into my English... 'Do you mean a *swing?*'"
English
Positive Memory: "I learned not to hear it as English, but as sense . . . I relaxed in this second language."

p. 51 Apply the Skills

1. Sample response: The teacher at Carol Morgan School took a more technical approach. She focused on teaching vocabulary and grammar.

2. Sample response: Her parents spoke English when they did not want the children to understand them. English kept Alvarez out of the conversation.

3. **Graphic Organizer**

Sample response:

Word Choice: "another strange tongue emerged from my papi's mouth or my mami's lips."

Attitude: "Supposing, just supposing . . . My mind would take off, soaring into possibilities . . ."

Sentence Structure: "I thought about the snow. I saw how it might fall on the hills. . . on people out late walking on the streets . . ."

4. Sample response: Her general purpose was to inform and entertain. She wanted readers to know what it was like to learn English. She also wanted them to enjoy reading about her experience.

Reading Informational Materials: Spanish/English Dictionaries

p. 56 Apply the Skills

Thinking About the Spanish/English Dictionary

1. Sample response: You would look under the heading Vowels in the Key to Spanish Pronunciation.

2. Sample response: The Note on Spanish Gender would give you this information.

Reading Skill

3. Sample response: The masculine form of the noun means *boundary mark* or *landmark*. The feminine form means *headless nail* or *brad*. Therefore, using one for the other would completely change the meaning.

4. Sample response: First, find the entry by looking up the keyword. Then, read the entry to find the part of speech. The italicized letter or letters immediately following the keyword show you what the part of speech is.

"The Secret Life of Walter Mitty" James Thurber

"Uncle Marcos" Isabel Allende

p. 57 Graphic Organizer

Sample response:

"The Secret Life of Walter Mitty"

Story Event or Detail: Walter Mitty forgets what his wife wants him to purchase.

Possible Importance: Walter Mitty is so involved in his daydreams that he has trouble remembering details about his real life.

Author's Purpose: to show that Walter Mitty is out of touch with real life

"Uncle Marcos"

Story Event or Detail: Uncle Marcos performs strange exercises at night. He sleeps during the day in a hammock.

Possible Importance: Uncle Marcos is an unusual person.

Author's Purpose: to reveal Uncle Marcos's unique character

p. 58 Reading/Writing Connection

Sample response: Daydreaming can enhance life by making it more interesting. A daydream might derive from real life events. Sometimes daydreams project my real-world experience into an imaginary world.

p. 58 Note-taking Guide

Sample response:

Daydream: Mitty is a surgeon saving a patient's life; Mitty is a criminal standing trial in a courtroom; Mitty is a pilot on a dangerous mission.

Reality: Mitty parks the car to buy overshoes; Mitty buys the biscuits and waits for his wife in a chair; Mrs. Mitty goes on another errand.

p. 59 Activate Prior Knowledge

Students may say they think about being a great athlete, singer, writer, actor, or mountaineer, or about becoming someone who is already famous.

p. 59 Literary Analysis

Students may say Mrs. Mitty is a flat character because readers only see her yelling at Walter Mitty. Students should underline "Not so fast!"; "What are you driving so fast for?"; "yelled at him"; and "You were up to fifty-five."

130 Reader's Notebook Teaching Guide

© Pearson Education, Inc., publishing as Pearson Prentice Hall.

p. 59 Reading Check
Students should circle "'Not so fast! You're driving too fast!'" and "What are you driving so fast for?"

p. 60 Reading Skill
Sample response: The author's purpose is to show that sometimes Mitty's daydreams cause him to be scatterbrained or to not pay attention to what he is doing in his real life.

p. 60 Build English Skills
Students should circle "buzz."

p. 60 Stop to Reflect
Sample response: Mitty may imagine himself to be a shooting expert because it is dangerous and exciting. His real life is not dangerous or exciting.

p. 60 Reading Check
Students should circle "Puppy biscuit."

p. 61 Read Fluently
Students should underline "I've been looking all over this hotel for you"; "Why did you have to hide in this old chair? How did you expect me to find you?"; "What?"; "Did you get the what's-its-name? The puppy biscuit? What's in the box?"; "Couldn't you have put them on in the store?"; and "I'm going to take your temperature when I get home." Students should circle "Things close in"; "Overshoes"; "I was thinking"; and "Does it ever occur to you that I am sometimes thinking?" Sample response: Quotation marks mean that a character is talking and authors will often tell you which character said it.

p. 61 Literary Analysis
Sample response: Walter Mitty is a dynamic character because some of his courage from his daydreams is coming into his real life.

p. 61 Reading Skill
Sample response: The author's purpose is to show the contrast between a man's exciting daydreams and his real life, which may seem boring. Thurber uses Mitty's daydreams to show the human desire for adventure and escape from everyday life.

p. 62 Apply the Skills
1. Sample response: In his imaginary life, Mitty is landing a plane, doing surgery, testifying in court, fighting a war, and facing a firing squad.

2. Sample response: The tasks of Mitty's daily life are boring and dull. The tasks of Mitty's fantasy life are exciting.
3. **Graphic Organizer**
Sample response:
Detail from Daydream:
2. "The other doctors are relieved that Walter can save the patient."
3. "Bravely, he stands ready to face his death."
Desired Character Trait:
2. Heroism
3. Fearlessness
4. Sample response: Thurber's purpose may have been to show the positive effects of imagination in the face of everyday troubles and defeats.

p. 64 Reading/Writing Connection
Sample response: One event that may evolve is my brother's skateboarding story. People might enhance the details of the story to make it seem more exciting. People might alter the reality of the event by exaggerating actual events.

p. 64 Note-taking Guide
Sample response:
Box 2: Marcos's flying machine carries him over the mountains.
Box 3: Marcos and Clara have great success telling fortunes.
Box 4: Marcos dies of an African plague during his travels.

p. 65 Apply the Skills
1. Sample response: Clara's reaction shows her faith and positive attitude. It may also suggest her innocence about death and her belief in her uncle's powers of magic.
2. Sample response: People can learn that their successes depend on their own attitudes. Be adventurous; be yourself; develop your sense of wonder; seek adventure; be unique.
3. **Graphic Organizer**
Sample response:
Project or Adventure: performs alchemy; takes trips around the world; builds flying machine
Character Traits: curiosity; adventurous; inventiveness
4. Sample response: Uncle Marcos never allows failure or the attitudes of others to discourage him. Allende's purpose may have been to encourage readers to be true to themselves.

"The Jade Peony"
Wayson Choy

p. 69 Note-taking Guide
Sample response:
Plot: Grandmama takes home remedies to treat her illness; Grandmama makes wind-chimes out of found objects; Grandmama and Sek-Lung hide collections under her bed until rest of family is out; Sek-Lung has missed school because he has been sick; Grandmama works on her last windchime; Grandmama dies; Sek-Lung discovers that she has left him her prize possession, a peony carved out of jade.
Conflict: Grandmama's collection process embarrasses other members of family; Sek-Lung's fear and sorrow at losing Grandmama; the family's ties to its Chinese heritage versus its desire to be modern and Canadian; the other children's dislike of studying Mandarin
Characters: Grandmama: 83; artistic; treasures memories of the past, particularly of the juggler who gave her the jade peony; believes in signs. Sek-Lung: 8; illness has kept him at home; close ties with Grandmama. Two brothers, sister, father, and stepmother.
Setting: Vancouver, Canada; Grandmama dies in September

p. 70 Activate Prior Knowledge
Sample response: An older adult can play a supportive role for a young person. He or she could teach the young person skills or lessons about the past.

p. 70 Short Story
Students should circle "Vancouver, Canada" and "modern Canadians."

p. 70 Culture Note
Students may mention such treatments as crystals, herbal tonics, green and black teas, bee pollen, and other natural remedies.

p. 71 Stop to Reflect
Sample response: Grandmama keeps the jade peony because it reminds her of the juggler. She can think of him and their time together every time she touches the pendant.

p. 71 Short Story
Sample response: She is important to them, and they love her. However, they are embarrassed about the way she acts.

p. 71 Reading Check
Students should underline "He promised to return to her one day."

p. 71 Short Story
Sample response: The older children are worried about what other people think of them. They are worried that their grandmother's garbage picking makes them look poor.

p. 72 Stop to Reflect
Sample response: They are sacred pieces because they are from a church. Also, Sek-Lung and his Grandmama had an abundance of beautiful pieces to choose from.

p. 72 Read Fluently
Sample response: We smelled like smoke and were covered in soot when we got home. We had a carton full of glass pieces with us. It was early, so we were able to sneak them into the house. We put them under Grandmama's bed.

p. 72 Vocabulary and Pronunciation
Students should choose letter "b."

p. 73 Stop to Reflect
Students may identify an object that they bought at a festival that reminds them of the event.

p. 73 Short Story
Grandmama says that her spirit will be drawn to the windchime after she dies. Then, she will be able to come back to the house and tell her family goodbye.

p. 73 Reading Check
Students should circle "She explains that it is because death is closing in on her."

p. 74 Short Story
Sample response: It shows that he loved his grandmother very much because he devoted so much time to her.

p. 74 Stop to Reflect
Sample response: She will remain in his memory. Every time he looks at the windchimes, he will remember her and what she taught him.

p. 74 Reading Check
Students should circle "It was all white and had pink eyes like sacred fire."

p. 75 Short Story

Sample response: The white cat symbolizes the juggler from Grandmama's past. He had white hair and pink eyes, as well. Grandmama thinks he has finally come back to her.

p. 75 Short Story

Sample response: The theme of this story is that family and traditions are important. A person must blend the past and the present together in order to be a complete person. Young people should honor older people for what they can teach. Sample response: The theme is implied. Choy never says that people should honor and respect the past. However, his deep relationship with his grandmother helps him understand who he is and what life is all about.

p. 76 Apply the Skills

1. Sample response: Making windchimes was a recreation of Grandmama's past. Not only was she maintaining tradition in creating the chimes, but she was also using fragments from the past to make them.
2. Sample response: Sek-Lung supports and understands Grandmama's activities. He is happy to be included in the process. The rest of the family is embarrassed by her activities.
3. **Graphic Organizer**
Sample response:
What It Says: The family waits for a sign.
What It Means: Grandmama's rest is peaceful, and her family is safe.
Why It Is Important: These signs or omens signify the attachment to and belief in the past.
4. Sample response: The theme is that the past is important because it forms people's characters and a culture's shared understanding. Students should explain how the chart did or did not affect their understanding of the story's theme.

"American History"
Judith Ortiz Cofer

"The Most Dangerous Game"
Richard Connell

p. 78 Graphic Organizer

Sample response:
"American History"
Detail: The door was painted green, the color of hope.

Question: Why might a writer describe a door as having the color of an emotion?
Inference: The door stands for opportunity.

"The Most Dangerous Game"
Detail: The island Rainsford swims to is described as forbidding.
Question: Why would an island be described this way?
Inference: This island must hold something evil.

p. 79 Reading/Writing Connection

Sample response:
1. A natural disaster can transform peoples' lives.
2. Bravery and kindness emerge when people go through a crisis.
3. People define themselves as survivors after living through a hurricane.

p. 79 Note-taking Guide

Sample response:
Story Detail 2: Even though she gets straight A's, the honors classes are not open to Elena.
Conflict 2: Elena is viewed as low class.
Story Detail 3: President Kennedy has just been killed, but Elena can't help but feel excited about the time she is going to spend with Eugene.
Conflict 3: Elena's mother thinks that Elena is disrespectful. She warns Elena that she is headed for heartbreak.
Story Detail 4: Eugene's mother asks Elena whether she lives "there" in the El Building.
Conflict 4: Eugene's mother does not want Elena spending time with her son.

p. 80 Apply the Skills

1. Sample response: Elena thinks her home is large and noisy. She thinks Eugene's home is quiet and comfortable.
2. Sample response: Elena's tears are just for herself because she feels her personal pain more than she feels the pain of the national tragedy.
3. **Graphic Organizer**
Sample response:
Elena vs. another person: Elena's conflict with her mother's expectations of her occurs when Elena chooses to go to Eugene's house instead of going to church.

4. Sample response: One inference is the love that people had for the president. This inference is based on their anguish.

p. 82 Reading/Writing Connection
Sample response:
1. I do not want to <u>contemplate</u> what could happen if a dangerous game became real.
2. Some people tried to <u>simulate</u> death and destruction.
3. Opponents might <u>utilize</u> real weapons to win the game.

p. 82 Note-taking Guide
Sample response:
Event 2: Rainsford meets Ivan and Zaroff on a nearby island.
Event 3: Rainsford refuses to hunt men and becomes the one who is hunted.
Final Event: Rainsford kills Zaroff.

p. 83 Activate Prior Knowledge
Students may suggest that playing a game with unfamiliar rules was confusing at first. They may say that they had to take time to learn how to play the game.

p. 83 Build English Skills
first-class cabin; hot-weather clothing; black-eyed jaguar

p. 83 Read Fluently
Students should underline "Don't talk rot, Whitney"; "Who cares how a jaguar feels?"; and "Bah! They've no understanding." Students should circle answer (c).

p. 84 Literary Analysis
Rainsford struggles for his life against the sea.

p. 84 Reading Skill
Students may infer that an animal is in trouble, perhaps fighting for its life.

p. 84 Culture Note
Sample response: People say "hi," "hello," and "how are you."

p. 84 Reading Check
Students should underline "I've read your book about hunting snow leopards in Tibet, you see."

p. 85 Reading Skill
Students may infer that Zaroff's "new animal" is human.

p. 85 Literary Analysis
Conflict develops over hunting men for sport. Zaroff considers the game ideal; Rainsford knows that this game is murder.

p. 85 Build English Skills
Students should circle "Verb."

p. 85 Reading Check
Students should underline: "If he cannot find the man in three days, then the man wins."

p. 86 Literary Analysis
Sample response: Either decision—to hunt or to face Ivan—is deadly. The internal conflict would be choosing whether to die quickly by Ivan's hands or whether to prolong their death in the hopes of escape.

p. 86 Reading Skill
Students may infer that Zaroff will give Rainsford the option of the hunt or Ivan's torture, and Rainsford will choose the hunt.

p. 86 Stop to Reflect
Zaroff hunts human beings. Students will probably say Zaroff is a demented, horrible person.

p. 87 Reading Skill
Students may infer that Zaroff is an excellent hunter. He is extremely strong and clever. He is able to track Rainsford and escape his trap alive. He is also extremely determined. He will come back for Rainsford.

p. 87 Stop to Reflect
Sample response: Rainsford most likely feels tension and fear, then relief, followed by new tension and fear.

p. 87 Literary Analysis
Rainsford's decision to jump into the sea was an internal conflict. He had to choose between being caught by Zaroff and his hounds or jumping into the sea. Either choice is almost certain death.

p. 88 Reading Skill
Students may infer that Rainsford does not feel like he has yet won the game. He still feels he is "a beast at bay." He thinks that the only way to win is to kill Zaroff.

p. 88 Literary Analysis
The conflict is resolved through a hands-on fight between the two men. Rainsford wins.

p. 88 Reading Skill
Students may infer that Rainsford is at peace. He has successfully overcome his enemy and won the game.

p. 89 Apply the Skills
1. Students may like Rainsford's courage, intelligence, and self-control under pressure. They may not like his attitude about hunting.
2. Sample response: Zaroff forces Rainsford to be the prey of a hunt. If Rainsford hunts, he will certainly think about the prey's experience.
3. **Graphic Organizer**
Sample response:
Rainsford vs. himself: not panicking when thrown from boat; controlling anxiety during hunt
4. Sample response: Whitney's desire to relate to the animals shows that he is a more sensitive man than Rainsford.

Reading Informational Materials: Signs and Instructions

p. 92 Reading Signs and Instructions
Students should circle the small falling person in the sign and underline the words "CAN CAUSE SERIOUS INJURIES OR DROWNING."

p. 92 Reading Skill
Sample response: Students may say that the picture does give a clear message because they can clearly see that a person is sucked under by a huge wave. They may say that the words "WARNING" and "HIGH SURF" should be as big as they are because they attract attention and relay the main message quickly.

p. 92 Reading Check
Students should circle "twenty-five feet plus" and "fifteen feet plus."

p. 92 Read Fluently
Students should circle "life" and "depend." Sample response: These words are the most important because they tell exactly what could be at risk if someone ignores the sign.

p. 93 Reading Signs and Instructions
Students should circle: "WARNING" and "STRONG CURRENT."
Warning; Strong Current

p. 93 Culture Note
Sample response: The people who live there would pay more attention to the signs. The people who live there know that high waves

and strong currents often hurt and kill people. The people who are on vacation may not realize how dangerous the water can be.

p. 93 Reading Informational Materials
Sample response: Signs and instructions should be easy to understand because everyone needs to be able to read the message. Some people cannot read difficult text. Some people will not take the time to read a sign with too many words.

p. 94 Apply the Skills
Thinking About the Sign and Instruction
1. Sample response: The simple pictures suggest danger without need for words.
2. Sample response: People who are very good surfers and who are familiar with big waves might be safe.

Reading Skill
3. Sample response: Large, powerful waves are the danger shown in the first sign.
4. Sample response: A "strong current" is water that is moving so quickly that it can overpower people who are trying to walk or swim against it. It is dangerous because people can be swept into deep water, and then they could drown or be seriously injured.

"The Gift of the Magi" O. Henry

"The Interlopers" Saki

p. 95 Graphic Organizer
Sample response:
"The Gift of the Magi"
Detail: Jim is shocked when he sees Della's hair.
My Experience: People are often speechless when something happens that they do not expect.
Inference: Jim was not expecting Della to cut her hair, so his gift may be something that she can use in her hair.

"The Interlopers"
Detail: The two men are alone when they get caught under the tree.
My Experience: It would take time to find people in a large forest. It would take even longer if you did not suspect that something was wrong.
Inference: The two men will not be rescued.

p. 96 Reading/Writing Connection
Sample response:

1. Some people might adjust the amount they spend on gifts.

2. A person can embody love simply by doing a special favor for a loved one.

3. Someone can emphasize love by giving a family member a treasured possession.

p. 96 Note-taking Guide
Sample response:

Della

Action: Della sells her hair to buy the chain.

Unexpected Result: Della receives combs for hair she no longer has.

Jim

Christmas Gift Idea: hair combs

Action: Jim sells his watch to buy the combs.

Unexpected Result: Jim receives a watch chain for a watch he no longer has.

p. 97 Activate Prior Knowledge
Students may list several types of sacrifices. For example, they may have sacrificed free time by taking a job to be able to afford something they wanted. They may have given up something they were accustomed to, such as new clothes or video games.

p. 97 Culture Note
Students may list things such as a pen, a small writing pad, or a couple of apples.

p. 97 Building English Skills
Students may say *Mrs.* and *Ms.*

p. 98 Read Fluently
Sample response: She let her hair down.

p. 98 Stop to Reflect
Students may say that people give expensive gifts because they think it shows how much they care. Others may say that people want to give expensive gifts because they want to show off.

p. 98 Vocabulary and Pronunciation
Sample response: impossible: not possible; impatient: not patient; immature: not mature

p. 98 Reading Check
Students should circle " 'Twenty dollars,' said Madame, lifting the mass with a practiced hand."

p. 99 Literary Analysis
Jim's gift is ironic because Della cannot use the combs on her short hair.

p. 99 Reading Skill
Sample response: He sees that what has happened is humorous. He appreciates how much she loves him.

p. 99 Literary Analysis
The ending is a surprise because neither Della nor the reader knows that Jim has sacrificed something, too.

p. 99 Reading Check
Students should circle "They gave up what they treasured most, out of love for each other."

p. 100 Apply the Skills
1. Della's action shows that she is generous and self-sacrificing.

2. Sample response: Wisdom is the understanding that some things, such as love and kindness, are more important than money or expensive things.

3. Sample response: This situational irony conveys the idea that life is not predictable. It also shows that gifts are not the best way for showing someone you love them.

4. Students may be familiar with characters who were in love from books, television, or movies. These characters were willing to sacrifice for each other, as well.

p. 102 Reading/Writing Connection
Sample response:

1. To end a feud, the groups involved could participate in a peace conference.

2. A court could verify which of the feuding parties owns the land.

3. Participants could focus more on ending rather than fighting the feud.

p. 102 Note-taking Guide
Sample response:

Detail: The two families have hated each other for three generations.

What the Reader Expects: Ulrich and Georg will never be able to resolve their conflict.

What Actually Happens: They resolve their conflict.

Detail: Ulrich offers to end the feud.

What the Reader Expects: Georg will refuse Ulrich's offer.

What Actually Happens: Georg agrees to end the feud. They decide to become friends.

Detail: Nine or ten figures respond to their cries for help.

What the Reader Expects: The men will be rescued. They will surprise everyone when they announce that they are friends.
What Actually Happens: The figures are wolves.

p. 103 Apply the Skills

1. Georg does not accept the court's decision.
2. Sample response: Their present situation makes the two men realize that their dispute is a waste of time.
3. Sample response: One message is that people should resolve their differences while they have the opportunity.
4. Sample response: Saki probably intended readers to infer that the men are proud and stubborn. He may have also wanted readers to infer that the unexpected situation makes the men see how good their lives could have been without the feud.

"The Necklace"
Guy de Maupassant

"Rules of the Game"
Amy Tan

p. 105 Graphic Organizer
Sample response:
"The Necklace"
Narrator's comments: "She would weep for whole days at a time from sorrow, regret, despair, and distress."
What They Show About the Character: Madame Loisel is unhappy with being poor.
Character's thoughts and words:
" . . . there's nothing more humiliating than to look poverty-stricken among a lot of rich women."
What They Show About the Character: She is very sensitive about her appearance and social status.
Character's actions: "She does all the hated household chores."
What They Show About the Character: She works hard to repay debts.
Character's appearance: "Disheveled, her skirts askew, with reddened hands, she spoke in a loud voice . . ."
What They Show About the Character: The hard work and poverty she endures have made her indifferent to her appearance.
What Others Say or Think About the Character: "Oh, my poor, poor Mathilde!"

What They Show About the Character: She really has changed.

"Rules of the Game"
Narrator's comments: " . . . she asked without a trace of knowing how wicked I was being"
What They Show About the Character: The narrator's comments reveal that Waverly is being sarcastic.
Character's thoughts and words: "I read the rules and looked up all the big words in a dictionary . . . I studied each chess piece, trying to absorb the power each contained." "By my ninth birthday, I was a national chess champion."
What They Show About the Character: Waverly's thoughts and words reveal her intelligence.
Character's actions: "I raced down the street, dashing between people, not looking back as my mother screamed shrilly, "Meimei! Meimei!"
What They Show About the Character: Waverly's actions show how Waverly argues with her mother.
Character's appearance: "In my crisp pink-and-white dress with scratchy lace at the neck, one of two my mother had sewn for these special occasions . . . "
What They Show About the Character: Waverly's special dresses for tournaments show her mother's involvement in her life.
What Others Say or Think About the Character: "Is shame you fall down nobody push you."
What They Show About the Character: Waverly's mother thinks that Waverly is talented enough to play in competitions.

p. 106 Reading/Writing Connection
Sample response:
1. Some people think expensive things identify them as having a successful and happy life.
2. Buying expensive items may cause some people to exceed their financial limits.
3. Many people think that expensive possessions will help them obtain admiration from others.

p. 106 Note-taking Guide
Sample response:
Box 2: She goes to the party and loses the necklace.

Box 3: The Loisels replace the necklace and work ten years to pay for it.
Final Event: Madame Loisel learns the secret of the necklace.

p. 107 Activate Prior Knowledge
Students may describe feeling upset, panicked, and regretful.

p. 107 Culture Note
She has no dowry.

p. 107 Reading Skill
Madame Loisel is unhappy because she is not rich.

p. 107 Reading Check
Students should circle the passage that begins with "She had a rich friend . . . " and ends with " . . . regret, despair, and distress."

p. 108 Read Fluently
Students should underline "Wait—you silly thing!" and "She danced enraptured—carried away . . . to the heart of a woman."

p. 108 Vocabulary and Pronunciation
Students should connect the words as follows: diamond–jewel; rich–wealthy; unhappy–sad; pretty–beautiful.

p. 108 Reading Check
Students should circle "Why don't you go and see Madame Forestier and ask her to lend you some jewelry."

p. 109 Build English Skills
Sample response: My mother aged five years when she saw my test score.

p. 109 Culture Note
Students may write *dollar, quarter, nickel, dime,* or *penny.*

p. 109 Literary Analysis
Sample response: This statement shows that Monsieur Loisel is honest and responsible.

p. 109 Read Fluently
Students should circle *old, strong, hard, coarse, disheveled, askew, reddened,* and *loud.*

p. 110 Literary Analysis
Sample response: Madame Loisel longs to be beautiful and admired again. This passage contains indirect characterization.

p. 110 Reading Skill
Madame Forestier is surprised by how much Mathilde has changed.

p. 110 Stop to Reflect
Sample response: Madame Forestier should sell the diamond necklace and repay Madame Loisel. Madame Loisel and her husband deserve to live comfortably after ten years of unnecessary work.

p. 110 Reading Check
Students should circle the passage beginning with "'You remember the diamond necklace . . .'" and ending with "'Anyway, I'm glad it's over and done with.'"

p. 111 Apply the Skills
1. Sample response: Monsieur Loisel is much less selfish and much more loving than his wife is.
2. Sample response: Madame Loisel loses her charm and beauty. She becomes old before her time. She also learns to work hard.
3. Sample response: Madame Loisel is interested in material possessions and appearances. An example of indirect characterization is her depression after she visits her rich friend.
4. **Graphic Organizer**
Sample response:
Causes: She is invited to a party.
Effects: She looks beautiful at the party.

p. 113 Reading/Writing Connection
Sample response: Games can induce feelings such as satisfaction, anger, or happiness. These feelings may initiate friendships that cross age or culture barriers. Games can also evoke conflicts that divide friends or family members.

p. 113 Note-taking Guide
Sample response:
Event 2: Waverly learns to play chess.
Event 3: Waverly wins many tournaments.
Climax: Waverly runs away when she and her mother quarrel.
Resolution: She thinks about her next move in this mother-daughter conflict.

p. 114 Apply the Skills
1. Sample response: She pretends to be weaker than she is.
2. Sample response: Waverly will win the game of doing what she wants to do. She has learned from her mother.
3. The conversation is an example of indirect characterization. Waverly's mother does not realize that Waverly is being wicked. Her

mother tells her that the Chinese do the best torture. These remarks show the cultural and generational differences between the two people.

4. **Graphic Organizer**
Sample response:
Causes: One cause for her success is her intelligence.
Effects: One effect of her success is that her self-confidence has increased.

"Blues Ain't No Mockin Bird"
Toni Cade Bambara

"The Invalid's Story"
Mark Twain

p. 116 Graphic Organizer
Sample response:
"Blues Ain't No Mockin Bird"
Cause: The twins ask whether the man in the story jumped.
Mental Picture: Granny stares at the twins.
Effect: Granny gets angry about the twins' responses to her story.

"The Invalid's Story"
Cause: The smell in the train becomes overwhelming.
Mental Picture: Thompson's face is buried in a handkerchief. The narrator's face has no color.
Effect: The men smoke cigars to try to cover up the smell.

p. 117 Reading/Writing Connection
Sample response: I would underline intervene if I saw someone abusing an animal. Laws should oblige people to respect animal rights. I write letters to a newspaper to promote the protection of endangered animals.

p. 117 Note-taking Guide
Sample response:
Beginning Event: The two men offend Granny.
Box 2: Granddaddy arrives.
Box 3: Granddaddy brings down the hawk.
Box 4: Granddaddy disables the camera.
Box 5: The cameramen back off.
Final Event: Granny goes back to making cakes.

p. 118 Activate Prior Knowledge
Students may describe a disapproving scowl or a glare that the older person has.

p. 118 Literary Analysis
The use of the words *ain't* and *no* and the dropping of the final *g* in words show that this story is written in dialect.

p. 118 Build English Skills
Students may underline "Me and Cathy look over toward the meadow where the men with the station wagon'd been roamin around all morning." Sample response: Cathy and I look over toward the meadow where the men with the station wagon had been roaming around all morning.

p. 119 Literary Analysis
No, the twins do not understand the lesson that Granny is trying to teach them. They are asking whether the man jumped. Instead, Granny wants them to think about why the photographer's actions were wrong.

p. 119 Read Fluently
Students have a choice of several words written in dialect. Students could underline "lookin," "Thanksgivin," and "visitin."

p. 119 Reading Skill
Students should underline "people wouldn't pay her for things like they said they would," "Mr. Judson bringin us boxes of old clothes and raggedy magazines," and "Mrs. Cooper comin in our kitchen and touchin everything and sayin how clean it all was."

p. 120 Reading Skill
Students should underline "Cathy say it's because he's so tall and quiet and like a king. And people just can't stand it."

p. 120 Vocabulary and Pronunciation
The definition of *duck* as it is used in the paragraph is "to bend down to avoid bumping into something, or to avoid getting hit by something." Sample response: The duck landed on the water.

p. 121 Reading Skill
Granddaddy stands straight and watches the hawk. Granddaddy does not appear to be afraid.

p. 121 Stop to Reflect
Students should look at "'Good day, gentlemen'" and circle "Like he'd invited them . . . it was time to go." Sample response: Granddaddy's greeting confuses the men because, although he is being calm and polite, he is still asking them to leave.

p. 121 Reading Skill

Sample response: By visualizing the scene, one can see the men trying to gather the spilled film as they back away. The men's reaction shows that Granddaddy's opening of the camera has made them nervous and afraid.

p. 122 Apply the Skills

1. Some students may choose Granddaddy because he is tall and dignified. Other students may choose the narrator because she sees things as they are.

2. **Graphic Organizer**

Sample response:

Hawks and Granddaddy: Granddaddy is threatening. He tries to protect his mate and drive away the threatening men.

What the Hawks Represent: The hawks represent Granny and Granddaddy. The intruders have walked onto Granny's property (as into a hawk's territory). Granddaddy, her mate, is trying to protect her.

3. The grammar shows dialect by the phrase "always got," instead of "have," and "teaches steady," instead of "steadily." The spelling shows dialect with the *g* dropped from "somethin."

4. Sample response: The men have taken motion pictures of his family.

p. 124 Reading/Writing Connection

Sample response: Seeing how characters analyze a problem might help readers deal with real-life situations. A reader might focus on how the characters find a solution. Finding humor in these stories can verify the importance of keeping a sense of humor.

p. 124 Note-taking Guide

Sample response:

2: The coffin is switched with a box of guns and a block of cheese.

3: The narrator and Thompson stand on the platform to avoid the smell.

p. 125 Apply the Skills

1. Thompson says that the corpse "wants to travel alone" because it is creating the bad smell.

2. The contrast between a serious and a harmless source of the odor is humorous.

3. **Graphic Organizer**

Sample response:

Humorous Details: The narrator and Thompson mistake the cheese odor for the smell of a dead body. Thompson gasps over the box near the cheese.

Evaluation: The story is funny because of all of the confusion and drama a simple cargo mix-up causes.

4. Students might say that the dialect makes the speaker come alive. The dialect makes the characters and setting more vivid because it makes them seem more realistic.

5. The smell makes the men leave the car.

Reading Informational Materials: Brochures

p. 128 Reading Skill

Students should circle the map and the hours and admission information. Sample response: They are located next to each other to help people easily find the information needed to visit the museum.

p. 128 Stop to Reflect

Brochures often are meant to persuade people to come to a place. The maps help people get to the place.

p. 128 Read Fluently

Students should circle the colons after Oct. 31 and Mar. 31. Students should underline the semicolon after 5 p.m.

p. 129 Reading Skill

Students should write "A" next to "The Museum." Students may write "B" next to "Barber Junction," "The Robert Julian Roundhouse," or "Historic Spencer Shops." Students may write "C" next to "Spencer Shops' mission was . . ." or "Southern Railway was one of the first U.S. rail systems . . ."

p. 129 Reading Check

Students should underline "While the museum is young—founded in 1977—the story of the Spencer Shops reaches back more than one hundred years."

p. 129 Culture Note

Sample response: In the 1800s, most people did not own automobiles. Now, many people do own them.

p. 129 Reading Informational Materials

Sample response: This brochure shows the reader the different activities that they could choose from when visiting the museum.

p. 130 Apply the Skills
Thinking About the Brochure
1. Sample response: Placing learning opportunities earlier would leave the reader wondering what there was to learn about.
2. Sample response: This building was chosen so that people could both learn history about trains and see train repairs taking place.

Reading Skill
3. Sample response: It is a good idea to put the map on the front page because it is easily and quickly seen there. The map is more useful to the reader on the first page.
4. You would look under the heading "Learning Opportunities."

"Before Hip-Hop Was Hip-Hop"
Rebecca Walker

p. 133 Note-taking Guide
Sample response:
Circle 1: Hip-hop helped bridge the gap between different cultures.
Circle 2: The revolution of hip-hop affected music, fashion, and dance.
Circle 3: Hip-hop created new words and slang.
Circle 4: Hip-hop taught her creativity, community, and self-confidence.

p. 134 Activate Prior Knowledge
Students may say that Ronald Reagan was President followed by George Bush. They may say that they think of slap bracelets, neon-colored clothing, home video and cable television, *Sixteen Candles* and *The Breakfast Club*, MTV, moonwalking, the Phillies winning their first World Series, the Rubik's Cube, video games, designer jeans, Smurfs, or Cabbage Patch dolls. Some of the music from the era includes Bruce Springsteen, Devo, Duran Duran, and Madonna.

p. 134 Nonfiction
Students should underline "EO," "ATL," "can't," "latest 'steelo,'" "cocked," "old school," and "sodas." Sample response: Walker may have chosen informal English because it seems more personal and fits better with the ideas of the story. It also reflects the language of hip-hop culture.

p. 134 Reading Check
Students should underline "The vast empire of hip-hop amazes me because I knew hip-hop before it was hip-hop. I was there when it all began."

p. 135 Nonfiction
Sample response: She wants readers to see how accepting and diverse hip-hop was when it began and also how flexible.

p. 135 Read Fluently
Students may underline "45s" as the unfamiliar word. Some may figure out by context that the word has something to do with music. Context clue definition: "Small records with two songs on them."

p. 135 Stop to Reflect
Students may say that they like many different kinds of music, just as Walker does. Students may say that they like country music because that is what they listen to at home. Some students may say that they like rap music because it is fast and they like to dance to it.

p. 136 Read Fluently
Students may underline "cliques" and "vicious." Sample response: "Cliques" are "small groups of people that stick together and remain aloof from others." "Vicious" means "spiteful" or "malicious."

p. 136 Nonfiction
Sample response: Both examples show the unexpectedness of what the author found in hip-hop culture. The author did not expect the reserved Asian American girl to sneak a bright red sweatsuit under her coat. In the same way, she did not expect the preppy boy to support all religions.

p. 136 Reading Check
Students should underline "how they talked and used words"; "how they used their hands while talking"; "how they walked and joked and what they wore."

p. 137 Nonfiction
Sample response: She uses expository, narrative, and descriptive writing. She wants to explain and inform about hip-hop culture. She also wants to tell the story of how after school and weekend activities led to its development. She describes the dancers so that readers will be able to "see" the dancers even if they have never seen breakdancing.

p. 137 Stop to Reflect
Students may agree with Walker and say that they do not like hip-hop music because it is sometimes violent and sometimes contains foul language. Students may describe hip-hop as a series of fast beats that repeat underneath one or more voices that are speaking very quickly and often in rhyme.

p. 138 Stop to Reflect
Sample response: People need something to bridge the differences in groups, and art can do this. Hip-hop was a kind of art because it

came from many different places and brought people together.

p. 138 Nonfiction

Students may underline "art could bring people together and make them forget their differences"; "I could express myself and communicate with others through what I wore and how I walked and what music I liked"; "loyalty, community, self-confidence, and creativity"; "She wants kids of today to know that when hip-hop started, it was not about expensive cars and clothes"; "It was created by kids that were doing what felt good to them"; "hopes kids today will do the same"; "She wants them to be honest and think how they can create their own exciting new culture." Sample response: Walker wants to inspire her young readers to create something like hip-hop in their own lives.

p. 138 Reading Check

Students should underline "Walker lived in the Bronx for only one year."

p. 139 Apply the Skills

1. Sample response: Hip-hop bridged the gap by giving Walker and her friends common interests.
2. Sample response: It was important for Walker and her friends to express themselves in this way because it taught them how to bring people together and how to communicate with others.
3. Sample response: The tone is personal, passionate, joyous, and nostalgic. Her tone comes through when she states that she was there when hip-hop began. It also comes through in her descriptions of the wonderful times she and her friends shared.
4. Sample response: Walker has an informal, direct, and friendly style.

Graphic Organizer
Sample response:
Level of Formality: talks about kids not knowing the impact of their ideas
Word Choice: slang, contractions; brand names; musical groups and their recordings; uses "I"
Sentence Patterns: direct, short sentences; tendency to provide multiple examples in one sentence; asks and answers her own questions

"A Celebration of Grandfathers"
Rudolfo A. Anaya

"On Summer"
Lorraine Hansberry

p. 141 Graphic Organizer

Sample response:
"A Celebration of Grandfathers"
Question: What does Anaya feel about old people?
Detail/Answer: Old people have much to teach us.
Main Idea? We should respect old people.

"On Summer"
Question: How do Hansberry's feelings about summer change as she grows older?
Detail/Answer: She begins to see the beauty of summer's gentle sunsets and long days.
Main Idea? Summer is "the noblest of seasons."

p. 142 Reading/Writing Connection

Sample response:
1. Older people can help people appreciate the values of the past.
2. Talking to older people can help people clarify their own values.
3. Older people often demonstrate a respect for the land.

p. 142 Note-taking Guide

Sample response:
What was the author's grandfather like?
Wise, spoke to the point, actively involved in life
Why are elders valuable? They work hard, are connected to the earth, have faith and inner strength, teach us valuable lessons
How are elders viewed now? They are supposed to look and act like young people.

p. 143 Activate Prior Knowledge

Students may say that a grandparent or older person has affected their lives by teaching them a respect for hard work and effort. Because life was not so easy in the past, a grandparent or older person may have taught them never to take life for granted or take for granted opportunities that have been presented to them.

p. 143 Literary Analysis
Students may say that the author creates a tone of admiration and respect for his elders.

p. 143 Reading Check
Students should underline "Buenos días le de Dios, abuelo."

p. 144 Read Fluently
Students should underline "Know where you stand." Sample response: The grandfather means that the boy should know where he is and what is happening around him.

p. 144 Stop to Reflect
Students may say that the advice could apply to them when they are faced with a difficult decision. It would help them make a choice to look at the circumstances surrounding them before coming to a decision.

p. 144 Reading Skill
Sample response: The main idea is that prayers are a meaningful action and wishing is not. When confronted with a problem, the grandfather wants Anaya to do meaningful things instead of wishing.

p. 145 Literary Analysis
Sample response: The repetition of the phrase "We need" puts the readers and Anaya into one group. His use of "need" means that the readers and Anaya must take certain actions.

p. 145 Reading Skill
Sample response: Some details are "the leaves falling from the tree"; "vision blurs, health wanes"; "the act of walking carries with it the painful reminder of the autumn of life."

p. 145 Build English Skills
Students should underline "vision blurs" and "health wanes."

p. 145 Reading Check
Students could circle "American society celebrates youth, but not old age. TV ads show older people as healthy and lively, but that is not the way it is for many of the elderly."

p. 146 Apply the Skills
1. Sample response: The old ones are strong, wise, and independent. Modern mass media show images of old people who appear youthful, lively, and healthy.

2. Sample response: Anaya believes that old people should be treated with patience and care because growing old can be painful and damaging.

3. **Graphic Organizer**
Sample response:
Diction: Buenos días le de Dios, abuelo; process of life; natural cycle of growth and change; transformation
Tone: admiration, respect, affection
Style: serious, thoughtful, informal
4. Sample response: Young people should respect old people because the elders are strong and wise and have something important to share.

p. 148 Reading/Writing Connection
Sample response:
1. The older members of my family embody stories from the past.
2. The pictures of our celebrations signify happy memories.
3. I react with pride when I see my family together.

p. 148 Note-taking Guide
Sample response:
As a Child: It is a mistake. It is excessive. It is an overstatement. It is too stark.
As an Adult: It is noble. It is life at its apex. It has the gentlest nights and the longest days. It is beauty. She has respect for it.

p. 149 Apply the Skills
1. Sample response: It is a memory of a specific summer. Hansberry's memories of her grandmother provide a contrast to her description of the woman in Maine.
2. Sample response: She considers summer noble because it represents life in its most complete form.
3. **Graphic Organizer**
Sample response:
Diction: "life at the apex," "gentlest nights," "noblest of the seasons"
Tone: respectful, admiring, affectionate
Style: thoughtful, solemn, formal
4. Sample response: Hansberry did not like summer as a young person, but she learned to appreciate it as an adult.

"The News"
Neil Postman

"Single Room, Earth View"
Sally Ride

p. 151 Graphic Organizer
Sample response:
"The News"
Details 1: Dramatic video is often shown to keep viewers' attention.
Details 2: The news anchor is chosen because he or she "looks" the part.
Main Idea: Television news cannot cover all of the news adequately because of its nature as entertainment.

"Single Room, Earth View"
Details 1: One moment she could see fires in Africa, and then she could see ice flowing in the Antarctic.
Details 2: The eddies and spirals in Earth's water eventually become visible.
Main Idea: Seeing the world from the space shuttle creates a new perspective on Earth.

p. 152 Reading/Writing Connection
Sample response: I rely on news Web sites to find out about current events. These sources clarify details and help me understand what is happening in the world. These sources also indicate how events will affect me in the future.

p. 152 Note-taking Guide
Sample response:
Newspapers: show many articles at the same time
Television News: shows stories in sequence
Both: supply news of the world

p. 153 Apply the Skills
1. Students may suggest that the comparison reveals that the news broadcast is an artificial order imposed on the real world. Real events appear "dramatized" on television news. This makes television news seem like a play.
2. Sample response: Time limits prevent the day's news from being covered sufficiently. The viewer gets only a series of impressions.
3. **Graphic Organizer**
Sample response:
Cause and Effect
Example: The need for television news stories to keep all viewers results in brief stories that have widespread appeal.

Effect: This example illustrates why it is impossible for television news to cover news stories adequately.
4. Sample response: The main idea of "The News" is that television news has time limitations and must appeal to a wide audience. As a result, it gives a false impression of the world.

p. 155 Reading/Writing Connection
Sample response:
1. I had to alter my feelings about the city when I saw it from the Empire State Building.
2. Looking at something up close can emphasize how complex it is.
3. The sight of the moon seems to contradict what I thought the moon's surface looked like.

p. 155 Note-taking Guide
Sample response:
Geographical Sites: Ganges River, Sahara
Human-Made Structures: cities
Natural Occurrences: typhoons forming; volcanoes smoldering
Environmental Problems: oil spills, air pollution, destruction of forests.

p. 156 Activate Prior Knowledge
Students may say that Earth is very blue because most of its surface is water. They might say that because they can see the landmasses, it looks just like a globe. They might also point out weather patterns such as hurricanes.

p. 156 Reading Skill
Sample response: The space traveler is a giant step farther away. A space traveler can see typhoons forming, volcanoes smoking, and meteors streaking through the atmosphere. An astronaut can see Africa and Antarctica in the same moment.

p. 156 Reading Check
Students should underline "During her space trip, Ride circled the Earth every 90 minutes."

p. 157 Vocabulary and Pronunciation
Sample response: Ride means that the expanses of North Africa are filled with sand.

p. 157 Stop to Reflect
Some students may say that seeing the Caribbean from space would be the most interesting. They may like to watch hurricanes form and move across the ocean.

p. 157 Literary Analysis

Sample response: She describes the effects of pollution. She is using the sense of sight to help readers realize the damage that pollution is doing to Earth.

p. 157 Reading Check

Students should circle "Then I realized they were obscured by a huge dust storm, a cloud of sand that enveloped the continent from Morocco to the Sudan."

p. 158 Read Fluently

Students may say that they have an image of the ocean, covered with swirls and mixing colors.

p. 158 Literary Analysis

Students should circle "It looks like bursting balls of light, like a fireworks show." Students should underline "Blue and orange bands would streak along the horizon." Sample response: The description appeals to the sense of sight.

p. 158 Build English Skills

Sample response: "Bands" in the underlined sentence means "long, thin strips."

p. 158 Reading Check

Students should circle "eddies" and "spirals."

p. 159 Apply the Skills

1. Sample response: Ride thought that she could almost see geological forces working in the way the theories say they work.
2. Students may say that the way they think about Earth is very different. The essay may have given them a new sense of the unity and fragility of the planet Earth.
3. **Graphic Organizer**
Sample response:
Comparison/Contrast: comparison of the appearance of Earth from space in 1973 with the view in 1983
Effect: The example emphasizes the changes that have taken place on Earth.
Cause and Effect: the effects of pollution on the Earth's environment
Effect: The example illustrates the various types of damage that have been done to the environment.
4. Sample response: The main idea is that space travel offers an amazing view of the world.

Reading Informational Materials: Technical Documents

p. 161 Graphic Organizer

Sample response:
Narrative text
Information Provided:
basic facts
Diagrams
Information Provided: names and locations of parts as well as an overall view of the shuttle
Lists or statistics
Examples: the *Shuttle Statistics* list

p. 162 Reading Technical Documents

Students should write the following:
1. Length; 2. Height; 3. Wingspan; 4. Weight; 5. Maximum cargo to orbit; 6. SRB separation; 7. External Tank Separation; 8. Orbit.

p. 162 Reading Skill

Sample response: At the end of a mission, the space shuttle weighs 104,326 kilograms (230,000 pounds).

p. 162 Stop to Reflect

Sample response: A technical document might start with history and background to help familiarize readers with the topic.

p. 162 Reading Check

Students may underline "The space shuttle is the world's first reusable spacecraft"; "The shuttle launches like a rocket"; "Each of the three space shuttle orbiters now in operation—Discovery, Atlantis and Endeavour—is designed to fly at least 100 missions."

p. 163 Read Fluently

Students should circle "The space shuttle consists of three major components." Students should underline "the orbiter which houses the crew"; "a large external fuel tank that holds fuel for the main engines"; "and two solid rocket boosters which provide most of the shuttle's lift during the first two minutes of flight."

p. 163 Reading Check

Students should circle "The longest the shuttle has stayed in orbit on any single mission is 17.5 days on mission STS-80 in November 1996."

p. 164 Reading Technical Documents
Sample response: By looking at the diagrams, one can tell that the space shuttle is made up of at least four separate large pieces.

p. 164 Reading Skill
Sample response: NASA has made engine system improvements that have increased the safety of the shuttle.

p. 164 Reading Informational Materials
Sample response: NASA has been doing very well with this goal. Although two shuttles have exploded and resulted in loss of life, most of the people who have traveled in space shuttles have returned safely.

p. 165 Apply the Skills
Thinking About the Technical Document
1. Sample response: The author probably discusses the shuttle's launch record because he or she previously mentioned accidents. The launch record shows that the space shuttle is largely a successful design. The author then mentions design improvements to show the progress being made to improve the shuttle.
2. Sample response: The text and the diagram give the reader different kinds of information about the shuttle parts. The text tells what the functions of the parts are. The diagram shows the reader where the parts are located.

Reading Skill
3. Sample response: *Discovery*, *Atlantis*, and *Endeavour* are now in use.
4. Sample response: The shuttle's wingspan is 23.79 meters (78.06 feet).

"Carry Your Own Skis"
Lian Dolan

"Libraries Face Sad Chapter"
Pete Hamill

p. 166 Graphic Organizer
Sample response:
"Carry Your Own Skis"
Claim: Be responsible for yourself and your stuff or you miss out.
Logical? yes
Evaluation: The author shows how being responsible leads to a fuller life.

"Libraries Face Sad Chapter"
Claim: Reading is not an assignment, it is a pleasure.
Logical? no

Evaluation: The author shows how losing library services would deprive children of access to information found in books.

p. 167 Reading/Writing Connection
Sample response: Activities that involve hardship would frustrate people who expect life to be easy. Some people, however, love the challenge of pushing themselves to extremes. They like to display their courage and their ability to face life's hardships.

p. 167 Note-taking Guide
Sample response:
Those Who Carry Their Own Skis: Are liked by others; Are asked to participate in other activities; Are responsible; Are not afraid to work hard
Those Who Do Not Carry Their Own Skis: Are not always liked by others; Are not always asked to participate in other activities; Are not responsible; Do not like to work hard

p. 168 Activate Prior Knowledge
Students may say that learning to write in cursive was difficult for them. They may say that they are glad now that they learned to do it because it looks nicer when they write.

p. 168 Reading Skill
Sample response: The details show that skiers used gear that did not keep them "dry and warm" and wooden skis that were "heavy" and "bulky." Lodges had no luxuries. The words Dolan uses show that skiing was uncomfortable and tiring.

p. 168 Literary Analysis
Students may point out the details "cold, wet, and tired" and "on our own." These details are so unpleasant that they make skiing seem like something a person would not want to do.

p. 169 Reading Skill
Sample response: Dolan gives examples of girls who did not help out with chores on camping trips.

p. 169 Read Fluently
Students should underline "provide food or do all the cleanup." Students may list CD or DVD as abbreviations they know.

p. 169 Reading Check
Students should circle "Be responsible for yourself and your stuff or you miss out."

p. 170 Literary Analysis

Sample response: Her motive might be to persuade other people to be responsible for themselves or to "carry their own skis." She might also be trying to tell people that those who do not take responsibility make life difficult for others.

p. 170 Reading Skill

Sample response: She shows how being forced to be responsible for her skis, even though she did not like it, taught her that she had to be responsible for other things in life. She would have to be responsible if she wanted to fully enjoy life.

p. 170 Stop to Reflect

Students may say that people who do not take responsibility for themselves annoy them. When others are not responsible, they make more work for responsible people.

p. 171 Apply the Skills

1. Sample response: This lesson guided her in getting a job and then working hard for the company that was providing her paycheck.
2. Some students may agree that taking personal responsibility leads to a fuller life because others are more likely to accept a person who does so. Other students may disagree, saying that avoiding responsibility may affect a person positively because others will do things for that person.
3. **Graphic Organizer**

Sample response:

Passage: Section beginning "The lesson was simple, really. Be responsible for yourself and your stuff or you miss out."

Reason or Emotion: She appeals to reason by explaining in a logical way why it was important to "carry your own skis."
4. Sample response: The author was convincing because she gave specific examples of people who do accept responsibility and people who do not accept responsibility.

p. 173 Reading/Writing Connection

Sample response: My first library visit did reveal that there are books on every topic. Seeing so many books helped me perceive that the world is a very big place. I knew then that I wanted to dedicate my life to reading books.

p. 173 Note-taking Guide

Sample response:

Circle 2: to check out books
Circle 3: to learn about jobs
Circle 5: to study to become a U.S. citizen

p. 174 Apply the Skills

1. Some students may say that they share Hamill's feelings because they had many happy experiences in a library as a child. Other students may not share Hamill's feelings, saying that people can get information by television, online, or by purchasing books.
2. Sample response: He believes that books feed the mind and imagination.
3. **Graphic Organizer**

Sample response:

Passage: paragraph beginning "We passed into that library . . ."; paragraph beginning "We could live in the South Seas . . ."

Reason or Emotion: He appeals to emotion by remembering how important libraries were to him as a child. He appeals to emotion by explaining how he liked to learn about history.
4. Students may say that Hamill's arguments are well reasoned and logical. He gives facts about how important libraries are to immigrants. He explains how the city government may be forced to cut services. He explains the importance of libraries today with the cost of books and the lack of good shows on television.

"I Have a Dream"
Martin Luther King, Jr.

"First Inaugural Address"
Franklin D. Roosevelt

p. 176 Graphic Organizer

Sample response:

"I Have a Dream"

Technique: restatement of "let freedom ring"

Purpose: to energize the audience and make them feel patriotic

Effect: makes listeners believe that there is support for them

"First Inaugural Address"

Technique: repetition of "stricken" in ". . . a stricken nation in the midst of a stricken world . . ."

Purpose: to show that it is not just this country that is having a problem

Effect: People will believe that they are not alone in the world.

p. 177 Reading/Writing Connection

Sample response:

1. When it comes to fairness, Americans embody the meaning of good sportsmanship.
2. Freedom and justice comprise two of the most important American ideals.
3. Most Americans define tolerance as the acceptance of other people and ideas.

p. 177 Note-taking Guide

Sample response:

Whom will it affect? everyone, regardless of race or religion

What will it take? faith in the cause of equality

What will it be like? Inequality will disappear; descendants of slaves and slave owners will be equal; people will be judged by their character, not by their skin color; all people will be truly free.

p. 178 Activate Prior Knowledge

Students may say that the United States celebrates the holiday because King was a great civil rights leader and national figure. Some students will be aware of his role in leading the Montgomery Bus Boycott, the protests in Selma, and the March on Washington. Some may be familiar with his philosophy of nonviolence and the fact that he was assassinated.

p. 178 Reading Skill

Students may say that they feel angry that people have been judged by the color of their skin. They may also say that they feel hopeful for the future because this is something that can be changed.

p. 178 Reading Check

Students should underline "sons of slaves" and "sons of slaveholders."

p. 179 Literary Analysis

Students should underline "Let freedom ring." Sample response: This parallelism emphasizes King's ideas that America is a nation of freedom and should live up to its ideals in every state.

p. 179 Vocabulary and Pronunciation

Students should circle "hilltops."

p. 179 Read Fluently

Sample response: King wants freedom and equality for all Americans. King finishes his speech by saying that all people will be free when the sound of freedom is everywhere.

p. 180 Apply the Skills

1. Sample response: He reminds everyone that the country was founded on a promise of liberty.
2. Sample response: The mention of these places ties in with his message of equality for everyone across the country.
3. **Graphic Organizer**

Sample response:

Example: "let freedom ring"

Effect: This emphasizes the hope that one day everyone will be free.

4. Students may say that King is effective because the rhetorical devices and emotion-charged language emphasize his ideas.

p. 182 Reading/Writing Connection

Sample response: A speaker's true excitement can evoke excitement in those who are listening. When I hear a person project his or her ideas, I think about what the ideas mean to me. Good ideas stimulate me to make changes.

p. 182 Note-taking Guide

Sample response:

Who is giving this speech? Franklin Delano Roosevelt, the thirty-second president of the United States

Why is he giving this speech? It is his first speech as president. All new presidents give a speech at the inauguration, or swearing-in.

In what year is he giving this speech? 1932

What is the greatest problem for the country at this time? Many people are unemployed and do not have any money to make a living.

What is the main promise that is made in the speech? Roosevelt wants to help people find jobs.

p. 183 Apply the Skills

1. Sample response: He sends the message that the people have been misled and cheated.
2. Sample response: His listeners probably felt encouraged.
3. **Graphic Organizer**

Sample response:

Repetition

Example: He repeats that he will perform his "duty."

Effect: The repetition helps give listeners a sense that he will do what they expect of a leader.

Parallelism
Example: "on honesty, on honor, on the sacredness of obligations, on faithful protection, on unselfish performance . . . ."
Effect: This listing of virtues gives readers a sense of momentum, or forward motion.

Analogy
Example: He compares the state of the nation today with its state in other dark times in the country's history, when good leadership and support of the people pulled the country through.
Effect: This analogy helps give listeners a sense that the country will pull through this tough time as it has in the past.

4. Sample response: Roosevelt plays to people's feelings when he says, "We are stricken by no plague of locusts. Compared with the perils which our forefathers conquered because they believed and were not afraid, we have still much to be thankful for."

Reading Informational Materials: Historical Research Study

p. 185 Graphic Organizer
Sample response:
Statement: "Only a foolish optimist can deny the dark realities of the moment."
Provable: no
Fact or Opinion: opinion
Statement: *Defending Your Life* was a 1991 movie written and directed by its star, Albert Brooks.
Provable: yes
Fact or Opinion: fact

p. 186 Reading Historical Research Studies
Sample response: This study begins with a quotation to capture the reader's attention. It reminds the readers that the study is about a speech. It includes the famous line, "The only thing we have to fear is fear itself."

p. 186 Stop to Reflect
Sample response: Axelrod starts the article with a description of a popular movie to catch the reader's attention.

p. 186 Reading Skill
Sample response: This statement is an opinion. It is not something that can be proved.

p. 186 Reading Check
Students should underline "First inaugural address, March 4, 1933."

p. 187 Reading Skill
Students may underline "In 1921 polio threatened first to kill him and then paralyzed him . . . ." Students may circle "He did not blink at the odds."

p. 187 Reading Historical Research Studies
Sample response: President Roosevelt is in a wheelchair and looks like he likes dogs. He also likes reaching out to people.

p. 187 Stop to Reflect
Sample response: Axelrod repeats the words "fog of fear" to tie ideas in the study together.

p. 188 Reading Historical Research Studies
Sample response: Axelrod used this quotation to show that Roosevelt did not lie to the nation. He wants to show how straightforward Roosevelt was and how determined he was to conquer the challenge of the high unemployment rate.

p. 188 Stop to Reflect
Students may say that Americans probably felt inspired by Roosevelt's attitude and as though they were moving toward ending the Depression.

p. 188 Reading Skill
Sample response: This statement is an opinion. It cannot be proved true.

p. 188 Reading Check
Students should underline "Lift the fog of fear and you could see that the Great Depression was not of natural, supernatural, or inevitable origin."

p. 189 Reading Historical Research Studies
Sample response: Axelrod is offering an explanation of the quote above.

p. 189 Reading Check
Students should underline "their efforts have been cast in the pattern of an outworn tradition."

p. 189 Reading Skill
Students should underline the word "always." This word warns that the sentence might be a generalization because it cannot be proved

that Roosevelt "always" navigated between the new and the age-old.

p. 190 Read Fluently
Sample response: I want to buy those sneakers, and yet I do not have enough money.

p. 190 Reading Skill
Students may underline "Happiness lies not in the mere possession of money; it lies in the joy of achievement, in the thrill of creative effort." Sample response: Roosevelt is stating an opinion. No one can prove what causes happiness.

p. 190 Reading Check
Students should underline "The measure of the restoration lies in the extent to which we apply social values more noble than mere monetary profit."

p. 191 Stop to Reflect
Students may point out the microphones for CBS and NBC on the edge of the podium. Roosevelt's words were reaching the people over the radio.

p. 191 Reading Historical Research Studies
Sample response: Axelrod is summarizing Roosevelt's speech and his comments on it.

p. 191 Reading Skill
Sample response: The phrase tells readers that the statement is an opinion. It cannot be proved true.

p. 191 Reading Informational Materials
Sample response: Axelrod did a good job of supporting his thesis with examples. He included many quotations from the speech. He tied those quotations to events in time.

p. 192 Apply the Skills
Thinking About the Historical Research Study
1. Sample response: Axelrod means that people can pay too much attention to their fear. Then, they do not face the problem. Focusing on fear can cause people to think less clearly about possible solutions.
2. Sample response: Axelrod points out how Roosevelt shows his radically new ideas. He connects these new ideas to Roosevelt's plans for the "New Deal." He also points out Roosevelt's age-old and unchanging beliefs with references to the Bible.

Reading Skill
3. Sample response: "Our kind has conquered worse in the past."
4. Sample response: "He began by asking the American people to sweep aside the 'nameless, unreasoning, unjustified terror.'"

"Uncoiling"
Pat Mora

"A Voice"
Pat Mora

p. 195 Note-taking Guide
Sample response:

What is the main image of the poem? a storm; giving a speech in front of people
What details support this image? "roars / and rivers leap," "howling / leaves off trees"; "lights on the stage unrelenting," "the only Mexican in the auditorium," "you wanted to hide from those strange faces"

p. 196 Activate Prior Knowledge
Students may compare a storm to an animal, a machine out of control, or an angry person. They might say that the storm might be cold if it were a machine and hot if it were an angry person.

p. 196 Poetry
Students should underline "scratches," "tosses her dark hair," "snares," "sighs," "spooks," and "spins."

p. 196 Reading Check
Students should circle "lightning," "cholla," "hawks," and "butterfly swarms."

p. 197 Build English Skills
Students should circle "other students."

p. 197 Poetry
Five stanzas are on the page. Each stanza has 4 lines.

p. 197 Vocabulary and Pronunciation
Students should circle "courtroom" and "flatbed."

p. 197 Poetry
Students should underline "You like," "You liked," "You liked," "all the," "all those," "How did I do it?" and "How did I do it."

p. 198 Stop to Reflect
Sample response: Mora means that families like to find similarities in their members, particularly over generations. By doing so, they preserve family characteristics, or blood.

p. 198 Read Fluently
For the stanzas that run from lines 29–36, students should bracket "You, who are never . . . like an ice cube."

p. 198 Reading Check
Students should underline "You, who are never at a loss / for words, felt your breath stick in your throat / like an ice cube. 'I can't,' you whispered. / 'I can't.'"

p. 199 Apply the Skills
1. The speaker is describing a desert storm.
2. Sample response: That day's failure taught Mora's mother that it was important to teach her children to use their voices.
3. Sample response: The storm is wild, powerful, and destructive. The women are frightened and timid but also protective.
4. **Graphic Organizer**
Sample response:
What It Says: The mother's breath sticks in her throat.
What It Means: The mother cannot make herself speak.
Effect: The image conveys a feeling of fright and helplessness.

Poetry Collection 1

Poetry Collection 2

p. 201 Graphic Organizer
Sample response:
Poetry Collection 1
Example: "Does it dry up / like a raisin in the sun?"
Type: simile
Meaning or Effect: The simile stresses that when dreams are pushed away they may lose their power and importance.

Poetry Collection 2
Example: "where mammals and computers / live together in mutually / programming harmony / like pure water / touching clear sky"
Type: simile
Meaning or Effect: The simile stresses how effortlessly the author wants mammals and computers to live together.

p. 202 Reading/Writing Connection
Sample response:
1. Dreams help people achieve their goals.
2. People can benefit from their dreams by taking steps to make them come true.
3. People who believe in dreams can maintain a positive attitude.

p. 202 Note-taking Guide
Sample response:
Dreams: to show that dreams should be followed
I Wandered Lonely as a Cloud: to lovingly recall an inspiring scene of nature
Meciendo: to compare rocking one's son to God's rocking of nature
Sonnet on Love XIII: to compare the poet's love to the idea of an inventor from long ago

p. 203 Activate Prior Knowledge
Sample response: Nature is a source of inspiration because of its beauty. Nature provides imagery to which most people can relate.

p. 203 Reading Check
Students should circle "What happens to a dream deferred?"; "Does it dry up / like a raisin in the sun?"; "Or fester like a sore— / And then run?"; "Does it stink like rotten meat?"; "Or crust and sugar over— / like a syrupy sweet?"; "Or does it explode?"

p. 203 Reading Skill
The first stanza contains one sentence.

p. 203 Literary Analysis
Sample response: One metaphor is "Life is a broken-winged bird / That cannot fly."

p. 204 Literary Analysis
The speaker compares the daffodils to stars in the Milky Way.

p. 204 Reading Skill
The reader should stop reading after "breeze," "dance," and "daffodils."

p. 204 Stop To Reflect
Students may circle "tossing their heads in sprightly dance." Sample response: This figurative language makes the reader think about little dancers tossing their heads around in happiness. The figurative language paints a vivid picture for the reader.

p. 205 Build English Skills
Students should circle "sea" and "wind."

p. 205 Reading Skill
This translation contains seven sentences.

p. 205 Literary Analysis
The wind is "wandering" and "loving," and it "rocks the wheat."

p. 205 Reading Check
Students should underline "I rock my son."

p. 206 Reading Skill
Sample response: Reading in sentences helps readers understand the poem because it keeps related ideas together, which makes the meaning clearer. It also keeps the rhythm natural.

p. 206 Literary Analysis
A paradox appears in the first stanza.

p. 206 Vocabulary and Pronunciation
The poet uses *remark* as a noun that means "a mention of something that deserves notice."

p. 206 Reading Check
Students should underline "'Give me a place to stand,' Archimedes said / 'and I can move the world.'"

p. 207 Read Fluently
Students should underline "from which to move a world out of joint." Sample response: I could tell that something was out of joint when my brother volunteered to clean the living room.

p. 207 Stop to Reflect
Sample response: The author connects his love with Archimedes' discovery because it is a strong and powerful love. Archimedes' lever could move the world, and the author is saying that his love could do the same.

p. 208 Apply the Skills
1. Sample response: Cherish your dreams. Life is meaningless without dreams.
2. Sample response: The sights and sounds fill the speakers with delight and comfort.
3. Sample response: One example is in "I Wandered Lonely as a Cloud": "A host, of golden daffodils . . . Fluttering and dancing in the breeze."
4. **Graphic Organizer**
Sample response:
Stanza: "The wind wandering by night / rocks the wheat. / Hearing the loving wind, / I rock my son."
Paragraph: The wind wandering by night rocks the wheat. Hearing the loving wind, I rock my son.

p. 210 Reading/Writing Connection
Sample response:
1. Computers minimize problems by helping people get organized.
2. E-mail allows us to accelerate communication.

3. Some choose to interact with computers instead of people.

p. 210 Note-taking Guide
Sample response:
"Hope" is the thing with feathers—: the characteristics of hope
Much Madness is divinest Sense—: the nature of sanity
The War Against the Trees: how progress destroys nature

p. 211 Apply the Skills
1. Sample response: The comparison suggests that the speaker feels comfortable and safe with computers.
2. Sample response: The image of war shows that the speaker feels that the trees are victims being unfairly attacked.
3. Sample response: The trees in "The War Against the Trees" are described as "great-grandfathers."
4. **Graphic Organizer**
Sample response:
Stanza: "I saw the ghosts of children at their games / Racing beyond their childhood in the shade, / And while the green world turned its death-foxed page / And a red wagon wheeled, / I watched them disappear / Into the suburbs of their grievous age."
Paragraph: I saw the ghosts of children at their games racing beyond their childhood in the shade, and while the green world turned its death-foxed page and a red wagon wheeled, I watched them disappear into the suburbs of their grievous age.

Reading Informational Materials: Case Studies

p. 213 Graphic Organizer
Sample response:
Details: Matt wants to study computer science and then become a professor; Gil wants to study robotics and explore other areas of robotics.
Generalization: Even people who have similar jobs at one point in their lives can go on to do different things in their futures.

p. 214 Reading Case Studies
Sample response: Readers learn that this case study examines the different paths that can be taken to a career in robotics.

p. 214 Reading Skill
Sample response: Matt, like other boys his age, needs to be motivated by a subject matter to be able to excel in it.

p. 214 Read Fluently
Students should circle "says Matt." Sample response: "I want to go to the movies," she said.

p. 214 Reading Check
Students should circle "Think you'll never use high school math? Think again . . ."

p. 215 Culture Note
Students may name Harvard or a college that is located near them.

p. 215 Reading Case Studies
Sample response: 1. He went to college to study political science; 2. He took an artificial intelligence class; 3. He took part in robotics competitions.

p. 215 Stop to Reflect
Sample response: It was worth it to give up their summers because they gained experience that helped them get jobs.

p. 216 Reading Case Studies
Sample response: Internships can often present opportunities for jobs.

p. 216 Reading Skill
Sample response: One detail that supports this generalization is "Often internships are the first step through the door."

p. 216 Reading Informational Materials
Students may say that this case study made them appreciate math class. Others may say that it had no effect on their feelings about math.

p. 216 Reading Check
Students should underline "variety" and "you usually get to learn something big and new every few weeks."

p. 217 Apply the Skills
Thinking About the Case Study
1. Sample response: Gil started working hard in high school. Matt did not start working hard until college.
2. Sample response: Yes; this case study's advice about pursuing a robotics career applies to other fields as well.

Reading Skill

3. Sample response: Matt took classes in psychology, philosophy, and anthropology.

4. Sample response: Matt did not do well in high school. But when he got to college and found a subject that he was interested in, he began to do well in school.

Poetry Collection 1

Poetry Collection 2

p. 218 Graphic Organizer

Sample response:

Poetry Collection 1: "Summer"
Sight: "old men sleeping"
Hearing: "bugs buzzin"
Smell: "daisies"
Taste: "juices dripping"
Touch: "hot"

Poetry Collection 2: "The Bells"
Sight: "twinkle"
Hearing: "tinkle, tinkle, tinkle"
Smell: none
Taste: "rust within their throats"
Touch: "balmy"

p. 219 Reading/Writing Connection

Sample response:

1. I anticipate summer because I love to go swimming.
2. During the fall, we are blessed with a display of colorful leaves.
3. When spring arrives, I can participate in baseball.

p. 219 Note-taking Guide

Sample response:

Summer
Two events: Bugs fly through the air. Old men sleep.
The Eagle
The Topic of the Poem: a look at an eagle
Two Events: An eagle stands on a mountain.
Analysis of Baseball
The Topic of the Poem: the basics of baseball
Two Events: The ball bounces. The fans cheer.

p. 220 Activate Prior Knowledge

Some students may say that winter is their favorite season because they love skiing. Other students may say that summer is their favorite season because they like swimming.

p. 220 Reading Skill

Sample response: "Summer" appeals to all five senses. "Juices dripping" appeals to the sense of taste. "Old men sleeping" appeals to the sense of sight. "Bugs buzzin" appeals to the sense of sound. "Daisies" appeals to the sense of smell. "Hot" appeals to the sense of touch.

p. 220 Literary Analysis

Students should circle "clasps," "crag," "crooked," "close," "lonely," and "lands."

p. 221 Literary Analysis

Students should circle "about," "bat," "mitt," "hits," "bat," "it," "hits," "mitt," "Bat," "doesn't," "hit," "bat," "meets," "it," bat," "it," "fits," and "mitt."

p. 221 Read Fluently

The stanza contains four sentences.

p. 221 Reading Check

Students should underline "to take bat's / bait."

p. 221 Build English Skills

Sample response: He was trying to trick Noah, but Noah wouldn't take the bait.

p. 222 Literary Analysis

Students should circle "pow."

p. 222 Vocabulary and Pronunciation

Sample response: distrust

p. 222 Reading Skill

The words "40,000 fans" appeal to the sense of sight because there are so many people. "Exploded" appeals to the sense of sound because the crowd sounds like an explosion.

p. 222 Stop to Reflect

Students may say that it is not necessary to know the rules of baseball in order to enjoy the poem. The sound devices and imagery make the poem enjoyable.

p. 223 Apply the Skills

1. Sweat or nectar may be dripping.
2. The eagle is probably watching for something to eat.
3. **Graphic Organizer**
Sample response:
Alliteration
Effect: makes the poem more rhythmic
Consonance
Effect: strengthens the feeling of wetness

Assonance

Example: "Summer": "daisies lay"

Effect: makes the daisies seem relaxed

4. Sample response: Fluent reading helps readers appreciate the musical quality that the sound devices give the poems.

p. 225 Reading/Writing Connection

Sample response: The buzz of my alarm clock is a trigger that gets me up and moving. It makes me appreciate my daily routine. My alarm clock helps me contemplate how valuable time is.

p. 225 Note-taking Guide

Sample response:

The Bells: different bells

Jabberwocky: the Jabberwock

p. 226 Apply the Skills

1. The ball dropping through the net makes the sound described.

2. Students may say that the poem is at least mocking stories of heroism.

3. **Graphic Organizer**

Sample response:

Alliteration

Effect: gives the poem a rhythmic quality

Consonance

Example: Slam, Dunk, & Hook: "but a hot"

Effect: quickens the reading pace

Assonance

Example: Jabberwocky: "left it dead"

Effect: makes this line sound depressing

4. Sample response: Fluent reading helps readers appreciate the musical qualities of the poems.

Poetry Collection 1

Poetry Collection 2

p. 228 Graphic Organizer

Sample response:

Poetry Collection 1

Lines of Poetry: "It looked extremely rocky for the Mudville nine that day; / The score stood two to four, with but an inning left to play."

Details in Lines of Poetry: The team is losing with one inning left to play.

Paraphrase: The Mudville team is losing by two runs. Only one inning remains in the game.

Poetry Collection 2

Lines of Poetry: "Ah, distinctly I remember it was in the bleak December, / And each separate dying ember wrought its ghost upon the floor."

Details in Lines of Poetry: The speaker clearly remembers a December night next to his fire.

Paraphrase: I remember a specific December evening when the fire was casting shadows on the floor.

p. 229 Reading/Writing Connection

Sample response:

1. Some events that evoke happiness are birthdays and graduations.

2. People respond to sad news by trying to stay positive.

3. People can reinforce happiness in others by being a giving person.

p. 229 Note-taking Guide

Sample response:

Casey at the Bat

What Happens Next: Casey gets two strikes.

Final Event: Casey strikes out.

Fifteen

What Happens Next: The boy imagines riding the motorcycle.

What Happens Next: Teenager finds the driver of the bike.

Final Event: The driver rides away.

Twister Hits Houston

Beginning Event: A bad storm is coming.

What Happens Next: The father and mother don't take shelter.

What Happens Next: The tornado rips through the yard.

Final Event: The family survives.

p. 230 Activate Prior Knowledge

Students may say that pressure improved their performance because it sharpened their ability to focus and got their adrenaline flowing. Others may say that they would have performed better without the added pressure.

p. 230 Reading Skill

Sample response: Some people get up to leave the game. But the ones who stayed were hopeful. They thought that if only Casey would get a chance to play, Mudville could still win the game.

p. 230 Reading Check

Students should underline "There was Blakey safe at second and Flynn a-huggin' third."

p. 231 Vocabulary and Pronunciation

Sample response: Students should circle (b). The clues that helped were "pride," "smile on Casey's face," and "responding to the cheers."

p. 231 Reading Skill

Students should underline "eyes were on him," "tongues applauded," and "pitcher ground the ball into his hip."

p. 231 Read Fluently

Sample response: Unheeded, the ball sped close by the sturdy batsman.

p. 232 Build English Skills

Students should underline "flew" and "two." Sample response: "Blue" rhymes with "flew" and "two."

p. 232 Literary Analysis

Sample response: The mood goes from optimistic to determined and tense. Casey is getting serious and wants to make sure that he gets the hit.

p. 232 Reading Check

Students should circle "And it's likely they'd have killed him had not Casey raised his hand" and "He stilled the rising tumult."

p. 233 Reading Skill

Sample response: Somewhere in the world everyone is happy. However, everyone in Mudville is sad because Casey struck out.

p. 233 Stop to Reflect

Sample response: Casey shows that he is a confident player when he lets the first two balls go by without swinging at them. Also, he calms the crowd and doesn't seem upset at the umpire for calling strikes.

p. 234 Build English Skills

Students should circle "lay," "led," and "was."

p. 234 Reading Skill

Sample response: The speaker means that he could ride the bike toward the horizon.

p. 234 Literary Analysis

The characters are the speaker and the owner of the motorcycle.

p. 234 Reading Check

Students should underline "South of the bridge on Seventeenth / I found back of the willows one summer / day a motorcycle with engine running."

p. 235 Literary Analysis

The poem takes place in a house in Houston. A tornado hits the house. The speaker is the son or daughter of the parents caught in the tornado.

p. 235 Reading Skill

Sample response: The tornado banged against the door like an angry cat.

p. 235 Reading Check

Students should underline "Papa was on the front porch. / Mama was in the kitchen."

p. 236 Apply the Skills

1. Sample response: He may have been overly confident. He let two pitches go by without swinging. He believes that he can get a hit when he wants.

2. Sample response: No, his behavior is not appropriate. A tornado is very dangerous. One would not sit calmly on the porch and watch it. One would take cover.

3. **Graphic Organizer**
Sample response:

Casey at the Bat
Plot: The ballgame is in the ninth inning. The opposing team is winning by two runs. Casey comes to bat. He strikes out.

Fifteen
Setting: the side of a road
Characters: a fifteen-year-old boy, a motorcycle rider
Plot: A fifteen-year-old boy finds an overturned motorcycle on the roadside. He pushes it back on the road. He imagines what it would be like to ride away on it. Instead, he helps the owner get back to his cycle.

Twister Hits Houston
Setting: a family home in Houston
Characters: Mama, Papa, the speaker
Plot: A speaker is retelling the story of a tornado that strikes the speaker's home. Papa sits on the front porch. Mama is in the kitchen. The storm uproots a big tree. It also drops a car in the yard and bangs the screen door.

4. Sample response: The baseball came flying, but Casey ignored it. He said that it wasn't his style. The umpire called strike one.

p. 238 Reading/Writing Connection

Sample response: Things in my life that evoke happy feelings include my family and friends. I respond to these feelings by spending more time with these people. When I am in a bad mood, I react by not talking.

p. 238 Note-taking Guide

Sample response:

The Horses
Event: The horses come.
Effect: The people are filled with hope.
The Writer
Event: The speaker hears his daughter typing.
Effect: The father stops in the hallway and thinks about his daughter and her life.

p. 239 Apply the Skills

1. Students might describe the speaker's state of mind as horrified or despairing.
2. Sample response: The sounds of his daughter's typing, trying to set her imagination free, remind him of the starling trying to gain its freedom.
3. **Graphic Organizer**
Sample response:
The Raven
Characters: the speaker and the raven
Plot: The speaker misses his lost love, Lenore. He grows more and more upset by a visiting raven. He asks the raven questions. The raven always answers "Nevermore."
The Horses
Characters: people living in the world and horses
Plot: After a war nearly destroys the world, a community abandons its tractors. The people farm with oxen and plows. Then, one day a herd of horses appears and gives the people hope of a new world.
The Writer
Characters: a girl, her father, a bird
Plot: A speaker is listening to his daughter struggle to type a story. He is reminded of when a starling was trapped in her room, struggling to find freedom through an open window.
4. Sample response: One gloomy night, while I tiredly pored over some old books . . .

Reading Informational Materials: Web Sites

p. 244 Apply the Skills
Thinking About the Web Site
1. The link "Nature's Most Violent Storms" provides information about measures schools can take to ensure the safety of students and teachers. The "You are in school" link on the "Weather Safety for Kids" page may also provide safety measures for schools.
2. Category F5 tornadoes have wind speeds greater than 260 mph and cause tremendous damage, such as houses lifted from their foundation and objects as large as cars thrown over 100 meters.

Reading Skill
3. The link "Storm Reports" has information on current storms.
4. It is a government-sponsored weather Web site.

Poetry Collection 1
Poetry Collection 2

p. 246 Graphic Organizer
Sample response:
Poetry Collection 1
Original Lines: "Two roads diverged in a yellow wood, / And sorry I could not travel both / And be one traveler, long I stood / And looked down one as far as I could / To where it bent in the undergrowth;"
Lines in Smaller Sentences: Two roads diverged in a yellow wood. I was sorry that I could not travel both. I was one traveler. I stood a long time. I looked down one as far as I could. I looked to where it bent in the undergrowth.
Paraphrase: There were two roads in the woods. I could not go down both roads. I stood and looked down one of the roads. I looked to where it curved into the bushes.

Poetry Collection 2
Original Lines: "But if I had to perish twice, / I think I know enough of hate / To say that for destruction ice / Is also great / And would suffice."
Lines in Smaller Sentences: But if I had to perish twice, I think I know enough of hate. For destruction ice is also great. It would suffice.

Paraphrase: If I had to die again, I know that hatred can be just as destructive.

p. 247 Reading/Writing Connection
Sample response:
1. People who challenge themselves can achieve great things.
2. Some people refuse to conform because they want to be different.
3. People like to distinguish themselves from those around them.

p. 247 Note-taking Guide
Sample response:
We never know how high we are: rising above fears to achieve wonderful things
Macavity: The Mystery Cat: a cat named Macavity who lives a life of crime

p. 248 Activate Prior Knowledge
Students may say that they like images the most in their favorite poems because they like vivid description. Other students may say that they like poems about subjects they are interested in.

p. 248 Literary Analysis
Students may underline "rise" and "skies."

p. 248 Reading Check
Students should circle "For fear to be a King—."

p. 249 Reading Skill
Sample response: The speaker takes the other path because it is just as pleasant and a little less worn.

p. 249 Literary Analysis
The rhyme scheme is *abaab.*

p. 249 Read Fluently
Students may circle "sigh," "ages and ages," "less traveled by," and "difference." Sample response: These words are the most important because they show the speaker's main idea.

p. 250 Build English Skills
Students should write (a) is not; (b) he will; (c) let us.

p. 250 Literary Analysis
Students should underline "Paw" and "Law" or "despair" and "there."

p. 250 Reading Check
Students should underline "He's broken every human law, he breaks the law of gravity / His powers of levitation would make a fakir stare."

p. 251 Reading Skill
Sample response: Macavity is unlike any other cat. He's a monster who happens to look like a cat. You might see him on the street. However, he is never at a crime scene.

p. 251 Literary Analysis
"Glass" and "past" are an example of both slant and internal rhyme. They both end with an "s" sound, and they are in the middle of the line instead of at the end of the line.

p. 251 Vocabulary and Pronunciation
Sample response: Another word that means the same as *larder* is *cupboard.*

p. 251 Reading Check
Students should circle "ginger," "tall," "thin," "sunken," "lined," "domed," "dusty," and "uncombed."

p. 252 Reading Skill
Sample response: Breaking down long sentences makes the text easier to read and gives the reader a better understanding of the subject matter.

p. 252 Stop to Reflect
Some students may say that their favorite animal is a dog. They may imagine a dog getting into an adventure near a lake because many dogs like to swim.

p. 252 Reading Check
Students should underline "Napoleon of Crime."

p. 253 Apply the Skills
1. **Graphic Organizer**
Sample response:
What Does It Mean? This choice might represent a choice of colleges to attend or a career to follow.
2. Sample response: Cats are mischievous and curious. They get into things, and they can move silently and quickly disappear.
3. Sample response: "We never know how high we are" has a more regular meter. Every other line has the same meter.
4. Sample response: Two roads diverged in a yellow wood. I was sorry I could not travel both and be one traveler. Long I stood and looked down one as far as I could. I saw where it bent in the undergrowth.

p. 255 Reading/Writing Connection

Sample response:

1. Childhood experiences help an individual acquire qualities such as patience.

2. As children grow older, they may alter their views and opinions.

3. Young adulthood is a time when most people cease to depend upon their parents.

p. 255 Note-taking Guide

Sample response:

Maggie and Milly and Molly and May: to describe the characters' self-discovery

The Seven Ages of Man: to describe a person's journey through life

p. 256 Apply the Skills

1. **Graphic Organizer**

Sample response:

What Does It Mean? Fire works as a metaphor for desire because desire "burns." Ice is fitting for hate because hate is a "cold" emotion.

2. Sample response: Each character is drawn to something that reflects her inner likes or fears.

3. Sample response: The words "severe" and "beard" show both slant rhyme and internal rhyme.

4. Sample response: Maggie found a shell that sang so sweetly she couldn't remember her troubles. Milly befriended a stranded star. Its rays were five languid fingers.

ANSWERS TO UNIT 5

from The Shakespeare Stealer
Gary Blackwood

p. 260 Note-taking Guide
Sample response:
Box 1: Dr. Bright discovers that Widge was caught stealing a sermon.
Box 2: Falconer buys Widge from Dr. Bright and takes him to Bass's house.

p. 261 Activate Prior Knowledge
Some students may not think copying music is a crime because music is available on the radio. Other students may give examples of when stealing seems acceptable—such as when a father steals diapers for a baby or a mother steals food to feed her children. Other students may say that in the past, perhaps there were reasons to steal. However, today, there is no reason to steal.

p. 261 Drama
Students should circle "Among these are the apothecary, or drug store, in the first scene. It also will represent Widge's living space and Simon Bass's home."

p. 261 Read Fluently
Students should circle "a florid, overweight man in his forties or fifties." Sample response: The details are important because they describe Dr. Bright.

p. 262 Drama
Sample response: The stage directions help the actor playing Widge know what actions to take in reaction to Dr. Bright's angry comments. The stage directions help readers of the play imagine what is happening on stage.

p. 262 Read Fluently
Sample response: The dots suggest a pause during which an upset and frustrated Dr. Bright is trying to think of names to call Widge. The dashes suggest that Widge is stuttering because he is so upset.

p. 262 Drama
Sample response: The dialogue shows the conflict between the two characters and how the characters feel about each other. Students may underline "clod-pated drivel," "simpleton," and "Have you let a hint drop to anyone of what you were up to?"

p. 263 Drama
Sample response: Widge is an orphan. Dr. Bright took him in and educated him. Widge is unhappy working for Dr. Bright.

p. 263 Vocabulary and Pronunciation
Students should circle "orphan."

p. 263 Drama
Sample response: Widge makes these comments to the audience so that Dr. Bright does not hear. The comments are probably funny to the audience but they would make Dr. Bright angrier.

p. 263 Reading Check
Students should circle "It is a book on charactery, or swift writing."

p. 264 Drama
Sample response: Falconer is interested in Widge's skills. He wants to use them for his own purposes.

p. 264 Drama
Students might suggest dimming the lights, raising and lowering the curtain, having some of the action go on in front of the lowered curtain, or using a revolving set.

p. 264 Drama
Sample response: It is possible that Falconer and Bass are the same person. Bass may pretend to be Falconer so that he can conduct business in secret.

p. 265 Drama
Sample response: Bass has an interest in theater and is not concerned about the possible issues involved with taking ideas from other people.

p. 265 Build English Skills
Students should circle "Noun."

p. 265 Reading Check
Students should underline "Widge says he has only seen plays at church, and they were not worth 'stealing.'"

p. 265 Drama
Sample response: Bass tells Widge that it is business. They are borrowing the work completely to make sure that it is something that the original author can be proud of.

p. 266 Stop to Reflect

Sample response: Dr. Bright used the copied sermons because he was too lazy to write his own. Bass admits that his reason is to make money.

p. 266 Drama

Sample response: Widge will copy the play and run into difficulty. Perhaps he will be caught by Shakespeare himself. Falconer will be there to protect him. Widge may learn about the negative consequence of swift writing.

p. 267 Apply the Skills

1. Sample response: Widge has an excellent memory and excellent skills. He was able to recall the sermon. He was able to produce a version good enough that Dr. Bright did not know about the incident until he received a letter from the bishop.

2. Sample response: Falconer does not trust Dr. Bright. He wants to see for himself whether the system works and whether Widge can do the job.

3. Sample response: Dr. Bright uses words such as "clod-pated drivel," and "halfwitted hoddypeak."

4. **Graphic Organizer**

Sample response:

Prop: Dr. Bright uses a walking stick.

How It Is Used: He uses it to scare Widge.

What It Shows: Dr. Bright likes to control others, but he yells more often than he hits with his stick.

Prop: Widge uses a notebook and pencil.

How It Is Used: He uses these to carry out tasks assigned by Dr. Bright, Falconer, and Samuel Bass.

What It Shows: These props represent his skill and his confidence in himself.

The Tragedy of Romeo and Juliet, Act I
William Shakespeare

p. 269 Graphic Organizer

Sample response:

Scene: one

Summary of Action: A fight breaks out between servants and relatives of the two families. The prince breaks up the fight. Benvolio finds out that Romeo is sad about a lost love.

p. 270 Reading/Writing Connection

Sample response:

1. Sad events inspire artists to <u>illustrate</u> people's tragic flaws.

2. To <u>contrast</u> perfection and reality, writers give readers detailed descriptions.

3. Composers can <u>emphasize</u> the pain of lost love by making their music sound dreary.

p. 270 Note-taking Guide

Sample response:

Box 2: Romeo and Benvolio attend the Capulets' feast.

Box 3: Romeo and Juliet meet and fall in love.

Final Outcome: Romeo and Juliet discover that their families are enemies.

p. 271 Apply the Skills

1. Sample response: Romeo is moody and romantic. Juliet is an obedient girl. Before meeting Romeo, she has not given much thought to love. They both fall in love easily.

2. Some students may say that Romeo's passion for Rosaline shows the deep feelings teenagers can have. Other students may say the fact that he forgets about Rosaline after meeting Juliet shows that teens' feelings can change quickly. Other students may say that Romeo is too violent in his passions and does not accurately portray teenagers in love.

3. **Graphic Organizer**

Sample response:

Character: Juliet

Dialogue: lines 97–99

Reveals: Juliet is an obedient daughter.

Character: Lady Capulet

Dialogue: lines 69–74

Reveals: Lady Capulet believes Juliet is not too young to marry.

4. Sample response: "Leave him alone. Who's in charge here, me or you? If you don't leave him alone, my guests will riot. But you want to act macho. Someday that's going to hurt you. Now, settle down!"

The Tragedy of Romeo and Juliet, Act II, Scene ii
William Shakespeare

p. 273 Graphic Organizer

Sample response:

Character: Juliet

Character's Speech: Formal

Character's Actions: Juliet wants to protect Romeo from her family.
Character's Rank: Important; Aristocrat

p. 274 Note-taking Guide
Sample response:
Effect/Cause: Romeo promises to send word about his plans to marry Juliet.
Effect/Cause: Romeo goes to ask the Friar for help.

p. 275 Activate Prior Knowledge
Students may say that they know that Romeo and Juliet are young lovers. Some may know their tragic end.

p. 275 Literary Analysis
Students should circle "thou," "maid," "far," "fair," and "she."

p. 275 Reading Skill
Students should circle "Deny" and "Capulet."

p. 275 Reading Check
Students should underline "In Act II, Scene ii, Romeo stands in the orchard outside Juliet's home. She appears at her balcony window above him."

p. 276 Build English Skills
Sample response: I take you at your word.

p. 276 Literary Analysis
Sample response: The stressed syllables draw attention to the words "I," "written," "I," "tear," and "word." These words strengthen Romeo's message that he hates his name.

p. 276 Reading Skill
Sample response: Romeo swears his love by the moon, but Juliet thinks that the changing moon is not a good choice. She suggests that he swear by his own self.

p. 276 Reading Check
Students should circle "My name, dear saint, is hateful to myself / Because it is an enemy to thee."

p. 277 Literary Analysis
Students should underline "words," "Rom-," "and "night," "-deed," "that," "bent," "love," "hon-," "-able," "pur-," "marr-," "send," "word," "-mor-," "one," "I'll," "-cure," "come," "thee," "and," "time," "wilt," "-form," "rite," "all," "for-," "at," "foot," "lay," "fol-," "thee," "lord," "-out," and "world."

p. 277 Read Fluently
Students should circle "Where and what time thou wilt perform the rite."

p. 277 Culture Note
Sample response: Shakespeare's culture probably had beliefs that women were not equal with men. A woman might have been expected to go everywhere with her husband and do what he told her to do.

p. 277 Reading Skill
Sample Response: It is almost daytime. I want you to leave. But I do not want to let you go. I am like a child that has a string tied to a bird. I let you go a little and then pull you back.

p. 278 Literary Analysis
Sample response: The splitting of the syllables between two characters shows that they are connected. This suggests that Romeo and Juliet are in a close relationship.

p. 278 Vocabulary and Pronunciation
Students should draw lines connecting evening—eve; beneath—neath; morning—morn.

p. 278 Reading Check
Students should circle "Then he leaves to tell his priest about Juliet. He plans to ask the priest for help."

p. 279 Apply the Skills
1. Sample response: The darkness hides Romeo from Juliet's relatives. It makes the lovers feel as if they are alone and can reveal their true feelings.
2. Sample response: Students may say that the romantic words and images, the vivid descriptions, and the expressions of devotion make the audience share the characters' emotions.
3. **Graphic Organizer**
Sample response:
Blank Verse Pattern: Stressed syllables are "words," "Rom-," "and," "night," "-deed." Unstressed syllables are "Three," "dear," "-eo," "good," and "in-".
Key Words: words, Romeo, night
Why are the stressed words important ones? They emphasize Juliet's request.
4. Students should say that there are 4 sentences.

The Tragedy of Romeo and Juliet, Act III
William Shakespeare

p. 281 Graphic Organizer
Sample response:
Allusion: "Gallop apace, you fiery-footed steeds, / Towards Phoebus' lodging!"
Refers to: the horses that pulled the sun chariot of the god of the sun, Phoebus
Purpose: refers to the sun moving more quickly across the sky; time moving more quickly

p. 282 Note-taking Guide
Sample response:
Effect/Cause: Romeo kills Tybalt.
Effect: Romeo is not allowed to come back to Verona.

p. 283 Apply the Skills
1. **Graphic Organizer**
Sample response:
What Does It Mean? Mercutio means the statement as a curse. He blames both sides for the fight.
2. Sample response: Romeo means that he is a victim of fate.
3. Sample response: Juliet is impatient for the night to arrive so she can be with Romeo.
4. Sample response: Banishment is torture, not mercy. Heaven is where Juliet lives. While every little creature may look upon Juliet, I cannot. I must go. Even flies have it better than I. They can hear Juliet speak. But I cannot hear Juliet's voice because I am banished. You say that exile is not death, but it is. The damned howl the word *banished* in hell. How can you torture me with the word *banished*?

The Tragedy of Romeo and Juliet, Act IV
William Shakespeare

p. 285 Graphic Organizer
Sample response:
Line of Dialogue: "I met the youthful lord at Lawrence' cell / And gave him what becomèd love I might, / Not stepping o'er the bounds of modesty."
Lines in Smaller Sentences: "I met the youthful lord at Lawrence' cell. I gave him what becomèd love I might. I did not step o'er the bounds of modesty."

Summary of Line: Juliet is telling her father that she met Paris and showed him appropriate affection.

p. 286 Note-taking Guide
Sample response:
What character does: Juliet takes a potion to escape marriage to Paris.
What character thinks: Juliet is sad because Romeo is gone and because she is being forced to marry Paris.
What others say about character: "A peevish self-willed harlotry it is." "How now, my headstrong?"

p. 287 Apply the Skills
1. Some students may find the advice risky and tricky and say that Romeo and Juliet should have admitted their marriage. Other students may say that, at the time, the plan seemed to be the only option.
2. Sample response: The soliloquy reveals that Juliet is fully aware of the great risks she is taking. However, she is still willing to take them.
3. **Graphic Organizer**
Sample response:
What Character Thinks: Capulet thinks Juliet is in her bed asleep.
What Audience Knows: The audience knows that Juliet is in a comatose state and cannot be awakened.
4. Sample response: Juliet tells Friar Lawrence that she will kill herself if he cannot help her. He must tell her something immediately or she will die.

The Tragedy of Romeo and Juliet, Act V
William Shakespeare

p. 289 Graphic Organizer
Sample response:
Cause: Friar John is unable to deliver the message to Romeo.
Effect/Cause: Romeo believes that Juliet is truly dead.
Effect: Romeo wants to kill himself.

p. 290 Note-taking Guide
Sample response:
Event 1: Romeo buys poison.
Event 2: Romeo goes to Juliet's grave in Verona.
Event 3: Romeo kills Paris.

Event 4: Romeo poisons himself.
Event 5: Juliet wakes to see Romeo.
Event 6: Juliet stabs herself.
Final Event: The Montagues and Capulets agree to stop fighting.

p. 291 Apply the Skills

1. Students may be surprised that Romeo kills Paris because it seems so sudden. Some students may be surprised that Lady Montague dies of grief because Romeo was not dead, he was only banished.
2. Some students will say it is not a fair exchange. The lovers might have stopped the fighting through their marriage. Others may say that two lives may save many more in the future.
3. **Graphic Organizer**
Sample response:
Fate or Chance: the accidental meeting of the two lovers; Tybalt's misunderstanding of Romeo's presence at the Capulets; the Friar's plan goes wrong
Other Causes: the feud between the Montagues and the Capulets
4. Sample response: Romeo hurries to Juliet's tomb and meets and kills Paris. Romeo kills himself because he believes Juliet is dead. Juliet awakens to find Romeo dead. She stabs herself. Families, servants, lawmen, and the Prince gather at the tomb. The Friar explains everything. The Prince, Capulet, and Montague meet at the tomb and the two families end their feud.

Reading Informational Materials: Atlases

p. 296 Apply the Skills
Thinking about the Atlas

1. Sample response: Palermo is the largest city in Sicily. No other city in Sicily uses a symbol that shows greater population.
2. Sample response: Sixteen percent of Italy's exports travel by sea.

Reading Skill

1. Students may list Rome, Florence, Venice, or Padova.
2. Sample response: Illegal immigration became a major issue in the 1993 election.

The Inspector-General
Anton Chekhov
Adapted by Michael Frayn

p. 297 Graphic Organizer
Sample response:
Information Provided: Traveler wants to talk about himself.
Conclusion: He thinks he is an important man.

p. 298 Reading/Writing Connection
Sample response: It can be difficult to interpret what others say. The person cannot respond because the person's identity is secret. If he or she chooses to ignore the conversation, he or she might miss something.

p. 298 Note-taking Guide
Sample response:
What character says: "Wheezes? That's not wheezing! That's the way he talks!" "He's never touched a drop!"
What character does: tries to sneak up on the towns; drinks vodka; wheezes when he talks; orders the driver to turn around when he realizes the town knows he is coming
What others say about the character: "We know everything about all of them up there!" The driver calls the new inspector-general good compared to the last one. The driver says the new inspector-general creeps into town trying to be sneaky. "He drinks, mind!" "Oh, like a hole in the ground. Famous for it." The driver says the new inspector-general hides his drinking. The driver explains that the people are more afraid of the inspector-general's housekeeper than of the inspector-general.

p. 299 Activate Prior Knowledge
Students may suggest feelings of anger or resentment. If they are doing what they should be doing, they might resent someone's distrusting them.

p. 299 Literary Analysis
Sample response: The inspector-general tries to take a town by surprise by hiding his identity. This is humorous because the town already knows who he is.

p. 299 Reading Skill
Students may underline "new inspector makes his visits very quietly" and "He travels in disguise." Sample response: The driver knows the traveler is the inspector-general.

p. 300 Reading Skill

Students may underline: "new inspector makes his visits very quietly" and "He travels in disguise." The driver knows the traveler is the inspector-general.

p. 300 Build English Skills

Sample response: I never touched a drop of her soda.

p. 300 Reading Check

Students should underline "The driver tells the traveler that the people tell many funny stories about the inspector-general."

p. 301 Reading Skill

Students should underline "The traveler discreetly pushes the traveling bag out of the driver's sight." Sample response: The traveler does not want the driver to see his traveling bag. It probably holds a bottle of vodka.

p. 301 Read Fluently

Students should underline "The driver says," "The driver says," and "the driver explains."

p. 301 Literary Analysis

Sample response: The traveler is trying to hide who he really is. The driver is pretending not to know that the traveler is the inspector-general.

p. 302 Vocabulary and Pronunciation

Sample response: He turns the cart around, and the traveler takes a long drink from his traveling bag.

p. 302 Reading Skill

Sample response: The inspector-general knows that his disguise has not fooled anyone.

p. 302 Culture Note

Sample response: This play would be fun to for students to perform because the speaking lines are simple, the story is funny, and the person who plays the inspector gets to be in "costume."

p. 303 Apply the Skills

1. Sample response: His identity is known and the people already know that he is coming. He is embarrassed to realize that he is not so clever after all.

2. **Graphic Organizer**
Sample response:
Questions: Who sent the anonymous letter?

Details: People in town seem to know that he is coming. Perhaps someone from the town sent the letter.
Understanding of the Play: Students' understanding may change because they understand why someone would want to contact the inspector-general.
Questions: Will the inspector-general ever visit the town again?
Details: The driver and everyone else in the town seem to know who he is and how he operates. The traveler turns around when he realizes that all the people know he is coming.
Understanding of the Play: Students' understanding may change because they understand why the driver might want to convince the inspector-general that he is expected.
Questions: Why does the driver not tell the traveler immediately that he knows who the traveler is?
Details: The traveler thinks he is being sneaky. The driver appears to enjoy the joke.
Understanding of the Play: Students' understanding may change because they realize that the driver could not have affected the traveler so strongly if the driver had been honest.

3. Sample response: The play ends happily because it's humorous the only harm done is to the inspector-general's pride. The driver's dialogue is witty when he insults the inspector-general to his face and the inspector-general is forced to sit quietly because the inspector-general wants to protect his identity. The situation is comic because the inspector-general tries to sneak into the town but everyone knows who he is.

4. Sample response: The driver is clever and has a sense of humor. He outsmarts the traveler and he is happy without letting the traveler know that he has been discovered.

Reading Informational Materials: Book Review

p. 305 Graphic Organizer

Sample response:
Intent or reasons for writing: to discuss the new translation of Chekov's plays
Bias toward the subject: The writer likes the plays of Chekov. The writer also thinks that

many of the translations are unreadable by Americans.

Thorough support for opinions: He uses excerpts from the other translations and the new translation to support his opinion that the new translation makes Chekov more accessible for American audiences.

p. 306 Reading Book Reviews
Sample response: He gives background and identifies a controversy.

p. 306 Read Fluently
Students should circle "Tolstoy voiced a common feeling. . . ."

p. 306 Reading Check
Students should circle "Uncle Vanya" and "Three Sisters."

p. 307 Reading Skill
Student may underline "But Chekhov's emphasis on tone and mood, and his faithful re-creation of ordinary conversation with all its hesitations, references, and silences. . . ."

p. 307 Stop to Reflect
Sample response: Including quotes is a good way to support his opinion that Schmidt's translation makes sense.

p. 307 Reading Book Reviews
Students may underline "The result is a surprisingly lively Chekov, colloquial and clear, which will come as a revelation to those who know the playwright through the widely read but rather stiff British translations of Constance Garnett and Elisaveta Fen." "The plays that emerge are funnier and more muscular than one might have expected."

p. 308 Stop to Reflect
Sample response: Yes, it is easier to understand. Americans would never say, "Who was it talking here just now?" But, Americans would say, "What's going on out there?"

p. 308 Reading Book Reviews
Sample response: Kirsch thinks it is a great translation. Americans should use this translation instead of older ones.

p. 308 Reading Informational Materials
Sample response: Chekhov's plays were first written in Russian. Chekhov's plays have been translated into British English.

p. 309 Apply the Skills
Thinking About the Book Review
1. Sample response: He thinks the starchy British English sounds awkward to Americans.
2. Sample response: The first translation does not sound like a typical American conversation. The second translation sounds more like an American conversation.

Reading Skill
3. Sample response: Kirsch's main purpose is to express an opinion about Schmidt's translation.
4. Some students may say that they believe Kirsch because he uses quotations from Schmidt, Tolstoy, and Chekov. Other students may that Kirsch's knowledge of Chekov and his works adds to his credibility.

**Play Hard; Play Together;
Play Smart**

from **the Carolina Way
Dean Smith with John Kilgo**

p. 312 Note-taking Guide
Sample response:
Attitude Toward Winning: making winning the main goal of a sport is a poor way to teach; many things happen that cannot be controlled, such as injuries or bad calls
How They Measure Success: by the things that players can control; whether players had fun and worked together
Play Hard: playing with the greatest effort, including practices
Play Together: game that counts on togetherness, playing unselfishly and sharing the ball
Play Smart: practicing the basics until they become automatic

p. 313 Activate Prior Knowledge
Students may say that playing a sport taught them that hard work and dedication could help them accomplish their goals in life.

p. 313 Themes in Literature
Students may say that Coach Smith's philosophy did surprise them because they think that winning would be the number one goal. Students may say that his philosophy stresses the strength of loyalty and the importance of heroism. Each player must be dedicated to the team by acting intelligently, unselfishly, and with courage. Each player must also act in the best interest of the team and show effort on the court.

p. 313 Reading Check
Students should underline "Hard meant with effort, determination, and courage."

p. 313 Culture Note
Students may list sports such as soccer, hockey, and basketball.

p. 314 Read Fluently
Students should circle "that" and "was." Sample response: That was out of his control in the course of any given game.

p. 314 Themes in Literature
Some students may react by saying that every player must do whatever it takes to help his teammates succeed. Other students may not like the idea of punishing the whole team because one person does not do what he or she is supposed to do.

p. 314 Stop to Reflect
Students may point out that all of his principles could apply to most things in life. Doing your best, working together, and behaving as though every task were the most important one would probably ensure success at most tasks.

p. 315 Build English Skills
Students should circle "unselfishly."

p. 315 Stop to Reflect
Students may suggest that developing good work habits is important in school or at a job.

p. 315 Reading Check
Students should underline "Smith worked on helping his players form good habits."

p. 315 Vocabulary and Pronunciation
Students should write *au to mat ic.*

p. 316 Apply the Skills
1. Sample response: If each player plays hard, plays smart, and plays together, they as a team should be able to deal with the unexpected. If they cannot deal with it effectively, then at least they have given it their best shot.
2. Sample response: Coach Smith probably feels that his career was successful because he was both a teacher and a coach. He believes that the two should be one and the same.
3. **Graphic Organizer**
Sample response:
Value: Play hard. Play together. Play smart.
Examples: Give your best effort, including in practice. Admit to being tired, and take a break. / Put the team before yourself, and do everything possible not to let them down. Do not be selfish. Trust your teammates. / Learn the basics, and practice them until they become automatic.
Application: Be the best you can be. Do not be ashamed to ask for help if you need it. / Workers in a company should put the company before themselves. With everyone working toward the same goal, everyone will benefit. / Treat each task you attempt as

important and essential. Use every resource you have to accomplish your goals.

4. Students will probably agree that sports are an important part of the cultural context of the United States. They may explain that team playing and working hard are a part of the American work ethic.

from The Odyssey, Part 1, The Cyclops
Homer

p. 318 Graphic Organizer
Sample response:
Historical/Cultural Detail: "We lit a fire, burnt an offering, / and took some cheese to eat . . ."
Background: Odysseus and his men offer a prayer of thanks to the gods and give a portion of their meal to the gods out of respect.
Analysis: Religion played an important role in ancient Greek culture. The gods appear in the *Odyssey*, often helping Odysseus or playing a part in his suffering. Ancient Greek beliefs and customs are reflected in Odysseus' offering.

p. 319 Reading/Writing Connection
Sample response: The journey involved an encounter with the local people. I had to interact with a new culture. The highlight of this experience was learning a new language.

p. 319 Note-taking Guide
Sample response:
Event 1: Odysseus and his men arrive at the land of the Cyclopes.
Event 2: Odysseus and his men are trapped in Polyphemus' cave.
Event 3: Odysseus finds an enormous club and turns it into a spike.
Event 4: Odysseus and his men blind Polyphemus with the spike.
Event 5: Odysseus hides his men under the Cyclops's sheep, and they escape.

p. 320 Activate Prior Knowledge
Students may say that an adventure story needs a hero whom readers can admire and villains against whom the hero must struggle.

p. 320 Reading Skill
Sample response: The Greeks valued a civilized society. They valued their laws and farming their land.

p. 320 Reading Check
Students should circle "the island of the Cyclopes."

p. 320 Vocabulary and Pronunciation
It means "wise."

p. 321 Stop to Reflect
Sample response: It was a bad decision for the men to stay in the cave. They were not invited, and they had no idea how the Cyclops would react to their presence.

p. 321 Literary Analysis
The Cyclops seals the opening of the cave with a huge rock. The men are now trapped and are at the mercy of the Cyclops.

p. 321 Reading Check
Students should circle "beat their brains out."

p. 322 Read Fluently
Students should circle "Eyelid and lash were seared; the pierced ball / hissed broiling, and the roots popped." Both parts describe what happens to the eye.

p. 322 Reading Skill
Sample response: This passage shows that the Greeks believed that the gods did what they wanted to do. A god had to correct what another god had done.

p. 322 Reading Check
Students should underline "Odysseus heats up the pole in the fire. He and his men jam the sharp end into the Cyclops' eye."

p. 323 Literary Analysis
Sample response: Odysseus is proud of how clever he is. He does not always act wisely.

p. 323 Reading Check
Students should underline "He ties the Cyclops' sheep together in groups of three. Then he ties his men to the bellies of the sheep."

p. 323 Literary Analysis
In the bracketed passage, Odysseus is taunting the giant. Students may say that Odysseus is allowing his anger to get the best of him. He is also acting boastfully in victory.

p. 324 Reading Skill
The ancient Greeks believed that the gods could be called to act on events in the mortal world. They might act for or against the people that call on them.

p. 324 Literary Analysis
The flashback allows the reader a more complete picture of Odysseus because all of his life experiences influence the stories he recounts.

p. 324 Build English Skills
blow—blew; fly—flew; grow—grew

p. 324 Reading Check
Students should circle "I slew him / by the seaside and burnt his long thighbones / to Zeus."

p. 325 Apply the Skills
1. Some students will say that they would like to have Odysseus as a leader because he is brave, clever, and resourceful. Others will say that they would not like to have him as a leader because he is boastful and lets his anger get the best of him. His mistakes often put his men in danger.

2. Students may say that the story is popular because of its adventures and remarkable characters.

3. **Graphic Organizer**
Sample response:
Action: Odysseus tricks the Cyclops in order to escape his cave. Odysseus taunts the Cyclops and receives Poseidon's wrath.
Trait: cleverness; pride or boldness

4. Sample response: Students may say that Odysseus would have benefited from a navigation system and a communication system.

from The Odyssey, Part 2
Homer

p. 327 Graphic Organizer
Sample response:
Detail in Text: Odysseus kills the suitors.
Meaning for Characters: The suitors had intruded on Odysseus' home and family. Trespassers deserved to die.
Meaning in My Culture: Killing is against the law. These murders were not committed in self-defense.

p. 328 Note-taking Guide
Sample response:
Conflict: Odysseus' home has been overrun by men who want to kill his son and marry his wife.
Exposition: The Greek hero Odysseus has just come home to Ithaca after twenty years and finds himself and his home in danger.

Event 3: Odysseus kills Antinous.
Climax: Odysseus removes his disguise.
Event 4: Odysseus, Telemachus, Athena, and the herdsmen kill the suitors.
Event 5: Penelope tests Odysseus.
Resolution: Odysseus and Penelope embrace.

p. 329 Activate Prior Knowledge
Students may say that a hero should be courageous, smart, and willing to sacrifice for others.

p. 329 Literary Analysis
The beggar is comparing Penelope with a good king.

p. 329 Reading Skill
Sample response: Her culture probably prizes kindness toward strangers.

p. 329 Reading Check
Students should underline "He is sad. He does not want to cry in her home. She may think he has had too many cups of wine."

p. 330 Reading Skill
Sample response: Greeks considered it important to honor the dead. They wove shrouds for them. Today it is still important to honor the dead. People hold memorial services to honor the dead.

p. 330 Stop to Reflect
Sample response: Penelope's actions show that she is brave and clever. She also does not wish to marry.

p. 330 Reading Check
Students should underline "Her parents want her to marry. Her son does not want the suitors to use up all the property he should inherit."

p. 331 Literary Analysis
Sample response: This epic simile shows Odysseus' skill with the bow and his grace in using it.

p. 331 Stop to Reflect
Sample response: The success with the bow and arrow signals that the old beggar is really Odysseus. Penelope probably set this test for her suitors because her husband was the only man she thought could pass the test.

p. 331 Reading Check
Students should underline "He draws an arrow and aims it at Antinous."

p. 332 Reading Skill

Sample response: Odysseus' explanation shows that a man's respect for the gods and his reputation are very important. It reveals the importance of property and marriage and how one man should respect what belongs to another man.

p. 332 Stop to Reflect

Students may say that the offer of repayment seems fair. However, the suitors cannot be trusted, and they will try to kill Odysseus at their first chance. Students may suggest that they would place the suitors in prison.

p. 332 Reading Check

Students should circle "He explains that Antinous led the suitors."

p. 333 Reading Skill

Sample response: Telemachus' joining the fight shows the importance of loyalty to the family. It also shows that a son should obey and support his father.

p. 333 Build English Skills

Sample response: He will get a pen when he runs out of pencils.

p. 333 Literary Analysis

The simile emphasizes the cold, twitching appearance of the dead men. They look like dead fish.

p. 333 Reading Check

Students should underline "Aided by Athena, Odysseus, Telemachus, Eumaeus, and other faithful herdsmen kill all of the suitors."

p. 334 Literary Analysis

Students may include details such as "gold infused / on silver by a craftsman, whose fine art / Hephaestus taught him, or Athena: one / whose work moves to delight."

p. 334 Stop to Reflect

Some students may point out that Odysseus has been gone for a long time and someone with great skill may be pretending to be him. They would also test him. Other students may say that they would have been satisfied with the arrow test and his actions in the house. They would not feel the need to test him further.

p. 334 Reading Check

Students should underline "He describes the way he had built the bed."

p. 335 Read Fluently

Students should circle "in joy, in joy." Sample response: The repeated phrase lets the reader know that the feeling is deep and powerful.

p. 335 Vocabulary and Pronunciation

Sample response: I have slain hundreds of flies.

p. 335 Reading Skill

Students may say that the epic ends the way that they expected. They may expect happy endings in stories. Others may not expect the ending. They may have expected Odysseus to experience punishment for the deaths of the suitors.

p. 336 Apply the Skills

1. Sample response: Odysseus faced many dangers, but Penelope suffered years of waiting, never knowing what had happened to Odysseus.
2. Her experience with the suitors has made Penelope act cautiously. She believes that she must be sure of his identity.
3. **Graphic Organizer**
Sample response:
Items Being Compared: Odysseus' longing for his wife is compared with a swimmer's longing for the shore.
Details of Epic Simile: "big surf," "clotted with brine," "kindly beaches," "knowing the abyss behind"
Purpose: to show the intensity of Odysseus' feelings as he returns to Penelope
4. Sample response: Many of Odysseus' values are universal. For instance, we still value hospitality and we can understand and sympathize with his longing for home. Many people may not share his belief that the gods participate and interfere in human affairs.

Reading Informational Materials: Applications

p. 341 Apply the Skills
Thinking About the Application

1. Sample response: The application asks for a personal essay so that the applicant can give more information about his or her reasons for applying. The applicant can also explain more about career plans and why he or she would be a good volunteer for this project.

2. Sample response: References can be more objective. References can also describe how well the applicant works with other people.

Reading Skill
3. Each volunteer is expected to take part in all excavation duties.
4. Applicants must list any archaeology and classics classes they have taken.

"Three Skeleton Key"
George G. Toudouze

"The Red-headed League"
Sir Arthur Conan Doyle

p. 342 Graphic Organizer
Sample response:
"Three Skeleton Key"
Protagonist: the narrator
Goals and Actions: He wants to get rid of the rats. He, Le Gleo, and Itchoua close all entrances to the lighthouse. They leave the lighthouse lantern unlit so that the outside world can see that they are in trouble.
Antagonist: the rats
Goals and Actions: The rats want to survive. They search for food. They take over a Dutch ship and eat the crew. Then, they overtake Three Skeleton Key and the lighthouse.
Conflict: The rats want to kill the men, and the men want to kill the rats.
Universal Motives or Struggles: the fight for survival

"The Red-headed League"
Protagonist: Sherlock Holmes
Goals and Actions: He wants to solve the mystery of the Red-headed League. He investigates the mystery.
Antagonist: John Clay
Goals and Actions: He plans to rob the bank. He digs a tunnel.
Conflict: Clay wants to rob the bank. Holmes wants to catch him.
Universal Motives or Struggles: the struggle of good against evil

p. 343 Reading/Writing Connection
Sample response: Lighthouse keepers often had more access to quiet simplicity. However, their duties often forced them to forgo social activities. Such isolation could induce loneliness.

p. 343 Note-taking Guide
Sample response:
Dangers at the Lighthouse: the sharks
Supporting Details: "the sea, which is patrolled by sharks"
Dangers at the Lighthouse: the rats
Supporting Details: "large, ferocious, and smart," "They also stick together," "If one is attacked, the others rush to defend it."

p. 344 Activate Prior Knowledge
Students may say that they are most frightened of snakes. If trapped and surrounded by snakes, they would probably panic and feel as though there were no escape.

p. 344 Literary Analysis
Students may underline "My most terrifying experience," "When I was a young man," and "I volunteered."

p. 344 Reading Check
Students should circle "The rocks are very slippery, so it is easy to slip and fall into the sea, which is patrolled by sharks."

p. 345 Vocabulary and Pronunciation
Students should circle "no one's aboard."

p. 345 Build English Skills
Students should circle "What's wrong with their crew? Are they all drunk or insane?" "What do you mean, Chief?" "Are you saying that she's the Flying Dutchman?" Students should underline "See us? No doubt—if there is a crew aboard!" "No, old man, that's not what I meant. If I say that no one's aboard, I mean she's derelict."

p. 345 Reading Skill
Le Gleo seems most frightened. He is afraid the ship is a ghost ship.

p. 345 Reading Check
Students should underline "Are you saying that she's the Flying Dutchman?"

p. 346 Read Fluently
Students may describe the vision of a ship in the distance. In their vision, they see the ship crossing back and forth across the water, the wind filling the sails and then the sails dropping each time the wind dies. Each time the ship changes direction, it comes closer to the lighthouse.

p. 346 Literary Analysis
Sample response: The details about the arrival of the abandoned ship, which looks as though it may crash into the lighthouse and bring some harm to the protagonist, may interest students in what will happen to the protagonist. The students may also be interested in the rats and how they drove out the crew of the ship. Students may want to know how the rats drove out the crew.

p. 346 Reading Check
Students should underline "They had been driven out by the rats."

p. 347 Vocabulary and Pronunciation
Students should circle "Verb."

p. 347 Stop to Reflect
Students may say that they would feel frightened or amazed. They may think that the sight of so many large, hungry rats would be intimidating.

p. 347 Literary Analysis
The protagonist and two other men are now in conflict with the rats. The rats want to eat them, and the men do not want to be eaten.

p. 347 Reading Check
Students should underline "The rats leap into the sea and swim strongly to the island."

p. 348 Literary Analysis
The rats are struggling to survive by trying to kill the men for food. The men struggle to stay alive by protecting themselves from the rats.

p. 348 Literary Analysis
Students should underline "without food or drink." The new antagonist is starvation or dehydration.

p. 348 Reading Check
Students should underline "They decide to signal for help by not lighting the lantern."

p. 349 Reading Skill
Le Gleo is more easily frightened. He begins to go crazy. The other two men stay mostly in control of themselves.

p. 349 Stop to Reflect
Students may say that they would bait the rats to another area with food and then set the rats on fire. This strategy would enable them to rescue the men.

p. 349 Reading Check
Students should underline "Using the dots and dashes . . ."

p. 350 Literary Analysis
Sample response: Readers are interested in what happens to the protagonist because they feel sympathy for the protagonist. They would not want to be attacked by rats. They can understand his need to fight for survival.

p. 350 Stop to Reflect
Some students may say that human intelligence won out because the rats were destroyed and the men escaped the island. Others may think that the humans did not win completely because one man dies and another loses his mind.

p. 350 Reading Check
Students should underline "the barge was filled with meat" or "the barge reeking with the scent of freshly cut meat."

p. 351 Apply the Skills
1. Sample response: The rats are dangerous and desperate. They did not give up and drown in the sea. They will probably not give up if they attack the men.
2. Sample response: Itchoua means that if the rats get into the lighthouse, the men will die. Then, three more skeletons could be added to the name of the island.
3. The conflict between the narrator and the rats represents the universal struggle for survival.
4. **Graphic Organizer**
Sample response:
End Only: The narrator has nearly died from the rat attack, and he has lost two friends. He is wiser now.
Beginning and End: He still enjoys the island and working in the lighthouse. He still does not believe the superstitions.

p. 353 Reading/Writing Connection
Sample response: You might perceive that a pencil is round, but most pencils have six sides. If you observe pencil lead closely, you can see that it has a rough surface. One way to differentiate between a pen and a pencil is to note that pencils often weigh less than pens.

p. 354 Note-taking Guide

Sample response:

Box 2: Wilson loses his job.

Box 3: Wilson asks Sherlock Holmes for help.

Box 4: Holmes uncovers the crime.

p. 354 Apply the Skills

1. Holmes finds Wilson's story interesting because it is different from any Holmes has heard before.

2. Spaulding's trousers showed that he had been digging in the cellar. The bank's property bordered Wilson's shop.

3. The protagonist is Sherlock Holmes. His goal is to solve the mystery and catch the criminal behind it.

4. **Graphic Organizer**

Sample response:

End Only: Holmes can take pride in capturing a known criminal.

Beginning and End: Holmes uses reasoning to solve crimes. He solves crimes to escape boredom. He waits for the next new crime.

Reading Informational Materials: Encyclopedia Entries

p. 359 Apply the Skills

Thinking About Encyclopedia Entries

1. Sample response: To "play fair" means that the author gives the reader the same information found by the detective. This information gives readers a fair chance to solve the mystery as they read.

2. The American style of mystery introduced in the 1920s focused on a tough detective as its hero. The mystery featured action and violence. It had a colorful narrative style.

Reading Skill

3. Sample response: to learn which writers are famous for writing detective stories

4. You would find this information in the section with the subhead "History."

"There Is a Longing"
Chief Dan George

"Glory and Hope"
Nelson Mandela

p. 360 Graphic Organizer

Sample response:

"There Is a Longing"

Philosophical Assumptions: The greatness of the Native American people is in the future

as well as in the past. The road to greatness will be difficult but will be worth it.

Evaluation: His beliefs support his purpose because they give Native Americans the power to improve their lives.

"Glory and Hope"

Philosophical Assumption: Democracy is a form of government that is better than apartheid.

Evaluation: This belief supports Mandela's purpose of bringing a message of hope and inspiration to the people of South Africa.

p. 361 Reading/Writing Connection

Sample response: Connecting with one's own heritage can reinforce a tolerance for other cultures. Contemporary culture does encourage the acceptance of other cultures. A blending of other cultures can produce a wide spectrum of beliefs and traditions.

p. 361 Note-taking Guide

Sample response:

The Speaker's Longings: for the young to become warriors in today's society; for his people to live without welfare and take their place in a society that is "rightly" theirs; for courage; for the ability to accept the "white man's" culture; to live in harmony with the new society, succeed in it, and move forward; to learn the skills of the white man so that he and his people can succeed in the white man's world; to see his people fill government positions so that they can rule themselves and change society

p. 362 Activate Prior Knowledge

Students may say that people need qualities such as determination, flexibility, and compassion in order to succeed in today's society.

p. 362 Reading Skill

Sample response: New warriors must learn different skills. They must go to school to learn these skills. The training will be more difficult than in the past.

p. 362 Build English Skills

Students should circle "man's" and "society's."

p. 362 Reading Check

Students should circle "His words are his only weapons now."

p. 363 Read Fluently

Sample response: When young warriors and leaders have better education and new skills, they will be in a position to make changes. Students should indicate pauses where commas are used.

p. 363 Literary Analysis

Sample response: He wants to guide other Native Americans. He wants to give them the power to become a great and proud people once again.

p. 363 Vocabulary and Pronunciation

Students should circle "Verb."

p. 364 Apply the Skills

1. Sample response: He thinks this training is necessary for his people to be able to work in law and in government. With this training, his people will be able to rule themselves and change society.
2. Sample response: He means that he must fight for the future of his people by speaking out for them. He will use reason and logic as his weapons to fight for their rights.
3. Students may say that his audience shared his faith and his belief in the potential of Native Americans. Students may support their answer with the following: "The young want to have a purpose in life. They want to be valuable to society."
4. **Graphic Organizer**

Sample response:

Past: Training to be great warriors was easier in the past. The olden Chiefs had power to make war.

Present: The people are filled with longing. They are faced with hard work and studying. The Chief has only the power to make speeches.

Future: His people can be great again. They can be leaders. They can be educated. They can rule themselves and be free. They can change society.

p. 366 Reading/Writing Connection

Sample response: A good speech from a leader can evoke emotions such as hope. People stand for the national anthem to signify their pride. The time people devote to learning about voting issues shows that they care.

p. 366 Note-taking Guide

Sample response:

Old South Africa: White people ran the government. Black people faced discrimination. The rest of the world looked down on South Africa. South Africa was a shameful country.

New South Africa: The government is a democracy. All citizens are equal and free. The world has a high opinion of South Africa. South Africa is a proud country.

p. 367 Apply the Skills

1. Students may point out such ideas as equality, dignity, and peace.
2. Sample response: Mandela believes that the present moment is glorious and that the future is hopeful.
3. Sample response: Mandela assumes that apartheid was wrong and that democracy is a good form of government. Also, Mandela believes that South Africa is a beautiful land with people who deserve freedom.
4. **Graphic Organizer**

Sample response:

Present: South Africa is experiencing "newborn liberty."

Future: South Africa faces many challenges on its way to becoming a democracy.

READER'S NOTEBOOK

Using a Dictionary

p. V8

1. Students should circle "n." The "v." stands for verb; "adv." stands for adverb; "adj." stands for adjective; and "prep." stands for preposition.
2. Students should underline "[ME *lymon* < Mfr *limon* < Ar *laimun* < Pers *limun*]." "MFr" stands for Middle French.
3. Students should draw a box around the pronunciation.
4. There are four noun definitions for the entry.
5. Definition four is slang.
6. Definition four is used in the sentence.

p. V9 Activity

1. **Pronunciation:** (lit′ ər ə chər)
Main Part of Speech: noun
Original Language(s): ME *litterature* < OFr < L *litteratura* < *littera*
1st Meaning: books, plays, etc. that are considered very good and that people have liked for a long time
Other Meanings: printed information produced by organizations that want to sell something or tell people about something
2. **Pronunciation:** (laŋ′ gwij)
Main Part of Speech: noun
Original Language(s): ME < OFr *langage* < *langue*, tongue < L *lingua*, tongue, language, altered (by assoc. with *lingere*, to lick) < OL *dingwa* < IE **dnghwa* > OE *tunge*, TONGUE
1st Meaning: a system of words, phrases, and grammar, used by people who live in a country or area to communicate with each other
Other Meanings: the use of words, grammar, etc. to communicate with other people; the kind of words that someone uses, or that are used when talking or writing about a particular subject; a system of instructions used in computer programs; any system of signs, movements, sounds, etc. that are used to express meanings or feelings

p. V9 Activity
Sample response:
Moment: A *moment* is a "short portion or point of time." The perfect moment passed me by.
Popular: *Popular* means "commonly liked or approved." Logan wanted to sit with the popular students during lunch.
Remedy: A *remedy* is "a medicine or treatment that cures an illness." Ariel discovered a remedy for her grandmother's illness.
Blur: A *blur* is "a stain or smear that obscures." I couldn't see through the window because of the blur on it.
Lazy: *Lazy* means "not energetic." My brother is lazy because he doesn't do any chores or his homework.

Denotation and Connotation

p. V12 A.
Sample response:
Inexpensive: The shirt I purchased was inexpensive.
Cheap: The cheap blouse I bought has already lost several buttons.
Bargain: You would not believe the bargain I found at the mall yesterday.

p. V12 B.
1. Sample response: Connotations for *slim* include "physically fit" or "delicate figure." A connotation of *skinny* is "undernourished."
2. Sample response: The word *horrifying* has a negative connotation, and *scary* has more of a neutral connotation. Something described as horrifying would be almost unbearable to watch or listen to.
3. Sample response: *Television* sounds more formal and neutral. *TV* has connotations of informality and familiarity.
4. Sample response: *Children* is a word that would be used in a more formal setting. The word *kids* suggests informality and playfulness.
5. Sample response: Connotations for *clever* include "intelligent" and "quick-thinking." Connotations for *sneaky* include "untrustworthy" and "criminal."

p. V13 C.

Graphic Organizer

Sample response:

Ask

Positive: inquire

Group

Positive: bunch

Attempt

Positive: try

Negative: none

Laugh

Negative: snicker

Neutral: funny

Positive: amusing

Negative: ridiculous

Neutral: small

Positive: cozy

Negative: cramped

Neutral: pushed

Positive: tapped

Negative: rammed

p. V13 D.

Graphic Organizer

Sample response:

Cheerful: friendly; sunny disposition; optimistic

Glad: pleased

Joyful: overflowing with happiness

Sample response: The general opinion of Alyssa was that she was a cheerful person. Neville was glad that his brother passed his science test. Laila was joyful when she heard that her sister got the job.

Unit 1: Academic Vocabulary Words

p. V14 A. True/False

1. F; Sample response: William Shakespeare is not considered to be a contemporary author.
2. T
3. T
4. F; Sample response: Life-or-death situations are not considered trivial.
5. F; Sample response: I do not appreciate it when my shoes are stolen from my locker.
6. T
7. F; Sample response: Most people will not display their faults in public.
8. T
9. T
10. F; Sample response: Alice was not being specific when she said she would be home around noon.

p. V15 B. Original Sentences

Sample response:

Appreciate: I appreciate everyone who helped me decorate for the dance.

Contemporary: My favorite contemporary author is J. K. Rowling.

Contribute: I plan to contribute some money to the charity.

Detect: Stephen detected a change in the tone of the article.

Display: I displayed my science fair project at school.

Involve: The class play will involve every student.

Participate: We will participate in extracurricular activities.

Specific: Please set a specific time for football practice.

Trivial: The teacher would not pay attention to his trivial question.

Vital: It is vital that you drink plenty of water.

Unit 2: Academic Vocabulary Words

p. V16 A. Completions

Sample response:

1. The scientist ran tests to *verify* the results of the experiment.
2. Please, *categorize* these facts into two groups.
3. The *circumstance* that would most likely make me scream would be failing my test.
4. His *motive* for stealing the car was that he was going to be late for his meeting.
5. The *aspect* of her personality that I like the most is her kindness.
6. You will get along with people better if you have an *attitude* that is positive and willing to compromise.
7. The most powerful *emotion* is happiness.
8. My favorite *topic* for group discussion is the environment.
9. When I got home, the front door was open, which *implies* that someone got home before me.
10. An example of a logical *sequence* is one, two, three.

p. V17 B. Original Sentences

Sample response:

Aspect: I knew every aspect of the project.

Attitude: Ori could not hide his negative attitude about the upcoming game.

Categorize: Please categorize the stories by genre.

Circumstance: The circumstances of the crime were not easily discovered.

Emotion: The result of the game produced mixed emotions among the players.

Imply: The tears on Austin's face implied the results of his audition.

Motive: My brother's motives for stealing my allowance were clear.

Sequence: The summary of the movie did not make sense because it was told out of sequence.

Topic: The topic of the essay is England.

Verify: I needed to verify the facts in my research report.

p. V17 C.

Sample response: The words *cringed, tangible,* and *lapses* were new to me. *Cringed* means "moved away from someone or something because of fear." *Tangible* means "real" or "able to be touched." *Lapses* are "short periods of time when a person forgets something, does not pay attention, or fails to do something he or she should have done."

Unit 3: Academic Vocabulary Words

p. V18 A. Code Name

1. texture
2. internal
3. abstract
4. hence
5. anticipate
6. derive
7. signify
8. illuminate
9. contemplate
10. equivalent

p. V19 B.

Sample response:

Abstract: Write an abstract of the article.

Anticipate: I anticipate the arrival of my brother for the holidays.

Contemplate: Mandy contemplated the symbolism of the flower in the poem.

Derive: I derived this information from an encyclopedia.

Equivalent: The word *attempt* is equivalent to the word *try*.

Hence: My family had an emergency last night; hence, my homework is unfinished.

Illuminate: The teacher illuminated the math problem.

Internal: The heart is an internal organ.

Signify: The sign signifies the upcoming sale at the store.

Texture: The fabric had a soft texture.

p. V19 C.

Sample response: The words *indisputable, aromas,* and *poised* were new to me. *Indisputable* means "definitely true." *Aromas* are "strong, pleasant smells." *Poised* means "prepared to do something."

Unit 4: Academic Vocabulary Words

p. V20 A. Completion

Sample response:

1. Two examples of *abstract* words are love and faith.
2. Careful *deliberation* is necessary before deciding to support one side of an argument.
3. When reading poetry, you should *emphasize* important words.
4. The teenage years are a *transition* from childhood to adulthood.
5. An object of *considerable* weight is worth noting in your class notes.
6. In science class, I learned the *concept* of Newton's Law.
7. The scientist invented a *mechanism* that would change the way we did work.
8. When giving a speech, you should demonstrate correct *usage* of grammar.
9. Part of my *distinct* style is my hair color.
10. An event that might cause a huge *impact* is a natural disaster.

p. V21 B.

Sample response:

Abstract: Liberty and justice are abstract words.

Considerable: The man had lost a considerable amount of weight.

Concept: I learned new concepts in geography.

Deliberation: It was important for the jury to make a careful deliberation.

Distinct: Some of the distinct features of the car are mentioned in the ad.

Emphasize: It is necessary to emphasize key points in a report.

Impact: The Internet has had an important impact on society.

Mechanism: I needed to fix the broken mechanism in the machine.

Transition: It is important to make transitions between paragraphs.

Usage: I needed to read the directions to discover the usage of the different pieces.

p. V21 C.

Sample response: The words *snares, pensive,* and *anthropology* were new to me. *Snares* means "catches in a trap." *Pensive* means "in deep or serious thought." *Anthropology* is "the scientific study of people, their societies, their beliefs, and so on."

Unit 5: Academic Vocabulary Words

pp. V22–V23 A.

Sample response:

1. An ambiguous question would not be clear because an ambiguous question would have many meanings.

2. A person would need to compile materials to put in his or her anthology. For example, if it were a literature anthology, the person would collect different stories, novels, or poems.

3. A heavily decorated room is elaborate because it has many details.

4. A condensed book would be shorter than the original because *condensed* means "shortened."

5. A book on raising tigers would not be relevant to my life because I do not raise tigers.

6. I would offer more details because *elaborate* means "to work out in detail."

7. A football game may require a strategy because a plan of action and defense would be needed.

8. I would reread my essay and correct any mistakes because that is what is meant by the word *revise.*

9. I might offer my brother some candy to leave me alone. This act may convince or persuade him.

10. An explanation could illuminate a question because it could make the question clear.

11. A general would not implement a flawed battle plan because he would want to win. A flawed, or imperfect, plan would not guarantee victory.

p. V23 B.

Sample response: The words *spectral, fond,* and *trundle* were new to me. *Spectral* means "like a phantom or ghost." *Fond* means "affectionate." *Trundle* means "to roll along."

Unit 6: Academic Vocabulary Words

p. V24 A. True/False

1. T
2. T
3. F; Sample response: Infants cannot complete complex tasks.
4. T
5. F; Sample response: The instructions were coherent, so I could easily build the model.
6. F; Sample response: There was no controversy about the new law, and everyone agreed that the government was right to pass it.
7. F; Sample response: To solve a problem, you should pay attention to the most significant parts of the issue.
8. T
9. F; Sample response: To appraise the value of a car, have someone determine the worth of it.
10. F; Sample response: The details in the story were compelling us to keep reading, so we continued until we finished the story.

p. V25 B.

Sample response:

1. I asked someone to appraise the house so that I could confirm its value.

2. The cogent speaker was compelling me to stay and listen.

3. There was a significant defect in the product.

4. There was controversy in the case because of the lack of coherent evidence.

5. The complex technique made the experiment difficult to complete.

p. V25 C.

Sample response: The words *poise, victuals,* and *ruses* were new to me. *Poise* means "balance." *Victuals* are "food or other provisions." *Ruses* are "tricks."

READER'S NOTEBOOK ADAPTED VERSION

Using a Dictionary

p. V8

1. Students should circle "n." The "v." stands for verb; "adv." stands for adverb; "adj." stands for adjective; and "prep." stands for preposition.
2. Students should underline "[ME *lymon* < Mfr *limon* < Ar *laimun* < Pers *limun*]." "MFr" stands for Middle French.
3. Students should draw a box around the pronunciation.
4. There are four noun definitions for the entry.
5. Definition four is slang.
6. Definition four is used in the sentence.

p. V9 Activity

1. **Pronunciation:** (lit′ ər ə chər)
Main Part of Speech: noun
Original Language(s): ME *litterature* < OFr < L *litteratura* < *littera*
1st Meaning: books, plays, etc. that are considered very good and that people have liked for a long time
Other Meanings: printed information produced by organizations that want to sell something or tell people about something
2. **Pronunciation:** (laŋ′ gwij)
Main Part of Speech: noun
Original Language(s): ME < OFr *langage* < *langue*, tongue < L *lingua*, tongue, language, altered (by assoc. with *lingere*, to lick) < OL *dingwa* < IE *dnghwa* > OE *tunge*, TONGUE
1st Meaning: a system of words, phrases, and grammar, used by people who live in a country or area to communicate with each other
Other Meanings: the use of words, grammar, etc. to communicate with other people; the kind of words that someone uses, or that are used when talking or writing about a particular subject; a system of instructions used in computer programs; any system of signs, movements, sounds, etc. that are used to express meanings or feelings

p. V9 Activity

Sample response:
Moment: A *moment* is a "short portion or point of time." The perfect moment passed me by.
Popular: *Popular* means "commonly liked or approved." Logan wanted to sit with the popular students during lunch.
Remedy: A *remedy* is "a medicine or treatment that cures an illness." Ariel discovered a remedy for her grandmother's illness.
Blur: A *blur* is "a stain or smear that obscures." I couldn't see through the window because of the blur on it.
Lazy: *Lazy* means "not energetic." My brother is lazy because he doesn't do any chores or his homework.

Denotation and Connotation

p. V12 A.

Sample response:
Inexpensive: The shirt I purchased was inexpensive.
Cheap: The cheap blouse I bought has already lost several buttons.
Bargain: You would not believe the bargain I found at the mall yesterday.

p. V12 B.

1. Sample response: Connotations for *slim* include "physically fit" or "delicate figure." A connotation of *skinny* is "undernourished."
2. Sample response: The word *horrifying* has a negative connotation, and *scary* has more of a neutral connotation. Something described as horrifying would be almost unbearable to watch or listen to.
3. Sample response: *Television* sounds more formal and neutral. *TV* has connotations of informality and familiarity.
4. Sample response: *Children* is a word that would be used in a more formal setting. The word *kids* suggests informality and playfulness.
5. Sample response: Connotations for *clever* include "intelligent" and "quick-thinking." Connotations for *sneaky* include "untrustworthy" and "criminal."

p. V13 C.
Graphic Organizer
Sample response:
Ask
Positive: inquire

Group
Positive: bunch
Attempt
Positive: try
Negative: none
Laugh
Negative: snicker
Neutral: funny
Positive: amusing
Negative: ridiculous
Neutral: small
Positive: cozy
Negative: cramped
Neutral: pushed
Positive: tapped
Negative: rammed

p. V13 D.
Graphic Organizer
Sample response:
Cheerful: friendly; sunny disposition; optimistic
Glad: pleased
Joyful: overflowing with happiness

Sample response: The general opinion of Alyssa was that she was a cheerful person. Neville was glad that his brother passed his science test. Laila was joyful when she heard that her sister got the job.

Unit 1: Academic Vocabulary Words

p. V14 A. True/False
1. F; Sample response: William Shakespeare is not considered to be a contemporary author.
2. T
3. F; Sample response: Life-or-death situations are not considered trivial.
4. T
5. F; Sample response: Alice was not being specific when she said she would be home around noon.

p. V15 B.
Sample response:
Contemporary/Writer: My favorite contemporary writer is J. K. Rowling.
Contribute/Money: I plan to contribute some money to the charity.
Specific/Time: Please set a specific time for football practice.
Trivial/Funny: The funny story was trivial, but entertaining nonetheless.

Vital/Water: It is vital that you drink plenty of water.

p. V15 C.
Sample response: The words *avalanche*, *admirable*, and *succession* were new to me. An *avalanche* is "the fall of a large amount of snow and ice down the side of a mountain." *Admirable* means "respectable; worthy of being admired." *Succession* means "following one after another."

Unit 2: Academic Vocabulary Words

p. V16
1. verify
2. sequence
3. imply
4. circumstance
5. motive

p. V17 B. Completions
Sample response:
1. The scientist ran tests to *verify* the results of the experiment.
2. The *circumstance* that would most likely make me scream would be failing my test.
3. His *motive* for stealing the car was that he was going to be late for his meeting.
4. When I got home, the front door was open, which *implies* that someone got home before me.
5. An example of a logical *sequence* is one, two, three.

p. V17 C.
Sample response: The words *pale*, *vitality*, and *burdened* were new to me. *Pale* means "without much color." *Vitality* means "energy." *Burdened* means "loaded down."

Unit 3: Academic Vocabulary Words

p. V18 A. Code Name
1. derive
2. signify
3. illuminate
4. contemplate
5. equivalent

p. V19 B.
Sample response:
Contemplate/Meaning: Mandy contemplated the meaning of the word.
Derive/Pleasure: I derived pleasure from reading the book.

Equivalent/Amount: I asked for an amount that was equivalent to the cost of my ruined sweater.
Illuminate/Idea: The teacher illuminated the confusing idea.
Signify/Importance: The poster signifies the importance of the new rules.

p. V19 C.
Sample response: The words *diversity*, *epidemics*, and *enveloped* were new to me. *Diversity* means "a range of different people and things." *Epidemics* are "widespread diseases." *Enveloped* means "covered completely."

Unit 4: Academic Vocabulary Words

p. V20 A. Completion
Sample response:
1. Two examples of *abstract* words are love and faith.
2. Careful *deliberation* is necessary before deciding to support one side of an argument.
3. In science class, I learned the *concept* of Newton's Law.
4. The scientist invented a *mechanism* that would change the way we did work.
5. When giving a speech, you should demonstrate correct *usage* of grammar.

p. V21 B.
Sample response:
Abstract/Art: My father enjoys abstract art.
Concept/Difficult: The new concept was difficult to grasp.
Deliberation/Jury: It was important for the jury to make a careful deliberation.
Mechanism/Car: The mechanism in the car's engine was broken.
Usage/Correct: I needed to read the directions to discover the correct usage of the different pieces.

p. V21 C.
Sample response: The words *snares*, *pensive*, and *anthropology* were new to me. *Snares* means "catches in a trap." *Pensive* means "in deep or serious thought." *Anthropology* is "the scientific study of people, their societies, their beliefs, and so on."

Unit 5: Academic Vocabulary Words

p. V22 A.
Sample response:
1. An ambiguous question would not be clear because an ambiguous question would have many meanings.
2. A person would need to compile materials to put in his or her anthology. For example, if it were a literature anthology, the person would collect different stories, novels, or poems.
3. A condensed book would be shorter than the original because *condensed* means "shortened."
4. I would reread my essay and correct any mistakes because that is what is meant by the word *revise*.
5. A general would not implement a flawed battle plan because he would want to win. A flawed, or imperfect, plan would not guarantee victory.

p. V23 B.
Sample response: The words *genial*, *inconstant*, and *valet* were new to me. *Genial* means "friendly." *Inconstant* means "changing." A *valet* is "a male servant."

Unit 6: Academic Vocabulary

p. V24 A. True/False
1. F; Sample response: Infants cannot complete complex tasks.
2. T
3. F; Sample response: There was no controversy about the new law, and everyone agreed that the government was right to pass it.
4. F; Sample response: To appraise the value of a car, have someone determine the worth of it.
5. F; Sample response: The details in the story were compelling us to keep reading, so we continued until we finished the story.

p. V25 B.
Sample response:
1. I needed someone to appraise the damage done to my car.
2. There was a defect in my new skirt, so it did not fit correctly.
3. The complex plan was full of many directions.

4. The public controversy over the film made the theater management decide not to show it.
5. My friend's reasons compelled me to go on the trip.

p. V25 C.
Sample response: The words *poise, solitude,* and *contempt* were new to me. *Poise* means "balance." *Solitude* means "aloneness." *Contempt* means "disdain or scorn."

Using a Dictionary

p. V8

1. Students should circle "n." The "v." stands for verb; "adv." stands for adverb; "adj." stands for adjective; and "prep." stands for preposition.
2. Students should underline "[ME *lymon* < Mfr *limon* < Ar *laimun* < Pers *limun*]." "MFr" stands for Middle French.
3. Students should draw a box around the pronunciation.
4. There are four noun definitions for the entry.
5. Definition four is slang.
6. Definition four is used in the sentence.

p. V9 Activity

1. **Pronunciation:** (lit′ ər ə chər)
Main Part of Speech: noun
Original Language(s): ME *litterature* < OFr < L *litteratura* < *littera*
1st Meaning: books, plays, etc. that are considered very good and that people have liked for a long time
Other Meanings: printed information produced by organizations that want to sell something or tell people about something
2. **Pronunciation:** (laŋ′ gwij)
Main Part of Speech: noun
Original Language(s): ME < OFr *langage* < *langue*, tongue < L *lingua*, tongue, language, altered (by assoc. with *lingere*, to lick) < OL *dingwa* < IE **dnghwa* > OE *tunge*, TONGUE
1st Meaning: a system of words, phrases, and grammar, used by people who live in a country or area to communicate with each other
Other Meanings: the use of words, grammar, etc. to communicate with other people; the kind of words that someone uses, or that are used when talking or writing about a particular subject; a system of instructions used in computer programs; any system of signs, movements, sounds, etc. that are used to express meanings or feelings

p. V9 Activity

Sample response:
Moment: A *moment* is a "short portion or point of time." The perfect moment passed me by.
Popular: *Popular* means "commonly liked or approved." Logan wanted to sit with the popular students during lunch.
Remedy: A *remedy* is "a medicine or treatment that cures an illness." Ariel discovered a remedy for her grandmother's illness.
Blur: A *blur* is "a stain or smear that obscures." I couldn't see through the window because of the blur on it.
Lazy: *Lazy* means "not energetic." My brother is lazy because he doesn't do any chores or his homework.

Denotation and Connotation

p. V12 A.

Sample response:
Inexpensive: The shirt I purchased was inexpensive.
Cheap: The cheap blouse I bought has already lost several buttons.
Bargain: You would not believe the bargain I found at the mall yesterday.

p. V12 B.

1. Sample response: Connotations for *slim* include "physically fit" or "delicate figure." A connotation of *skinny* is "undernourished."
2. Sample response: The word *horrifying* has a negative connotation, and *scary* has more of a neutral connotation. Something described as horrifying would be almost unbearable to watch or listen to.
3. Sample response: *Television* sounds more formal and neutral. *TV* has connotations of informality and familiarity.
4. Sample response: *Children* is a word that would be used in a more formal setting. The word *kids* suggests informality and playfulness.
5. Sample response: Connotations for *clever* include "intelligent" and "quick-thinking." Connotations for *sneaky* include "untrustworthy" and "criminal."

p. V13 C.
Graphic Organizer
Sample response:
Ask
Positive: inquire

Group
Positive: bunch
Attempt
Positive: try
Negative: none
Laugh
Negative: snicker
Neutral: funny
Positive: amusing
Negative: ridiculous
Neutral: small
Positive: cozy
Negative: cramped
Neutral: pushed
Positive: tapped
Negative: rammed

p. V13 D.
Graphic Organizer
Sample response:
Cheerful: friendly; sunny disposition; optimistic
Glad: pleased
Joyful: overflowing with happiness

Sample response: The general opinion of Alyssa was that she was a cheerful person. Neville was glad that his brother passed his science test. Laila was joyful when she heard that her sister got the job.

Unit 1: Academic Vocabulary Words

p. V14 A. True/False
1. F; Sample response: William Shakespeare is not considered to be a contemporary author.
2. T
3. F; Sample response: Life-or-death situations are not considered trivial.
4. T
5. F; Sample response: Alice was not being specific when she said she would be home around noon.

p. V15 B.
Sample response:
Contemporary/Writer: My favorite contemporary writer is J. K. Rowling.
Contribute/Money: I plan to contribute some money to the charity.
Specific/Time: Please set a specific time for football practice.
Trivial/Funny: The funny story was trivial, but entertaining nonetheless.

Vital/Water: It is vital that you drink plenty of water.

p. V15 C.
Sample response: The words *avalanche*, *admirable*, and *succession* were new to me. An *avalanche* is "the fall of a large amount of snow and ice down the side of a mountain." *Admirable* means "respectable; worthy of being admired." *Succession* means "following one after another."

Unit 2: Academic Vocabulary Words

p. V16
1. verify
2. sequence
3. imply
4. circumstance
5. motive

p. V17 B. Completions
Sample response:
1. The scientist ran tests to *verify* the results of the experiment.
2. The *circumstance* that would most likely make me scream would be failing my test.
3. His *motive* for stealing the car was that he was going to be late for his meeting.
4. When I got home, the front door was open, which *implies* that someone got home before me.
5. An example of a logical *sequence* is one, two, three.

p. V17 C.
Sample response: The words *pale*, *vitality*, and *burdened* were new to me. *Pale* means "without much color." *Vitality* means "energy." *Burdened* means "loaded down."

Unit 3: Academic Vocabulary Words

p. V18 A. Code Name
1. derive
2. signify
3. illuminate
4. contemplate
5. equivalent

p. V19 B.
Sample response:
Contemplate/Meaning: Mandy contemplated the meaning of the word.
Derive/Pleasure: I derived pleasure from reading the book.

Equivalent/Amount: I asked for an amount that was equivalent to the cost of my ruined sweater.
Illuminate/Idea: The teacher illuminated the confusing idea.
Signify/Importance: The poster signifies the importance of the new rules.

p. V19 C.

Sample response: The words *diversity*, *epidemics*, and *enveloped* were new to me. *Diversity* means "a range of different people and things." *Epidemics* are "widespread diseases." *Enveloped* means "covered completely."

Unit 4: Academic Vocabulary Words

p. V20 A. Completion

Sample response:
1. Two examples of *abstract* words are love and faith.
2. Careful *deliberation* is necessary before deciding to support one side of an argument.
3. In science class, I learned the *concept* of Newton's Law.
4. The scientist invented a *mechanism* that would change the way we did work.
5. When giving a speech, you should demonstrate correct *usage* of grammar.

p. V21 B.

Sample response:
Abstract/Art: My father enjoys abstract art.
Concept/Difficult: The new concept was difficult to grasp.
Deliberation/Jury: It was important for the jury to make a careful deliberation.
Mechanism/Car: The mechanism in the car's engine was broken.
Usage/Correct: I needed to read the directions to discover the correct usage of the different pieces.

p. V21 C.

Sample response: The words *snares, pensive,* and *anthropology* were new to me. *Snares* means "catches in a trap." *Pensive* means "in deep or serious thought." *Anthropology* is "the scientific study of people, their societies, their beliefs, and so on."

Unit 5: Academic Vocabulary Words

p. V22 A.

Sample response:
1. An ambiguous question would not be clear because an ambiguous question would have many meanings.
2. A person would need to compile materials to put in his or her anthology. For example, if it were a literature anthology, the person would collect different stories, novels, or poems.
3. A condensed book would be shorter than the original because *condensed* means "shortened."
4. I would reread my essay and correct any mistakes because that is what is meant by the word *revise.*
5. A general would not implement a flawed battle plan because he would want to win. A flawed, or imperfect, plan would not guarantee victory.

p. V23 B.

Sample response: The words *genial, inconstant,* and *valet* were new to me. *Genial* means "friendly." *Inconstant* means "changing." A *valet* is "a male servant."

Unit 6: Academic Vocabulary

p. V24 A. True/False

1. F; Sample response: Infants cannot complete complex tasks.
2. T
3. F; Sample response: There was no controversy about the new law, and everyone agreed that the government was right to pass it.
4. F; Sample response: To appraise the value of a car, have someone determine the worth of it.
5. F; Sample response: The details in the story were compelling us to keep reading, so we continued until we finished the story.

p. V25 B.

Sample response:
1. I needed someone to appraise the damage done to my car.
2. There was a defect in my new skirt, so it did not fit correctly.
3. The complex plan was full of many directions.

4. The public controversy over the film made the theater management decide not to show it.

5. My friend's reasons compelled me to go on the trip.

p. V25 C.

Sample response: The words *poise, solitude,* and *contempt* were new to me. *Poise* means "balance." *Solitude* means "aloneness." *Contempt* means "disdain or scorn."

Idioms

p. V48 A. Hypothesize

1. If a person gets "cold feet," the person suddenly feels that he or she is not brave enough to do something.

2. If someone did not "lift a finger," he or she did no work.

3. If Maria "put her foot down," she said very firmly what she would or would not do.

4. If a person has a "green thumb," he or she is good at growing and tending to plants.

5. If a relationship "gets off on the wrong foot," it begins badly, often with an argument.

p. V49 Graphic Organizer

Sample response:

Idiom: break your heart

Explanation: This idiom means that some event or someone inspires sadness or sympathy in another.

Sample Sentence: The children's situation could break your heart.

Idiom: his heart tried to shake itself loose in his chest

Explanation: This idiom is used to express fear.

Sample Sentence: My heart tried to shake itself loose in my chest when I heard the footsteps in the attic.

Idiom: face his death

Explanation: This idiom means that a person is prepared to die.

Sample Sentence: He sat in his hospital bed, ready to face his death.

Idiom: household held its breath

Explanation: This idiom means that a person or people are anxiously waiting for some event or someone.

Sample Sentence: When I heard a car pull up outside I held my breath.

Idiom: she will always be with him

Explanation: The grandmother will not literally be with the narrator. This idiom means that one person will be with another in spirit and in memories.

Sample Sentence: My grandfather told me that he would always be with me.

Idiom: our hearts were racing

Explanation: If a person's heart is racing, his or her heart is beating quickly.

Sample Sentence: Our hearts were racing after we found the perfect piece for our windchime.

Idiom: death is closing in

Explanation: This idiom means that a person is quickly approaching death.

Sample Sentence: Emma knew that death was closing in on her.

Idiom: make or break you

Explanation: This idiom is used to express how good and bad events can change a person's life. A good event could lead to a life of success and luxury. A bad event could lead to a life of poverty.

Sample Sentence: Tomorrow's meeting could make or break me.

Idiom: spell out

Explanation: If someone "spells out" something to another, he or she is thoroughly explaining something. The person may also be stating expectations.

Sample Sentence: Gemma spelled out what she expected of her team.